"This is a great study on the Book of Romans! I love the expeditionary metaphor! I was freshly inspired at a personal level."

—Joel Kruggel
Senior Pastor
Bethany Covenant Church
Bedford, NH

"The Divine Expedition is a fresh look at the book of Romans. The personal examples from the authors' lives and excerpts from great expeditions in history make it both practical and compelling. It is a missional guide to join God in the incredible adventure of restoring all creation to Himself, and it clarifies the amazing part God has for us to play in the grander story of the Kingdom. I gladly recommend it."

—Dan Larsen
Executive Pastor and World & Local Outreach
Cedar Mill Bible Church
Portland, Oregon

"If you have ever questioned your life-purpose or wondered if there isn't more to life than you have experienced on the road you are traveling, then this book is for you. The Divine Expedition can take you on a life-changing journey to find answers you have been seeking. It fully awakens your spirit of adventure. Along the way, it changes you. It challenges you. It deepens your relationship with your Guide. Prepare yourself for what could be a trip of a lifetime!"

—Ruth Craig
Educator, Founder/Owner
CI International
Denver, Colorado

"Years ago, as a 'green' church planter, I asked Linus Sr. what kept him from burning out in Christian ministry. He answered that it was always going back to and studying the Scriptures. Both he and his son walk that talk! This book is a wonderful expression of the wisdom and experience that come from years of engaging with the powerful, energizing, and Holy Word of God!"

—Ungars Gulbis
Lead Pastor
Riga Reformed Church
Riga, Latvia

*"The Divine Expedition: Where Are You in the Book of Romans?*will illuminate God's grand redemptive plan and help you find your role within it; you will begin to discover exactly how God wants to use you in the story of history He is authoring. Journey through Romans and discover the divine destiny for your life."

—Kevin Palau
President
Luis Palau Association

"The Divine Expedition reflects countless hours of humble exploration in Romans by Linus Sr. and Linus Jr. Using an expedition motif and filled with stories of practical application, they breathe life into Paul's letter to the Romans. Join the Linus and Linus' team in an adventure that leads to the expanded panorama of the Gospel of Christ ever more widely known in all the world."

—Richard Wallace
Senior Pastor
Mountainview International Church
Madrid, Spain

"Grab your bible, turn to Romans, slide on your favorite hiking boots, and get ready for an adventure. *The Divine Expedition* will captivate your heart and blow a fresh breeze of faith and hope across your soul. It will encourage you as you traverse God's plan for your life."

—Tim Holt
Lead Pastor, Seacoast Vineyard
Myrtle Beach, South Carolina

"Linus and Linus venture into bold territory with their claim that God intends life with Him to be an adventure on par with the greatest expeditions of all time. Their book is an inspiration for people around the world to launch out on their God-given mission to explore, rescue and restore on behalf of an eternal kingdom."

—Jane Hawkins
Founder, Sampa Community Church
São Paulo, Brazil

"What do Christopher Columbus, Lewis and Clark, and the two Linus Morrises have in common? They are all explorers. You are holding in your hand a book written by a father and son who have been blazing trails in the missional community for over a generation. Now they have left us with a map that charts a course from the lost paradise of Eden all the way to the New Jerusalem. *The Divine Expedition* will guide you and encourage you as you pursue life's Greatest Adventure."

—Dr. Gary Brandenburg
Lead Pastor
Fellowship Bible Church Dallas

"What a wonderful metaphor for the book of Romans as our own personal expedition through life! This book will challenge and incite the reader to spiritual growth in a powerful way."

—Rita Warren
Author, Chairman of the Board
Christian Associates International

"Every Christian and non-Christian should read *The Divine Expedition*. Whether you are a believers or a non-believer you will be captivated by the epic tales shared by Linus Sr. and Linus, Jr. I was particularly taken with Linus Jr.'s story about the "big green monster," a wave he once encountered while surfing. We all encounter "big green monsters" that tend to suck the life out of us. I certainly have. But there is something even more powerful than the "big green monster"— the love and the saving grace of a Savior. May this book lead many on a divine expedition toward the Savior Jesus Christ. I am confident that it will. Thank you Linus and Linus, Jr. for leading us on this expedition."

—Ross M. "Buddy" Lindsay
C.P.A., J.D., L.L.M., Ph. D.
Lindsay and Shroff, Attorneys and Counsellors at Law
Hampton Inn & Suites Oceanfront Resort
Radical Ropes Family Adventure Park
Myrtle Beach, South Carolina

THE
DIVINE
EXPEDITION

Where are you in the book of Romans?

A GUIDE TO
SPIRITUAL DISCOVERY, EMPOWERMENT,
TRANSFORMATION, AND MISSION

By
Linus J. Morris, Sr.
and Linus J. Morris, Jr.

PRESS

The Divine Expedition
Where are you in the book of Romans?
by Linus J. Morris Sr. and Linus J. Morris Jr.

Printed in the United States of America

ISBN 9781619042780

FOR MORE INFORMATION

For more information about Divine Expedition workbook and seminars, go to www.onexpedition.org or email Linus Morris at linus@onexpedition.org

Also available: The High-Impact Church by Linus Morris Sr.

Cover Design by Linus Morris Jr.

www.xulonpress.com

TABLE OF CONTENTS

PART I
THE NEED
FOR THE DIVINE EXPEDITION

PART II
THE LOSS AND RESTORATION
OF THE DIVINE DESIGN

PART III
THE LOSS AND RESTORATION
OF THE DIVINE EXPEDITION

FOREWORD

I think it is fair to say that *The Divine Expedition: Where Are You in the Book of Romans?* is a very unusual book: It is a unique concoction of personal journal, Bible study, spiritual guide, and missional journey, woven together by the father and son combination of the two Linuses—Linus Sr. and Linus Jr. The inter-generational aspect alone gives it a unique twist. It is difficult to point to many other books with the same features.

Because it includes personal testimony, it will be of particular interest to those who have participated in the kind of organization that Linus Sr. found and led for over 30 years. Linus Jr. was born into this ministry, but subsequently chose to embark upon the Roman's expedition for himself.

There is no doubt the book of Romans has played a major role in the unfolding of the history of the world—particularly that of Western culture and its identity. Its impact on us can be felt via highly influential persons such as Augustine, Luther, Wesley, Barth, and countless others. The book of Romans contains nothing less than the formula for the wholesale renewal of persons, society, and church. Its message, in a phrase, is "dynamite," a term Paul explicitly uses to describe the power (*dynamis*) contained within the Gospel (Romans 1:16).

I have long felt the gravity of the message of Romans, and think it is fair to say that apart from the Gospels themselves, it is *the* New Testament book to grapple with. The two Linuses (or is it the two Morrises?) have wisely chosen to construct their story around it. The theme of spiritual and missional journey looms large in their book, and is certainly a favorite theme in my own thinking.

We have tended to domesticate the Gospel and make it into a religious ideology, a tame churchly phenomenon, rather than the call of God to the dangerous journey we call discipleship. God continues to be actively involved in our world through Jesus Christ. Not only are we personally called to enter His Story and make it our own but we must also acknowledge that we exist to extend the Divine Expedition, that is, the Gospel.

Paul's spiritual journey informs and directs the story of the two Linuses, and theirs, in turn, is a life-map to inform ours. They are guides to help us to see the Gospel in a new light. By interweaving Paul's story, thinking, and experience with that of their own, they invite us all to engage in the divine expedition that is the Gospel of Jesus our Lord. Bon voyage!

Alan Hirsch
Writer, Dreamer, Activist
www.theforgottenways.org

INTRODUCTION

HOW TO READ THIS BOOK

EXPEDITIONS

This book is written by two Linus Morrises—Linus Morris Sr. and Linus Morris Jr., father and son. We both believe it is our divine design to be on an expedition. Expeditions are the undertaking of an adventuresome journey with a mission. We love the idea that in such endeavors there are voyages to embark upon, horizons to sail toward, lands to explore, mountains to summit, rivers to traverse, and things of great value to accomplish. Expeditions shake us from the humdrum routine of life and give us a sense of purpose and excitement.

It is our divine design to be on an expedition.

Expeditions are different from cruises, where every comfort is provided, others wait on you, and all you have to do is sit back, relax, and enjoy the ride. Whereas cruises soothe and pamper us, expeditions challenge and stretch us. They require preparation, training, diligence, and even hardship. They take us into the unknown and push us beyond our comfort. Although demanding, expeditions are rewarding as we make new discoveries, reach new heights, and accomplish things we would never otherwise achieve.

Expeditions reveal our strengths and weaknesses. Their rigors and demands show us areas of our lives that must be developed if we are to attain our objectives. We become better persons and better leaders as a result. Moreover, by undertaking such noble challenges we can look back at lives of fulfilling accomplishments.

Expeditions show us that we need others. Their complexities and challenges require teams that work together to accomplish the common goal. Such endeavors lead to a deeper sense of camaraderie and life-long bonds.

I (Linus Sr.) have engaged in a number of adventures in my life: hunting, fishing, hiking, mountain climbing, white-water rafting, and more. I have lived in six countries, traveled to many more, and played basketball internationally against national, Olympic, and professional teams. One summer, our team won fifty-four games without a defeat. None of these adventures, however, compares to the challenge, excitement, and fulfillment I have experienced in the adventure of the Divine Expedition.

> The greatest adventure of all time is revealed in the Bible in the book of Romans.

I (Linus Jr.) have also embarked upon numerous adventures: surfing, kite boarding, stand-up paddling, scuba diving, snow boarding, rock and mountain climbing, white-water rafting, and playing basketball abroad. I was born in Canada and spent ten of my first fourteen years living in Europe. I mountaineered for a month in the Olympic wilderness as part of the National Outdoor Leadership School (NOLS). We summated mountains, traversed glaciers, and navigated pitfalls and storms common in the mountain wilderness. I also spent ten days in New Zealand for a National Geographic photo shoot, during which the New Zealand Tourist Board flew us to remote sites by helicopters and ski planes. While many seek their life's meaning in such experiences, participating in the Divine Expedition transcends them all. It alone points to the real purpose of life.

THE GREATEST EXPEDITION

Both of us believe that the greatest adventure of all time is revealed in the Bible in the book of Romans. In it, we are invited to embark upon an adventure that leads far beyond where we could otherwise journey in life. It is a Divine Expedition with a divine mission: to rescue people stranded in life and restore to them that which was lost. Embarking upon this mission rescues us from spiritual deadness and restores to us the design and purpose for which God created us.

The Divine Expedition is not unlike a trip a friend of ours took to help those who survived the tsunami disaster that swept Southeast Asia on December 26, 2004. He was part of a team resourced and sent out by a group of Christ-followers. Their mission was to help rebuild and restore a portion of that which the devastating tsunami swept away. The Divine Expedition is likewise a mission to rescue, rebuild, and restore damaged and devastated lives.

The expedition outlined in Romans was not written as a cerebral, esoteric, theoretical, or theological treatise. Its purpose was and is to lead us to spiritual discovery, empowerment, transformation, and action. Thus, we do not write *The Divine Expedition: Where Are You in the Book of Romans?* as a technical commentary (although we have carefully studied the book of Romans, read many commentaries on Romans, and have taught Romans verse by verse). We write as those seeking to grasp its intent and fully activate the reality of what is revealed in its pages. Our desire is that our work might serve as a practical action guide to help others understand and implement the life-transforming message of Romans.

We write with two audiences in mind: both those just starting out on the expedition, and those who have already been on the journey for some time. In the early chapters we give attention to explaining concepts that a not-yet or new believer needs to comprehend. As we proceed in later chapters, those who are more mature are in view.

> We seek to unveil the intentionally sequential nature of Romans.

INTENTIONALLY SEQUENTIAL

Our hope is that you will join us on the expedition that unfolds in the book of Romans. We want to make the transforming, empowering, and missional message of this first century epistle accessible to every person and practical to everyday life. We seek to unveil what we believe is the intentionally sequential nature of the message of Romans, convinced that it is a divinely charted map to guide us into the reality of God's design and purpose for us on earth. That purpose is the Divine Expedition.

Because the book of Romans is deliberately sequential, each chapter builds on the previous one(s) and can be implemented in a practical, step-by-step way. As we access and apply what is revealed in one chapter, it becomes the building block for the next step of the expedition. As you work through this book, it is imperative to keep in view its overall sequential flow, at the same time digesting and applying each unfolding chapter-by-chapter dimension of the journey.

We encourage the reader first to grasp the overarching sequence of the book before working through each chapter in more detail. Once the overview is obtained, then the next step is to progressively discern, embrace, apply, and enter into the theme of each successive chapter.

The Divine Expedition is not meant to be a book that one reads and sets aside; it is an expedition to embark upon. Each element is to be reflected upon, absorbed consciously, experienced in community with others, and acted upon in the world around us. The power of its message will be unleashed by doing so. Embarking upon the Divine Expedition leads to dynamic personal empowerment, renewed sense of purpose, and effective ministry and mission in our families, friendships, community, and society.

> Each element is to be reflected upon, absorbed internally, experienced in community with others, and acted upon in the world around us.

WHERE TO START

To begin, we suggest you take a spin through the whole epistle of Romans before reading our comments about each chapter. Get a feel for the whole. As you do, ask God to speak to you and make its message real in your life experience. We encourage being part of a group that is interactively seeking to grasp and live out the Romans' expedition in community. The likelihood of carrying out the Divine Expedition increases when joining with others. A *Divine Expedition Guidebook* is available in which we present reflection and action questions to help you interact with the ideas of each chapter and implement more fully what is read.

Throughout this work, we refer to stories from some of the great expeditions in history to illustrate elements and practices of the Divine Expedition. We do so knowing that a great feat in an age gone-by may be critiqued as less than noble, ethical, or ideal through the lens of contemporary culture. Nevertheless, the historical expeditions chosen illustrate the desire of people in all ages to accomplish something great and live lives that transcend the mundane existence of mere survival, safety, or pleasure.

Ask God to speak to you and make its message real in your life experience.

_____

We also draw from personal experiences to illustrate our own attempts to live out the Divine Expedition. We write with humility, realizing that no one, apart from Jesus himself, has perfectly lived out the Divine Expedition. Even the apostle Paul acknowledged that his effort to draw from God's divine power and live out His divine purposes was imperfect, saying, "Not that I have already obtained all this, or am living it out perfectly" (Philippians 3:12). Notwithstanding, like Paul, we are committed and excited to be on the journey.

We encourage you to read *The Divine Expedition* expectantly and thoughtfully. Meditate upon it—alone and together with others—until you grasp, integrate, and experience each and every element in a life-transforming way. Take hold of it like Jacob did when he wrestled with God and wouldn't let go until God blessed him (Genesis 32:22-30). Just as this encounter changed Jacob's destiny, so wrestling with the Divine Expedition will change your life. You will have to go back over certain concepts multiple times to fully reap their intended effect in your life. It is our desire that you not be content until you experience the fullness of the Divine Expedition, discovering and carrying out your intended role in it.

GRATITUDE

LINUS JR.

I dedicate this book to my friend Sean Hershey, who was fully engaged in the Divine Expedition before his life was cut short in a tragic accident on a Sierra Nevada Mountain road. Sean reminds me of William Borden (called Borden of Yale) who lived passionately and missionally at the beginning of the twentieth-century. Upon completing his undergraduate studies at Yale University and graduate work at Princeton Seminary, Borden sailed for China, stopping first in Egypt to study Arabic. While there, he contracted spinal meningitis, and at 25-years of age was dead. Written in Borden's Bible were the words "No reserves. No retreats. No regrets." Sean exhibited this same spirit and like Borden, died young but without reserves, retreats or regrets.

LINUS SR.

I want to thank my dear wife Sharon, who persevered with me before I knew Jesus. She embarked upon the Divine Expedition as a young girl and clung to it faithfully despite my antagonism toward her faith for the first three-and-a-half years of our marriage. Over the years, she has faithfully, sacrificially, and courageously partnered with me on our Divine Expedition journey together. She has played an incredible role in imparting God's love, kindness, and grace to our children, neighbors, and friends, both at home and abroad. She is evidence of God's goodness and mercy toward me, and continues to be my life partner and close companion in the adventure of the Divine Expedition.

TOGETHER

We wish to thank those who proof read, made writing places available, and provided funding for us to work on and publish *The Divine Expedition: Where Are You in the Book of Romans*? Hoping that we have not missed anyone, we especially thank Michael and Rita Warren, Leslie Colgin, Dag and Lynn Larson, Larry and Beccy DeWitt, Buddy Lindsay, Scott Watt, Bob and Pat Levings, Bill Boyd, Brad Bailey and the Westside Vineyard, Tim Holt and Seacoast Vineyard, Patricia Taylor, John Conley, and Maurius Jeffery. We also wish to thank the unnamed myriad of others who have partnered with and supported us along the way.

PART I

THE NEED FOR THE DIVINE EXPEDITION

CHAPTER 1

OVERVIEW

THE LIFE-MAP OF
THE DIVINE EXPEDITION

Nicolo, Maffeo, and MarcoPolo…, undismayed by perils or difficulties (to which they had long been inured), passed the borders of Armenia, and prosecuted their journey. After crossing deserts of several days' march, and passing many dangerous defiles, they advanced so far, in a direction between north-east and north, that at length they gained information of the Grand Kahn, who then had his residence in a large and magnificent city named Cle-men-fu (near where Peking now stands). Their whole journey to this place occupied no less than three years and a half; but, during the winter months, their progress had been inconsiderable.
—*The Travels of Marco Polo*[1]

Many of the most influential Castilian officers, and even the Portuguese pilots, were convinced that their fierce and rigid Captain General was leading them all to their deaths in his zeal to find the Spice Islands. Few among them had confidence that Magellan could lead them to the edge of the world and beyond with a reasonable chance of survival.
—*Over the Edge of the World*[2]

I am obligated...I am eager...I am not ashamed....
—Romans 1:14-16

TRANSCENDING TIME

Marco Polo[3] and Ferdinand Magellan[4] each embarked upon grand expeditions never before imagined. In the 1200s, Polo trekked from Venice to Peking (now called Beijing) and back. A merchant from the Venetian Republic, Marco Polo, along with his father and uncle, Niccolo and Maffeo, embarked upon an epic 24-year journey to Asia. Marco wrote of their travel adventures to China, throughout Asia on behalf of Kublai Khan, and their eventual return to Venice, in all covering a distance of 15,000 miles (24,140 km). His writings introduced Europeans to the lands of Central Asia and China.

In the early part of the 1500s, Magellan led five ships and 251 sailors in an attempt to do something no other ship had done before: find a westerly route to the Spice Islands. Although the expedition met with mutiny, his voyage took him west from Spain, along the eastern coast of Brazil and around the tip of South America, known today as the Straight of Magellan, until they reached the Spice Islands (an archipelago of Indonesia).

Following the death of Magellan, his ship, *Victoria*, continued in the same westerly direction and was the first to sail in one continuous direction and reach the same port it left, thus, circumnavigating the globe. It was perhaps the most important maritime voyage ever undertaken, altering the Western world's ideas about the geography of the world, ascertaining that the earth was round, that the Americas were not part of India but were actually a separate continent, and that the oceans covered most of the earth's surface.[5]

> Such adventure and discovery awaits each of us in the Divine Expedition....

Marco Polo and Ferdinand Magellan exemplify a desire in all of us for exploration and adventure. Such adventure and discovery awaits each of us in the Divine Expedition revealed in the book of Romans. This expedition transcends every culture, is relevant for every age, and is meant for every person. It is an adventure that connects us to God and His ultimate design and purpose for our lives.

REARVIEW MIRROR

Periodically, events take place that significantly impact history and serve as markers for the rest of our lives. Three that occurred in the first decade of the twenty-first century were the destruction of New York City's Twin Towers on September 11, 2001, the Southeast Asia tsunami, December 26, 2004, and the worldwide economic crisis of 2008 and beyond. These three great shocks impacted both our global and personal consciousness.

One of these crises was perpetrated by the hostility of men, the second by the fury of nature, and the third by unwise lending policies. As the news of each of these crises became known, God, who was fading in the rearview mirror of the western world's consciousness, flashed briefly into view again, at least for some. We realized afresh that we are vulnerable to such forces as evil, disaster, and greed. We awakened, even if only momentarily, to the fact that life is short, relationships are not to be taken for granted, humankind is somehow bound together, and God and goodness matter.

I (Linus Sr.) especially remember 9/11. Driving to my office in the early morning (Pacific Standard Time), I tuned in to my favorite sports information station only to find the topic was not the world of sports. Instead, it was the news that two hijacked jetliners had crashed into the Twin Towers of New York City. One of the four commercial planes commandeered by Islamic terrorists was a flight from Washington's Dulles airport scheduled to fly to Los Angeles.

My daughter, Leslie, and her husband, Sean, were returning from their honeymoon on the same airline, on the same day, on the same Washington to LA route. It wasn't until three a.m. the next morning that we knew what happened to Leslie and Sean. They called from a payphone in Halifax, Nova Scotia, Canada. Their plane, along with 65 other jumbo jets, was diverted mid-flight to Halifax. Upon landing, they sat on the airport tarmac for seventeen hours before Canadian immigration could process them and they could get to a phone to notify us that they were safe. By then all hotel rooms in Halifax were full, so they were bussed two hours north and spent the next five days in Canadian military barrack bunk beds before flights resumed and could return home.

When events like this happen, they mark us. We are prompted to reflect anew on the meaning of life. Why are we here? What is life all about? Is this all there is? Is there a greater purpose to life? Where can we find it? These questions are often suppressed into our subconscious minds, as we are absorbed with everyday matters. They resurface, however, in times of crisis. The book of Romans addresses these questions and reveals the meaning and mission for which God created us. The message of Romans is that God has designed us to play a role in a grander story.

THE DIVINE EXPEDITION AND THE APOSTLE PAUL

The person God used to unfold the Divine Expedition was the apostle Paul (then called Saul, his Hebraic or Aramaic name). Paul was Jewish by birth and religion but Roman by citizenship. He was fluent in Aramaic and Greek and probably spoke Latin as well.

Paul was entrenched in the values and worldview of his first century Jewish religion and culture, and thus held a rigid interpretive framework to life. He lived during the lifetime of Jesus Christ[6] and the initial spread of the predominantly Jewish movement of Jesus' followers. But unlike these followers of Jesus, Paul was adamant that Jesus was a fraud and not the promised Messiah His followers believed Him to be. Paul believed that Jesus was guilty of sedition and deserved the violent death he suffered. He saw the movement of Christ's followers as a devious threat to his religious and cultural worldview, so he began to aggressively persecute Christians with a goal of stamping out this fledgling, cultish movement.

Unexpectedly, however, Paul's worldview was jolted as he encountered Jesus on the road to the Syrian capital, Damascus. This encounter made him conscious that the crucified, dead, and buried Jesus was now resurrected and alive. The impact on Paul was immediate, altering the direction of his life. It took several years for him to fully grasp the implications of his encounter with Jesus—and it took the rest of his life to live them out. His whole life was transformed from being one of the greatest antagonists to the Christian movement to becoming one of its greatest advocates.[7]

The first thing Paul did after encountering Jesus was to withdraw and rethink his culturally-bound Jewish understanding of the Old Testament Scriptures and what they said about a coming Messiah. Encountering Jesus transformed his interpretation of Old Testament prophecies, comprehending that they were fulfilled in Jesus. He realized that the longings, salvation, and future of the Jewish people, indeed those of all humanity, were wrapped up in a belief in and relationship with Messiah-Jesus. Grasping all of this catapulted Paul to proclaim the message of hope and salvation in Jesus.

LETTER TO ROME

It was to this same Paul that God revealed the details of the Divine Expedition. Paul referred to it as "the good news" or "the gospel." Wherever he traveled, he verbally presented its message, doing so in shortened or expanded form, depending upon the time he had to deliver it. He penned the basic outline of the Divine Expedition and sent it in advance of his visit to the followers of Jesus in Rome. In his letter to these Roman Christians, Paul presents God's Master Plan for each person's rescue, transformation, empowerment, and purpose in life.

My own (Linus Sr.) breakthrough understanding of the message of Romans came during a trip to Gordon College in Wenham, Massachusetts. Upon a late afternoon arrival, I was informed that I was to give a presentation to a class of youth leaders the following morning. Not aware of this earlier, I felt a surge of anxiety. I was not prepared and had no idea what to talk about. It was already late, and without my normal study resources, I decided to go to bed early and wait until the next morning to gather my thoughts. I drifted off to sleep offering up a prayer of anxiety: "GOD, HELP!"

> It was to this same Paul that God revealed the details of the Divine Expedition.

When I awoke, a thought popped into my mind in the form of a question: "Where are you in the Book of Romans?" I heard this asked many years before by someone speaking on Paul's epistle to the Romans. The question had burrowed somewhere into my sub-conscious and resurfaced that morning. I quickly reread Paul's letter to the Romans, jotting down an outline of what might be relevant to a group of youth leaders. God not only gave me the message I needed that morning, but also unfolded to me a fresh understanding of Romans as The Divine Expedition.

RESCUE AND RESTORE

What is the Divine Expedition? It is a mission of rescue and restoration. It is, in fact, the good news of God's mission to rescue and restore us. He rescues us from our lostness and brokenness and restores to us His Divine design and purpose. This rescue and restoration is accomplished through the redemptive, transforming, resurrection power of Jesus Christ. Once rescued and restored ourselves, we are enlisted to rescue and restore others.

This rescue and restore mission in Romans is presented as an intentionally sequential and progressive expedition for us to embark upon. It is a life-map that guides us on a journey, leading us from one point of discovery, transformation, and action to the next. The expedition revealed in Romans begins with the first chapter of Romans, unfolds throughout the book, and culminates in the final chapter (Romans chapter sixteen).

> The Divine Expedition is the good news of God's mission to rescue and restore us.

I (Linus Jr.) spent a month in the Olympic Mountain wilderness as a part of a NOLS (National Outdoor Leadership School) course. The Olympic Wilderness is one of the most diverse wilderness areas in the United States, the heart of which is made up of the rugged Olympic Mountains and some of the most pristine forests left south of the 49th Parallel. The temperate rainforest valleys of the west and south flanks of the mountains receive 140 to 180 inches of precipitation annually. The Olympic Wilderness also contains 48 miles of wilderness coast with its beaches, rugged headlands, tide pools, seastacks and coastal rainforests.

During my Olympic Wilderness expedition, our team had to constantly consult a map of the Olympic wilderness, without which we risked losing our bearings, becoming lost, and placing ourselves at risk. A successful expedition requires an ability not only to follow a map, but also discernment and judgment to navigate the map in relation to the team, the surrounding conditions, the weight of the load being carried, the time of day or night, and many other variables. Without the map we become lost; without discernment and judgment we can't make sense of the map and get to the destination we are seeking.

Following my Olympic Mountain adventure, I was with a fellow surfer who possessed considerable wealth, owned a million dollar Malibu, California home, and had unlimited time and resources to pursue his interests. While he had all these things going for him, his life was empty. He lacked a life-map. Instead, he was searching for an "Aha" moment that would give clarity and meaning to his life. Perhaps it would be the perfect wave. Maybe it would be a new possession. Just possibly it would be a new relationship. Unfortunately, he was living without the life-map of the Divine Expedition. He lacked direction and discernment to know what his life was all about.

As I interacted with my surfer friend, I couldn't help contrast the meaning and purpose I have because of the life-map of the Divine Expedition with my friend's sense of uncertainty about the meaning of his life. I don't possess the wealth or possessions of my friend, but I have a deep sense of why I am here and the meaning of my life. The Divine Expedition is the map that has kept me from becoming lost, and with it has come the direction and discernment I need to navigate life.

As we embark upon the Divine Expedition, we discover the purpose for which God created us and develop into the people God designed us to be. The farther we journey along the Divine Expedition, the more purposeful and fulfilled we become. We are transformed as we connect with Jesus and experience God's work in us. We increasingly shed the cynicism, selfishness, hopelessness, and helplessness that cripple us and keep us from making a positive impact in our world.

FINDING OUR HEARTS

Sadly, there is an underlying despair in our world as so many people lack the life-map revealed in Romans. Eighteenth century philosopher Henry David Thoreau captured this, reportedly saying, "most men (people) live lives of quiet desperation." Poet T.S. Eliot pointed to the emptiness and despair of Western culture in his poem "Hollow Men," writing: "This is the way the world ends, this is the way the world ends, this is the way the world ends, not with a bang but a whimper." John Eldredge noted in his book *Wild at Heart* that most men (Eldredge was writing specifically to men) live lives of boredom and duty. They are separated from their hearts and need a deeper sense of purpose.[8]

In contrast to lives of desperation, emptiness, hollowness, purposelessness, and lives separated from our hearts, God reveals to us in Romans the adventure and purpose each of us seek. Eldredge says that in the heart of every man is a desperate desire for a "battle to fight," "an adventure to live," and "a beauty to rescue."[9] John and Stasi Eldredge address together the mystery of a woman's heart in their book Captivating, pointing out that in the heart of each woman is also a desire to play an irreplaceable role in a great adventure.[10] The adventure begins with encountering Jesus and journeying on the Divine Expedition. Encountering Jesus and embarking upon the Divine Expedition reveal the pathway to fulfill these desires and become the kind of man or woman who lives from the heart.

> The adventure begins with encountering Jesus.

MY JOURNEY-OUR JOURNEY

I (Linus Sr.) had no concept of my life's meaning and purpose until I was 23-years-old. I didn't believe in God and reasoned that if I needed religion, I could invent my own. Deep down inside me, however, was a sense of emptiness that nothing satisfied. I was married, had a child, was about to graduate with an electrical engineering degree from Oregon State University, and had a lucrative career ahead of me—yet something was still missing. Everything looked promising from the outside, but at the core of my being was the hollowness T.S. Eliot wrote about. I was living for myself and by my own means. My marriage was a mess because of my insecurity, self-centeredness, and compulsion to control. In my reflective moments (which I tried to block out), something within me queried, "So what?" "Is this all there is?" "Is there some deeper and greater purpose other than that we are born, live, and die?"

Fortunately, some friends introduced me to Jesus and the message of the Divine Expedition. I entered into this new adventure, gradually experiencing the restoration of God's design in my life, and launching farther and farther on the journey of the Divine Expedition. I continue to activate further and further the sequential parts of the expedition unfolding in Romans.

In the pages that follow we are more concerned about illuminating the overall flow of the message of Romans than we are in elaborating its every detail. We seek to give an aerial view of the stages and themes of the life-map of the Divine Expedition so that the reader can activate each and every stage. One step leads to the next, and then the next step leads to the next. It is a step-by-step journey as each chapter is the staging point for the next.

The Divine Expedition is like journeying through a passageway or portal. It is a journey in time and space, leading to a new connectedness with God, an inner personal transformation, a closer sense of community with others, and a life-long, transcending purpose for our lives. As we enter into the various aspects of the Expedition we increasingly journey from death to life, from darkness to light, from the temporal to the eternal, from meaninglessness to meaningfulness, from self-reliance to God-reliance, from impotence to empowerment, from despair to hope, from isolation to community, and from self-absorption to a passionate sense of mission.

> "Where am I in the book of Romans?"

THE QUESTION TO ASK

As the Divine Expedition unfolds, each of us must ask the question, "Where am I in this Expedition; where am I in the book of Romans?" The answer to this question will determine our personal, even eternal, wellbeing. It will determine whether or not we find the true and ultimate meaning of our lives. The question of where we are in the book of Romans can also be asked collectively of our family, our workplace, our community, our organization, our church, and our ministry. "Where are *we* in the book of Romans?" "Have *we* embarked upon the Divine Expedition?" "Where are *we* in that journey?"

We, the two Linuses, believe that the Divine Expedition is meant not only as a guide-map for each individual, but also as a template for our families and communities. Our response to the Divine Expedition not only determines our individual future and well-being, but also that of our families, ministries, churches, society—and our entire world. It is our hope that you, the reader, will make it your goal to grasp and lean into every part of the Expedition from beginning to end. The ultimate purpose and fulfillment of your life depends upon it. It is your destiny.

CHAPTER 2

SETTING
THE FOCUS OF
THE DIVINE EXPEDITION

Two books became my climbing inspiration. One was "Camp Six" by Frank Smythe, and the other "Nanda Devi" by Eric Shipton. With Smythe I climbed every weary foot of the way up the North side of Everest. I don't think I have ever lived a book more vividly. I suffered with Smythe the driving wind and the bitter cold and the dreadful fight for breath in the thin air. And when he was finally turned back at 28,000 feet, I didn't regard it as a defeat but a triumph.

Shipton's story struck a different chord—one that I could more readily understand. For Shipton in his Himalayan explorations and climbs epitomized for the New Zealander the ideal in mountaineering. His problems, although on a larger scale, were the same as ours: the problems of limited finance, of the difficulty in moving too quickly through tough, inaccessible country, of the need to carry all your own supplies, and of the constant battle against rain and weather and sheer misery.

—Sir Edmund Hillary[1]

As for preparations, his main tasks were threefold: The first was to find good men for the journey....
— *Shackleton's Way*[2]

Rather, as it is written: 'Those who were not told about him will see, and those who have not heard will understand.'
— Romans 15:21

ARDUOUS ADVENTURE

New Zealander Edmund Hillary was sixteen before he ever saw a mountain, having never been more than fifty miles (80 kilometers) outside of Auckland. He describes himself as a tall, bony, clumsy-looking youth, far from being the brightest lad in his class.[3] Yet Hillary was inspired by the exploits and writings of others, such as British mountaineer Frank Smythe and British explorer Eric Shipton. Inspired thusly, Hillary and his Nepalese fellow climber, Tenzing Norgay, went on to become the first men to reach the top of Mt. Everest, the world's highest point, at a height of 29,035 feet or 8,850 meters.

Hillary's first expedition to the Himalayas was from August 28 to November 17, 1951. This led to the discovery of the southern route up Everest, although his mountaineering party did not ascend it. His second trip was from April 19 to June 8, 1952, when he participated in grueling Himalayan training, awaiting the outcome of a failed Swiss team's attempt on Everest. His third and finally successful assault on the mountain was part of a 1953 expedition led by Colonel John Hunt.

The book Hillary later wrote, *High Adventure: The True Story of the First Ascent of Everest,* describes his trek and near mishaps in unforgiving conditions up Everest. He faced brutal weather shifts over chaotic icefalls and unstable snow ledges as he and his climbing partner ascended the mountain. His memoir points to the human drive to explore, to understand, to risk, and to conquer.

FROM CITY TO CITY

The book of Romans introduces us to an adventure no less challenging—the Divine Expedition. Contained in its pages is a venture that God intends for every person and every community of mankind. Its message is an outline of what the apostle Paul presented as he traveled from city to city. When forced to move on quickly, as in Thessalonica[4], Paul gave a condensed version, leaving behind or later sending a close companion to assist those who embraced the Expedition message.[5] When afforded more time, as in Ephesus, where Paul taught for two years[6], he elaborated more fully the Divine Expedition, grounding people in its concepts, mentoring them in its practices, and establishing an ongoing community made up of those who responded. He trained leaders to nurture others and further spread the message. He also paid return visits and wrote letters to address questions or problems that surfaced.

The message of the Divine Expedition had a tremendous impact wherever it spread—but the cost to Paul and those like him who proclaimed its message was severe. Like the near mishaps and unforgiving conditions up Everest experienced by Hillary and his fellow climbers, Paul speaks of the ardors of imprisonments, beatings, and ship-wreck. His list of hardships included frequent journeys, danger from rivers, danger from robbers, danger from his own people (Jews), danger from Gentiles (non-Jews), danger in the city, danger in the wilderness, danger at sea, and danger from false brothers. Paul experienced toil, sleepless nights, hunger, thirst, cold, and exposure. In spite of these hardships, like a parent concerned for a child, he expressed a constant concern for the well-being of the communities he started.[7]

> The message of the Divine Expedition had a tremendous impact wherever it spread.

BEGINNINGS IN ROME

Paul had not visited Rome before writing his letter of Romans. The first followers of Jesus in Rome were Jews and converts to Judaism who had visited Jerusalem for the Jewish festival of Pentecost[8] fifty days after Jesus ascended. These pilgrims saw strange Holy Spirit phenomena and heard Peter proclaim that Jesus was both Lord and Christ. Peter grounded his declaration upon Jesus' fulfillment of Old

Testament prophecies, His performing of miracles, signs, and wonders, and His resurrection from the dead.[9]

Hearing Peter's message, these visitors to Jerusalem from Rome, along with many others from around the Roman Empire (3000 in all), embraced Jesus as the promised Old Testament Messiah.[10] The new followers of Jesus from Rome returned to their home city where they began to meet together, forming the nucleus of a new community of Christ-followers and a Divine Expedition missional outpost.

Virtually all of the earliest followers of Jesus were Jewish. Roman authorities viewed the young community of Christ-followers as a Jewish sect, which afforded the fledgling movement the same legal rights and privileges as those of the larger Jewish community. As part of an officially recognized religion, Jews were exempt from the state-enforced emperor worship.

Over time, more and more non-Jews embraced Jesus as Messiah and joined the colony of predominantly Jewish Christ-followers. Within this now mixed community, two factions developed. Both groups believed Jesus was the promised Jewish Messiah but held different views of which Old Testament religious practices were binding. Those from non-Jewish backgrounds believed you could follow Jesus without being bound to Jewish culture. Those with Jewish roots, in contrast, were convinced it was essential to observe Jewish customs and laws and in effect remain (or become) culturally Jewish. This latter group reasoned that since God revealed Himself originally to Israel, the customs and laws He gave Moses were binding for all believers for all time.

The outcome of this dispute was critical to this new outpost of Christ's followers in Rome (and elsewhere). If following Jesus meant you must become culturally Jewish, then participation in the Divine Expedition would be limited to those willing to assimilate into the culture of Judaism, embracing its dietary laws, Sabbath regulations, and other rules and observances. Contrastingly, if to follow Jesus you could remain

> Those from non-Jewish backgrounds believed you could follow Jesus without being bound to Jewish culture.

culturally Roman (or some other culture), and not be bound by Jewish laws and culture, then the Jesus mission could spread rapidly, adapting to, permeating, and impacting multiple cultures.

AN EVEN BIGGER CONFLICT

The internal dispute between Jewish and non-Jewish followers of Jesus was eclipsed by an even greater conflict between Christ-followers (both Jew and non-Jew) and the larger Jewish community residing in Rome. Traditional Judaic leaders argued that to embrace Jesus as Messiah meant you ceased to be Jewish altogether and were not, therefore, entitled to the legal privileges Rome afforded to Judaism. The Judaic religious leadership was so adamant in this stance that they took their case to the Roman authorities in hopes of officially disconnecting Jesus' followers from Judaism and eliminating their rights under Roman law. This dispute was put before the Roman emperor Claudius himself, who, rather than take sides, responded by expelling *all* Jews from Rome, regardless of whether they believed in Jesus as Messiah or not.

> Claudius rather than take sides, responded by expelling all Jews from Rome.

The expulsion of Jews from Rome in 49 A.D. was a mixed blessing to the non-Jewish followers of Jesus remaining behind. Since Jewish Christians made up a substantial part of the Roman church, their departure meant the loss of mature leadership well grounded in the Old Testament Scriptures. At the same time, the exodus of Jews had a positive effect on the young church, giving it a respite from the hostile pressure of traditional Jews. A more subtle benefit was that the departure of culturally conservative Jewish followers of Jesus allowed the church to take on a more distinctly non-Jewish Roman cultural flavor. Consequently, the now twenty-plus-years-old body of Christ-followers began to morph in style, becoming more culturally attractive to the predominantly non-Jewish (Gentile) population of Rome.

> The returning Jewish followers of Jesus discovered a different church than the one they left.

This respite lasted seven years until Claudius' death in 56 A.D. (Some scholars put this at 54 A.D.), after which his edict lapsed. As the expelled Jewish community filtered back to Rome, the returning Jewish followers of Jesus discovered a different church than the one they left. During the seven years of their absence, the church underwent a significant shift in cultural feel and style of ministry. This resulted in a fresh tension between those who wanted the church to return to the way it had been and those who preferred to keep the changes.

NEED TO REFOCUS

One of Paul's underlying purposes in writing to the Roman church was to help the Roman followers of Jesus, Jew and non-Jew alike, to shift their focus from divisive cultural issues to the unifying core message and mission of the Divine Expedition. His concern was that they grasp afresh the essentials of the faith and mission they shared in common. It was imperative that they do so in order to have a greater impact on others in Rome and beyond.

Similarly, many Christians today miss the essence of what it means to be a Christ-follower. They have a skewed perspective of their purpose and mission that is shaped either by the dominant culture around them or a particular Christian subculture of which they are a part. They slide between the poles of not being much different in values and behavior from the surrounding culture or being strangely different because they have been absorbed by a Christian subculture that the dominant culture finds repulsive.

Jesus' call is for us to make an impact on the world! While many good churches and vibrant Christians do make a difference, the sad reality is that many do not. The latter are often oblivious to how much of their thinking and behavior is permeated by the dominant culture around them. They are like fish floating downstream, drifting with the culture in terms of their values, aspirations, and behavior. At the same time, many of those seeking to swim upstream are caught up in living from a particular Christian subculture. The result is that their focus is spent trying to preserve or maintain a subculture, rendering them ineffective in terms of impacting the world beyond their sub-cultural enclave.

Every group has a tendency to pick out certain external and superficial boundary markers, such as what we wear, what we do, and what we don't do, that reflect the cultural identity of the group. These identify who belongs and who does not, who is in and who is out. All of us are part of one culture (and subculture) or another. The error is, however, applying these external markers to spirituality and salvation. Jesus bypassed the Pharisaic sub-cultural boundary markers of his day (Sabbath rules, etc) and instead emphasized the condition of the heart. He declared that God desired inner spiritual and moral transformation, not external cosmetic alteration.

It is imperative that we ask are we really following Jesus or are we following a boundary marker approach to life or religion? Are we more identified by the conventions of the overarching dominant culture or some particular Christian subculture to which we belong, or are we reflecting Christ's transforming power and purposes? It is only the latter that will result in Christianity once again becoming a grassroots movement that impacts and changes the surrounding world.

LETTER TO THE CHURCH

Several years ago, I (Linus Sr.) wrote to the leadership of a church and made some observations about the entrenched subculture that I believed inhibited its ability to impact the surrounding community. Like the conservative branch of the church at Rome, this church was more bent on preserving its cultural preferences than it was in reaching the community around it. The same letter could be written to many churches in the western world. Leaving out my introduction and closing remarks, I have included the essential part of the letter and put in bold letters the main points I wanted to get across:

Let me say that I have a deep love for the church and respect its leadership. I frame my comments with the knowledge that I have a clear missional bias for what I think the focus of the church ought to be. **I believe that a major function of the church is to reach lost people for Christ.** I understand and have written about the multiple purposes of the church, so I know that outreach is not the sole ministry of the church. At the same time, I believe that in today's increasingly post-Christian American society, it is important that the church recapture the New Testament apostolic or missional mind-set.

I believe **the community around us is seeking spiritually**. After attending the church service a few Sundays ago, I walked home, and enroute strolled through the Self Realization Fellowship campus [a Western expression of Hinduism]. The parking lot and services were full. So was the overflow parking lot. I scouted out the service and observed many people listening intently. (Please understand that I know that SRF is a universalistic form of Eastern/ Hindu philosophy. Some years ago I did a series in the church adult class critiquing world religions and cults and included SRF in this. I was not there to validate SRF but to check it out.)

What my visit told me is that people are seeking spiritually although I believe they are looking in the wrong places. I am convinced that some of these could be reached for Christ, and that God has, as Paul put it, "many people in this city." In other words, there are many more people within reach of the gospel and our church.

To impact our surrounding community with the gospel, **the issue of the church's culture and its underlying values has to be addressed.** I am not talking about core values such as belief that the Bible is God's authoritative word, or our belief that Jesus Christ is God's one and only Son, or that the gospel is the power of God for salvation, or that Jesus was born of a virgin, etc. I am talking about other values which are more subtle, involving the attitudes of its staff and members, the ambiance of its ministries and services, and the way we do things at the church.

Every nation, organization, ministry, church, family, and person is steeped in culture, which is made up of a set of behaviors, values, beliefs, and atmosphere that we share in common with some and that also set us apart from others. While I see a number of positives about the church, **there** are a number of factors that I believe inhibit the church from being more effective in having a greater impact in the surrounding community.

First, there is a formal, religious feel to the church. The fact that ushers and elders dress up in professional attire gives the feel of formality rather than accessibility in the casual beach culture setting we are in. While this may appeal to those who have a traditional church background (where people dress up to go to church), it is off-putting to those who did not grow up in that culture.

Second, there is an unfriendly feel to the church. I do not mean that people in the church are unfriendly. It has some wonderfully friendly people. The problem is that they are friendly to those whom they already know. As a result, there is a cliquish feel to the church as members are passive toward newcomers. Members gravitate toward those they already know. Greeters and ushers do not appear to be on the lookout for new people, apart from handing out a brochure during the service.

Third, there is a non-emotive, overly cognitive, controlled feel to the church. The messages are predominantly informational in orientation. The worship leader talks between every song. There seems to be an overly Greek influence in the church's understanding of spirituality and maturity; that is, spiritual growth occurs by educating the mind, or knowing and believing certain information or truth. Sermons are primarily cognitive and informational. Seldom are there personal illustrations of the points that would touch the heart and move the emotions. There appears to be a distrust of emotions, feelings, and experience. My guess is that this comes in part from the influence of the Enlightenment that discounts anything that cannot be rationally explained. It may also be an overreaction to the Pentecostal and Charismatic movement's overemphasis on experience.

Fourth, the church is excessively believer-centered and insular. It appears to me that outreach to the community is minimal. Even the primary outreach vehicle of the church (a Christian school) is oriented in large part toward meeting believers' needs and protecting members' children from the influence of the surrounding culture. I commend the vision the church has for this, but believe more emphasis needs to be placed on outreach and creating mutiple contact points with the community and multiple entry points into the church. An example of the kind of shift I believe is needed relates to a sermon you gave following the September 11th tragedy. The emphasis of that sermon was on comforting church members. I felt a tremendous opportunity was missed to mobilize church members to reach out to those in the community around us who are "without God and without hope."

Lastly, the church is primarily clergy and teaching dominated. Sunday School classes are mostly taught by the pastoral staff. Small group ministry is minimal. Reproduction of leadership and new churches appears to be minimal as well. The church is not sufficiently mobilizing its lay people. It is more a teaching center than an equipping center. Because it does not sufficiently mobilize lay people, impart vision, and equip them for ministry, church members are prone to be passive. Members apear to attend church to learn, but do not seem to have a vision to reach the community around them or discover and use their spiritual gifts.

I am encouraged to say that the pastor took to heart some of my observations and significant changes have taken place. This has not been easy for some and some have left the church due to the changes made.

MISSION NOT MAINTENANCE

One of the challenges of the Divine Expedition is to be clear about our mission. Just as Hillary knew his goal was to summit Everest and Shackleton's knew his objective was to reach the South Pole, so our mission is the rescue of those not-yet connected to Jesus so that God's design can be restored to them. Too many organizations (including churches) and individuals descend into self-preservation and lose their sense of purpose. Our mission is not the maintenance of a subculture, organization, or a life-style, but the transformation of lives around us. It is to rescue people and restore them to the fullness of God's design that sadly has been marred and lost.

> Our mission is not the maintenance of a sub-culture but the transformation of lives around us.

Throughout history, whenever people grasp and embrace the message of the Divine Expedition, they are transformed within and turn outward in love and compassion toward others. I (Linus Sr.) am an example of this as I was immersed in my own wants and needs as a soon-to-graduate university student. Upon grasping the core message of the Divine Expedition and opening my life to Jesus, I experienced His transforming power in my life and turned outward with a sense of mission and purpose. Over time, the nuances of the Divine Expedition became clearer and clearer, challenging me to follow Jesus as the Lord of my life. Embarking upon this journey changed my marriage (which was in jeopardy), my worldview, the direction of my life, and the way I treated others. It realigned the focus of my life from centering on self to caring for and reaching out to others. My journey on the Divine Expedition has been a great adventure that continues to unfold. It has led me to take risks (including writing the letter to the church above) and continually open myself to what God wants to do in and through me.

I (Linus Jr.) embarked upon the Divine Expedition at a small, conservative (that's my nice way of saying legalistic), Christian, liberal arts school. Being on my own for the first time was an exciting time of life for me—but I was confused. Too many who claimed to be Christians didn't appear to have much vibrancy in their faith. Their focus was on keeping rules, not "messing up," and playing it safe (they called this "being holy"). It appeared to me that they were missing the adventure that following Jesus is meant to lead to. There was more of an emphasis on *staying away from* the world than there was in *engaging* those in it with the good news of Jesus. Being around such a pseudo-Christian subculture caused me to think, "I believe in God and Jesus—but there is no way I want to live like that." Fortunately, I grew to realize that Jesus invites us into a larger adventure than keeping rules and playing it safe.

God's plan for us is not static. He wants to use us in the lives of others. This includes sharing the good news of the Divine Expedition with those around us. Our family has lived this way and has seen many others experience spiritual transformation, healing, wholeness, and new meaning in their lives.

Part of the adventure God has for us is to summit the *tough, inaccessible country* of skepticism and cultural bias with the message of the good news of Jesus. Although challenging, a life bent rescuing and restoring others to God's design and purpose results in joy, satisfaction, and fulfillment. God invites us into a much bigger story and mission. He invites us into the great Expedition of collaborating with Him into the adventurous unknown.

CHAPTER 3

ROMANS 1:1-15
THE MINDSET OF
THE DIVINE EXPEDITION

I want to go as far as I think it possible for man to go.
—Captain James Cook[1]

After months in the wilderness, harsh jungle conditions and the river's punishing rapids had left the expedition on the verge of disaster. Roosevelt and his men had already lost five of their seven canoes and most of their provisions, and one man had perished. What lay around the next bend was anyone's guess. Even Colonel Candido Rondon, the expedition's Brazilian co-commander, who had explored more of the Amazon than any other man alive, had no idea where the uncharted river would take them.
—*The River of Doubt*[2]

Paul, a servant of Christ Jesus, called to be an apostle and set apart for the good news of God...
—Romans 1:1

Through Him and for His name's sake, we received grace and apostleship....

—Romans 1:5[3]

PURSUIT OF ADVENTURE

Martin Dugard, writing about the legendary English explorer Captain James Cook and his sea-going exploits, asks, "Why do people who are otherwise deeply content feel the need to risk all—family, career, and even life—to pursue adventure?" The gist of his question predates Cook and is so very evident in today's world in which people crave to scale sheer rock faces, hang glide high above the earth, sail the globe, or cling to inflatable rafts through white water rapids. According to Dugard, adventurers hold life in higher esteem than the general populace. By pushing limits and confronting fears, "life becomes sweeter, more easily savored moment by moment."[4]

> Adventurers hold life in higher esteem than the general populace.

Cook exemplifies the desire to push limits. While serving in the British Navy in North America as master of the ship *Pembroke*, Cook mapped much of the St Lawrence River entrance and the rugged Newfoundland coastline. On his first voyage commanding the ship *Endeavor*, from 1768-1771, Cook surveyed the complete New Zealand coastline before reaching the southeastern coast of the Australian continent. His expedition then became the first from Europe to encounter Australia's eastern coastline. Continuing northward from there, he passed (and became stuck upon for seven weeks) the Great Barrier Reef. He subsequently returned to England via Batavia (modern Jakarta, Indonesia), the Cape of Good Hope, and the island of Saint Helena. Two more voyages followed, the last of which cost Cook his life at the hands of the native Hawaiians.

Another limit-pusher, Theodore Roosevelt, the twenty-sixth President of the United States (1901-1909), pushed limits and confronted fears throughout his life, turning to intense physical exertion as a means of overcoming setbacks and sorrow. From his earliest childhood, Roosevelt chose action over inaction and championed what he termed the "strenuous life." This approach compelled him forward in public life and lifted him above a succession of personal tragedies and disappointments.[5]

Frail and sickly as a child and plagued by life-threatening asthma, Roosevelt engaged in a regimen of harsh physical exercise to overcome his weakness. To deal with his grief upon the death of his mother and his wife, he set out for the Dakota Badlands, where he spent himself in the unfamiliar world of danger on the American frontier.[6]

Roosevelt's impulse to defy hardship became a fundamental part of his character and lay behind his decision to go to Brazil to explore the Rio da Duvida, the River of Doubt, a previously unmapped, 1000-mile (1600-kilometer), churning, ink-black tributary of the Amazon River. Suffering defeat in his effort to return to the White House in 1912, he could not rest until he found some physically demanding adventure. What could be more challenging than venturing into the dense jungles of the Amazon and exploring a river in its vast, tangled expanse![7]

GREATER CAUSES

Like Cook and Roosevelt, there is something that beckons all of us beyond mere human survival, personal peace, or affluence. Each of us is designed to embark upon the Divine Expedition. This expedition orients us outside ourselves to a greater purpose and a higher cause. It releases us from the grip of navel-gazing, self-absorption, and self-centeredness. Instead of seeking to align everything in the universe to us, the Divine Expedition aligns us with God and the universe He created. It connects us to the larger cosmic story playing out in history, a story in which Jesus, history's greatest hero, comes to rescue and restore us from the damage a sinister dark lord has wrought in and around us. But this is more than a story—it is the reality in which the drama of our lives is played out.

Eastern philosophy directs us to detach ourselves from the world and contemplate within. In contrast, the Divine Expedition summons us to engage the world around us with a divine purpose. Many endeavors that occupy people's everyday lives are self-centered in their purpose, such as personal thrill seeking, hope for fame and wealth, a search to be loved and accepted, and many more. The Divine Expedition, however, orients us to live beyond self and seek the wellbeing of others, not unlike the motto of the Coast Guard seen in the movie *The Guardian*: "That others may live."

The more we orient ourselves to the Divine Expedition, the more we are moved to love others and reach out to them in life-giving ways. The less we embrace and engage in it, the more likely we are to be consumed by our own selves, struggles, problems, desires, and needs. The statement "The smallest package in the world is the person all wrapped up in him- or herself!" applies here.

> The more we orient ourselves to the Divine Expedition, the more we are moved to love others. . .

As part of our family's journey to be on expedition, we moved to Amsterdam to start a new Christ-following community called the Crossroads International Church. One woman who became a part of our work was named Fineke. She is a young Dutch woman who was raised in a family that tried to find identity and significance through religion and sex. Her parents exposed her to such things as Buddhism, New Age, and Rosicrucianism. Part of her initiation along the way was to experience a heightened level of sexual stimulation and indulgence. She was told that love didn't matter.

Fortunately, Fineke began reading the Bible and saw that Jesus said, "Love one another." She also met some Christ-followers who were not self-absorbed, seeking meaning through some deeper spiritual or sexual experience, like her parents and their friends. Instead, these Christians were full of love, joy, kindness, and compassion toward others. Fineke felt her personhood was violated in the world in which she grew up, but she found in Jesus and her new Christian friends a fresh identity and sense of wellbeing. As she embraced Jesus and embarked upon the Divine Expedition, she felt release from the anxiety and self-doubt that dominated her. Her sense of humor emerged and she found joy in a gift of hospitality, which she is learning to develop and express.

APOSTOLIC/MISSIONAL PASSION

In Romans chapter one, Paul calls us to an outward "that others may live" mindset. He comprehends his own life in terms of service and apostleship (1:1). The word "apostle" means "one who is sent." An apostle is a person who is sent on a mission with a message. This Greek word *apostolos* was later translated into Latin by the word, *missionary.* Paul is passionately "apostolic" or "missional" in his mindset. He has a sense that he has been called and sent to be a part of a greater cause. This cause is to rescue those who are lost, restore to them the Divine Design, and help them find God's purpose for their lives, so that they too might embark upon the Divine Expedition.

Paul writes in his letter to Timothy: "Christ Jesus came into the world to save [rescue] sinners."[8] He says to the fledgling Galatians Christian community, "Grace and peace to you from God our Father and the Lord Jesus Christ, who gave himself for our sins to rescue us from this present evil age" (Galatians 1:3). This passion to rescue and save others is also seen in Paul's letter to the Christ-following community in Corinth: "To the weak I became weak, to win the weak. I have become all things to all men so that by all possible means I might save some. I do all this for the sake of the gospel."[9] This apostolic mindset is exhibited in the first chapter of Romans where Paul speaks of serving with his whole heart in telling others the good news of God's Son (1:9).

Just as the Royal Society of London sent Cook to explore the Pacific Ocean, and the Brazilian government and, in part, the American Museum of Natural History sponsored Roosevelt and Rondon's expedition down the Rio da Duvida, so we are sent on a mission. The biblical meta-story is about God sending His messengers—and ultimately His Son—with a mission to rescue us.

> The biblical meta-story is about God sending His messengers and ultimately His Son, Jesus, to rescue us.

TRAPPED

Like the thirty-three gold and copper miners entombed half a mile below ground in Chile for sixty-nine days from August 5 to

October 13, 2010, humanity needs to be rescued. Jesus is, figuratively speaking, the bullet-shaped capsule that was lowered into our world to rescue us. When we entrust ourselves to Him, He lifts us to new life. He is the rescuer, and once we are rescued we become part of the rescue team He uses to rescue others. This is the message and mission of the Divine Expedition.

The Bible only makes sense when it is read *relationally*, *redemptively*, and *missionally*. Its message is *relational* in that Jesus puts us in right relationship with God and with others. Its message is *redemptive* in that we are redeemed and restored to God's design for us through Jesus. Its message is apostolic or *missional* in that it calls us to engage in the rescue and restoration mission of Jesus.

> The Bible only makes sense when it is read relationally, redemptively, and missionally.

Paul saw himself as sent to communicate the message of the Divine Expedition and to enlist others to do the same. He makes it clear that the Christ-followers in Rome are also called to apostolic mission, saying, "Through him and for his name sake, we (both Paul and those to whom he was writing) received grace and apostleship to call people...to belong to Jesus Christ " (1:5). The Divine Expedition calls and orients each person and every community to participate in reaching out to rescue and restore others. Any person, family, church, or organization focused only upon his, her, or its own self falls short of the apostolic call to join the greater call of the Divine Expedition.

CALLED TO MISSION

I (Linus Sr.) remember being called to the mission of the Divine Expedition. Prior to graduating with my university degree, I was tendered several financially attractive job offers from large engineering companies. Before accepting, I was asked to consider joining the staff of the student ministry that introduced me to Christ. Unsure of which offer to take, I made a list of pros and cons for each option. One of the biggest differences was in the area of salary. The engineering option would pay me twice the money, not counting stock options. To choose student ministry, I would have to raise the funds needed to pay my salary. I went back-and-forth trying to decide which option to take until one evening I attended a ministry leadership-training event. As I stepped across the threshold of the meeting place, I had an incredible inner-sense that God wanted me to pursue the student ministry option. While not as lucrative from a financial standpoint, I have never been sorry I chose this path.

Most Christ-followers are not called to pursue a path of paid ministry—but all are called to the rescue and restoration ministry of the Divine Expedition. I (Linus Jr.) have chosen to use my training in graphic design and media production to support myself. I also have a standup paddleboard (SUP) business. In my line of work, I have many opportunities to point others to Jesus and encourage them to live out their faith just as I seek to live out mine in the everyday, work-a-day world. I am no less engaged in the Divine Expedition than someone in paid ministry. The Apostle Paul acknowledges that he had the right to be supported financially for his apostolic ministry, but he chose instead to support himself by his skill as a tent-maker.[10] I have chosen this path as well. Whether paid or not, we are enlisted to reach beyond ourselves to rescue and restore others.

> Throughout his letter to the Romans, Paul lays out the passionate, outward, apostolic, missional plan God has for us.

Paul wrote to the outpost of Christ-followers in Rome expressing his hope to visit them. His purpose was to clarify the message of the Divine Expedition and strengthen and engage them in it (1:11). He believed his upcoming visit to Rome would result in a spiritual harvest as he mobilized believers to more fully participate in rescuing others in Rome who were yet to know Christ (1:12-13). Once his mission in Rome was complete, he communicated his desire to take the good news of Jesus to faraway Spain, engaging the Roman Christians to assist him in mission there (see Romans 15:23-24).

Throughout his letter to the Romans, Paul lays out the passionate, outward, apostolic, missional plan God has for us. God initiated this plan by sending His unique Son, Jesus, to rekindle His awesome love, mercy, and purpose in our world. God's plan is that through the life-transforming grace, love, and power of Jesus, His Divine Design be restored to us, empowering us to reflect His love and reach, rescue, and restore others.

The Divine Expedition begins when we embrace Jesus as Rescuer. By doing so, His divine power is released within us and we begin the relational, redemptive, and missional expedition to which God calls us. Through His transforming power at work within us, as well as the outward, missional mindset of the Divine Expedition, we can go beyond Cook's desire "go as far as it possible for man to go." We can go "as far as it is possible for God to take us."

CHAPTER 4

ROMANS 1:16-17

THE DOORWAY OF THE DIVINE EXPEDITION

Surely the best thing Jefferson ever did as President was the Louisiana Purchase. The next-best thing Jefferson did as President was to organize, set the objectives, and write the orders for an exploring expedition across the country. He then picked Meriwether Lewis to command it and, at Lewis' insistence, William Clark became co-commander.

—Undaunted Courage[1]

Meriwether Lewis resolved: "in future, to live for mankind as I have heretofore lived for myself."

—Undaunted Courage[2]

I am not ashamed of the gospel, because it is the power of God for the salvation of everyone who believes...

—Romans 1:16

COMMISSIONED

American President Thomas Jefferson commissioned Meriwether Lewis to lead an expedition that took him westward across the

North American Continent from the Atlantic Seaboard to the Pacific Ocean. On July 4, 1803 Jefferson announced that the United States had purchased from France's Napoleon the territory of "Louisiana." This included all the country that was drained from the west by the Mississippi River, an area of 825,000 square miles, doubling the size of the country for a price of fifteen million dollars.[3]

The next day, July 5, 1803, Lewis set off. His mission was to look for an all-water route across the western two-thirds of the continent, and to discover what Jefferson had bought from Napoleon. William Clark joined Lewis in October 1803 at Clarksville, Indiana Territory, across the Ohio River from Louisville, Kentucky. Thus, it was Lewis who became the first man ever to cross the North American continent that today makes up the United States. It was Clark who on November 7, 1805 wrote the immortal line, "Ocean in view! O! The joy" upon seeing the Pacific Ocean after their trek of thousands of miles through the wild and rugged Northwest.[4]

In their exploration, Lewis and his partner, Clark, explored Missouri, Kansas, Iowa, Nebraska, the Dakotas, and Montana, all part of the Louisiana Purchase. The expedition then took Lewis and Clark across, and made possible the American acquisition of the great Northwest Empire of Idaho, Washington, and Oregon. In all, it took two years and four months to complete their expedition.

> The mission is this: to connect our world to Jesus, who rescues us....

In the same way that Jefferson enlisted Lewis and Clark for their grand exploration, God enlists us for the grand mission of the Divine Expedition. The mission is this: to connect our world to Jesus, who rescues us from spiritual deadness and restores to us God's divine design and purpose (Romans 1:1-4, 16-17).

MESSIAH-SON-KING JESUS

The Divine Expedition is God's plan to rescue us, to connect us back into relationship with Him, and to impart to us His power to make a difference in our world. The rescuer and connector is Jesus. He is the Messiah/Christ, promised hundreds of years beforehand by the Old Testament prophets. The messianic proclamation of the prophets was that God would send a rescuer of mankind. This prophetic proclamation goes back to the beginning of recorded history—to the time of Abraham and Sarah—even earlier—to the time of Adam and Eve.[5]

> The messianic proclamation was that God would send a rescuer of mankind.

In Romans chapter one, Paul connects the messianic expectation to the prophetic indication that God would send His Son (1:1-3). A thousand years before Jesus, the Psalmist wrote that the Anointed One (Messiah) would be God's unique Son. Psalm 2 quotes God as saying, "You are my Son; today I have become your Father...and I will make the nations your inheritance..." (Psalm 2:7). According to this same prophetic Psalm, the Son would also be a King who would rule the nations. They are warned in Psalm 2 to "Kiss the Son, lest he be angry." The Psalmist then adds, "Blessed are those who take refuge in him."[6]

Jesus is the prophesied Messiah-Son-King. Paul highlights two indicators as verifications of this. The first is that Jesus fits the prophetic criteria that the Messiah would be a descendent of the Israelite King David (Romans 1:2-3). The genealogies of the Gospel writers Matthew and Luke bear record to the fact that Jesus descended from David. Nathan, a Jewish prophet who lived at the time of king David, a thousand years before Jesus, prophesied that an offspring of David would come whose kingdom God would establish forever.[7] This is one of many prophecies Jesus fulfilled (for others, see endnotes).[8]

The second indicator Paul references that verifies Jesus is the promised Messiah-Son-King is the resurrection of Jesus from the dead. Paul notes that, following His brutal execution foretold by the Old Testament prophets[9], Jesus "was declared with power to be the Son of God by his resurrection from the dead" (1:3-4).[10] This too was prophesied in the Old Testament and is supported by the first century eyewitness testimony of the Gospel writers who documented Jesus' resurrection appearances.

Paul summarizes the resurrection appearances of Jesus in 1 Corinthians saying,

> "For what I received I passed on to you as of first importance: that Christ died for our sins according to the Scriptures, that he was buried, that he was raised on the third day according to the Scriptures, and that he appeared to Peter, and then to the Twelve. After that, he appeared to more than five hundred of the brothers at the same time, most of whom are still living, though some have fallen asleep. Then he appeared to James, then to all the apostles, and last of all he appeared to me also, as to one abnormally born."[11]

Various theories have been put forth attempting to explain away that Jesus was truly raised from the dead (the passionate conviction of Jesus' followers). Upon scrutiny, these theories do not adequately counter the eyewitness testimony coming to us from the first century, nor do they sufficiently explain the dramatic spread of the early Christian movement at incredible cost to the followers of Jesus. The skeptical alternative theories are speculative and lack historical verification, unlike the eyewitness testimony of the New Testament documents originating from the first century.

Prior to embracing Jesus in my own life, I (Linus Sr.) thought that Christianity was a matter of wishful thinking based on a "blind leap" of faith. I was surprised, then, when I attended a meeting where the speaker talked about "the historical evidence for the resurrection of Jesus." Prior to this, my mindset was like that of a history professor who told a student friend of mine that he couldn't write a paper on the resurrection of Jesus because, as the professor said, "There is no evidence for the resurrection of Christ!" The position of the professor was not that research has already shown conclusively that the resurrection of Jesus didn't happen. It was based on an underlying rationalistic premise that "miracles like the resurrection don't happen, because miracles can't happen." Both this professor as well as my attitude was, "my mind's made up so don't confuse me with the facts." I was stunned to learn that there was a historical reality to Jesus' life, death, and resurrection. Upon looking into the historical eyewitness testimony, I became convinced that Jesus was alive. As a result, I opened my life to Him and encountered Him as the living Messiah-Son-King.

Paul's two indicators are from the beginning and the end of Jesus' life. He could well have included the character, teaching, miracles and ministry of Jesus, but he instead chooses to compress all of this into the two primary verifiers that Jesus is the afore-told and now living Messiah-Son-King. He is the promised descendant of David and He rose from the dead. The two indicators he highlights in Romans 1:2-4 are part of a litany of compelling testimony that Jesus is the promised Messiah (Hebrew) or Christ (Greek), the Son sent from heaven, and the rightful heir to the throne of David.

LORD JESUS

Paul goes on to tell us that Jesus is more than Messiah-Son-King; He is also Lord (1:4). He states this clearly in the beginning of his letter to the Romans declaring, "Jesus Christ our Lord" (1:4). This too was foretold as the prophet Isaiah declared:

> "For to us a child is born, to us a son is given, and the government will be on his shoulders. And he will be called Wonderful Counselor, Mighty God, Everlasting Father, Prince of Peace. Of the increase of his government and peace there will be no end. He will reign on David's throne and over his kingdom, establishing and upholding it with justice and righteousness from that time on and forever. The zeal of the LORD Almighty will accomplish this."[12]

The New Testament followers of Jesus held this radical belief, proclaiming Jesus as Lord:

> "In the past God spoke to our forefathers through the prophets at many times and in various ways, but in these last days he has spoken to us by his Son, whom he appointed

heir of all things, and through whom he made the universe. The Son is the radiance of God's glory and the exact representation of his being, sustaining all things by his powerful word. After he had provided purification for sins, he sat down at the right hand of the Majesty in heaven" (Hebrews 1:1-3).

Paul reiterates this in his letter to the Colossians:

"He (Jesus) is the image of the invisible God, the firstborn over all creation. For by him all things were created: things in heaven and on earth, visible and invisible, whether thrones or powers or rulers or authorities; all things were created by him and for him. He is before all things, and in him all things hold together. And he is head of the body, the church; he is the beginning and the firstborn from among the dead, so that in everything he might have supremacy. For God was pleased to have all his fullness dwell in him (Jesus), and through him to reconcile to himself all things, whether on earth or things in heaven, by making peace through his blood on the cross." (Colossians 1:15-20)

Thus, Paul proclaims Jesus as Messiah, Son, King, and Lord. By citing Jesus as Messiah/Christ, he connects Jesus to the Old Testament messianic expectation of the Jews. By referring to Jesus as Son, Paul highlights Jesus' unique relationship with God, pre-existing with and coming from God. By connecting Jesus genealogically to David, Paul points to Jesus as the rightful King of Israel who inherits the eternal throne promised to David by the prophet Samuel (2 Samuel 7:12-14). By calling Jesus 'Lord,' Paul declares that He alone is worthy of our complete trust and allegiance.

> Paul proclaims Jesus as Messiah, Son, King, and Lord

When Paul was physically present, he assuredly elaborated upon the many Old Testament prophecies and evidences for the resurrection that point to Jesus as Messiah-Son-King-Lord. In his letter to the Romans, however, he only touches on them briefly, yet drawing attention to the fact that the fulfillment of prophecy along with the body of credible, historical, eyewitness testimony to the life, claims, ministry, death, and resurrection of Jesus commend Him as Messiah, unique Son of God, heir to the throne of David, and Lord over all. Faith in Jesus is not an irrational blind leap disconnected from reality. It is rooted in multiple prophecies and well-documented history. It actually takes more faith *not* to believe that Jesus is the Messianic risen-Christ than it does *to believe* He is.

WHY JESUS?

On a flight from Portland to Los Angeles I (Linus Sr.) sat next to a young woman who engaged me in conversation. Airplane flights are where I get most of my reading done, but it was not to be on this flight. We talked from take-off to landing. During our conversation the subject of God came up and my seatmate stated, "I believe in God; I just don't believe in Jesus."

> This Good News [about Jesus] tells us how God makes us right....

I asked, "What is it that don't you believe about Him?"

She listed things like His being born of a virgin, dying for our sins, and rising from the dead.

I replied that I didn't believe in God until I came to know Jesus and explained briefly how the things she thought didn't make sense actually fit into the grand action of God's sending His Son to rescue us.

I added, "Once we comprehend the full picture of God's action to send Jesus to rescue us, the things that don't make sense begin to do so. They are, in fact, compelling."

Departing from the plane, my flight-mate asked me to email her the name of a good book about Jesus, which I subsequently did.

What's so great about Jesus? It is not only who He is (as Paul emphasizes in the first few verses of Romans); it is also what He did and what He makes available to us. Paul says, "This Good News (about Jesus) tells us how God makes us right in his sight. This is accomplished from start to finish by faith" (1:17).[13] Jesus is the Messiah-Son-King-Lord who rescues us. He brings us into a relationship of right standing with God when we put our trust in what He did for us. Being right with God through Jesus opens the door for us to experience His life-transforming power.

THE JESUS MISSION

This is the mission of the Divine Expedition: to help others connect to God, become right in His sight, and experience His transforming power in our lives. Being made right with God through Jesus includes more than just wiping clean the slate of past failures. It opens the way for intimacy and closeness with God as Father, and it empowers us to make things right with others and the world around us. As we place our trust in Jesus, something supernatural occurs within us. We experience the presence and power of God in our lives as Jesus enters our lives and restores us to what we were designed to be.

> As we place our trust in Jesus, something supernatural occurs.

Grasping the significance of Jesus as the door to a relationship with God is transforming. As He rescues us and as we walk with Him, He restores us to His Divine Design and empowers us to love and serve others. A right relationship with God dissolves our self-centeredness and connects us with others. Instead of being isolated, often the result of the individualism of Western society, we connect to others through the love of Christ working in us. Paul points to this when he speaks of being "mutually encouraged by each other's faith" (1:12). His relationship with those following Christ in Rome is not one-sided, as teacher to pupil, but one of mutual interdependence and encouragement. It is not top-down but alongside.

A relationship with God through Jesus reorients us to the world around us, especially as we engage in the Divine Expedition. It is a new compass that allows us to navigate through life. When I (Linus Jr.) trekked the Olympic wilderness, we relied upon a compass as well as a map. The compass allowed us to know the direction we were headed. Without both compass and map, we would have lost our way—or worse. The Divine Expedition is the map that directs us, and the inner transforming work of Christ is the compass that keeps us going in the right direction.

Embracing and following Jesus point us away from self-absorption to a concern for others. Paul reflects this in his deep sense of obligation to both "Greeks and non Greeks, both to the wise and the foolish" (1:14). The first century world divided people into us/them categories: Greek/non-Greek, Roman/Barbarian, Jew/Gentile, and wise/foolish (1:15). In contrast, Paul speaks of the gospel being the power of God for the salvation of "*everyone* who believes" (1:16). This was a huge shift from the cultural pride and exclusiveness of Paul's life before he encountered Jesus.

The ultimate meaning of our lives is rooted in a relationship to Jesus and the message and mission of the Divine Expedition. Can we find meaning in life without knowing Jesus and participating in the Divine Expedition? Yes, but we will fall short of the grandeur of the grander, *ultimate* purpose for which God created us. Can we be successful in life without the Divine Expedition? Yes, relatively speaking, but we will fall short of a God-designed significance that is meant for us both now and into eternity.

> The ultimate meaning of our lives is rooted in a relationship to Jesus and the message and mission of the Divine Expedition.

GOD SHAPED VACUUM AND SPIRITUAL PAUL POTTS

Augustine of Hippo (present-day Annaba, Algeria) also known as Saint Augustine (354-430 A.D.) expressed the essence of true identity and meaning when he proclaimed, "You have made us for yourself, O God, and our hearts are restless until they find their rest in you." Pascal, the French physicist and philosopher, stated similarly, ""There is a God shaped vacuum in the heart of every man which cannot be filled by any created thing, but only by God, the Creator, made known through Jesus"[14] The Divine Expedition begins with connecting to God through Jesus Christ. Sadly, many people are trapped within the confines of skepticism and popular belief and miss the greatest purpose of life.

The story of Paul Potts, winner of "Britain's Got Talent" competition, is just one example of how true identity can be stifled. An unpolished, overweight, mobile car-phone salesman from south

Wales, Potts was bullied and lacked self-confidence growing up. Appearing before the audience and panel of judges assembled for the competition, there was little expectation for his singing until his amazing performance of the extremely difficult opera aria - Puccini's "Nessun Dorma."

As Potts began to sing, his demeanor was transformed, and the audience and judges were shocked and transfixed. His tenor voice was as good as any professional opera singer, thereafter winning the "Britain's Got Talent" competition. Potts' performance epitomized the vision of the creators of the British show to find "someone doing an ordinary job, very unassuming, quietly having an amazing talent we could provide a platform to show the world what they could do."[15] There is a spiritual Paul Potts inside each of us in terms of the design and purpose of God that is meant to emerge, and will upon embracing and following Jesus.

> There is a spiritual Paul Potts inside each of us....

Embracing the Good News about Jesus opens the doorway to a new identity and a new trajectory in life. This trajectory is the path to radiate God's love and glory and extend His mission of grace and peace to others (1:5-7). This new sense of purpose and passion that emerges is expressed in Paul's own life in the phrases: "I thank my God through Jesus Christ for all of you because your faith is being reported all over the world" (1:8); "God whom I serve with my whole heart" (1:9); "Constantly I remember you in my prayers at all times" (1:10); "I long to see you so that I may impart to you some spiritual gift to make you strong...in order that I might have a harvest among you" (1:11-13); I am obligated...I am eager...I am not ashamed.... (1:14-16). These are words of passion and purpose. They are the language of the Divine Expedition.

What is Paul so passionate about? Why does he keep referring to "good news" or "gospel?" He is passionate about the incredible good news that Jesus rescues us, connects us and restores us to intimacy with God (similar to when the first man and woman, Adam and Eve, walked with God), and empowers us to be and do that for which we are designed. When we embrace Messiah-Son-King-Lord Jesus, the same power that raised Him from the dead begins to work in us, catapulting us on an expedition greater than the one set out upon by Lewis and Clark.

Paul expands this further in the loss and restoration of the Divine Design to follow.

PART II

THE LOSS
AND RESTORATION
OF THE
DIVINE DESIGN

CHAPTER 5

ROMANS 1:18-32
THE LOSS
AND RESTORATION
OF THE DIVINE DESIGN

I felt a terrible sense of fear and loneliness. 'What was the sense of it all? A man was a fool to put up with it! And for what? Shuddering with the cold, I tried to put such unprofitable thoughts aside, and compose my mind so that the time might pass a little more quickly.
—Sir Edmund Hillary[1]

Life on polar expeditions, however, wasn't for dreamers. Antarctica is the coldest, windiest, and driest continent on earth, covered by a layer of ice up to three miles thick. It snows only one or two inches a year in the frozen desert. Fierce winds consistently whip up the dry snow, which feels more like sand. The lowest temperature ever recorded on earth was in the Antarctic, -128.6 degrees Fahrenheit (-89.2 degrees Celsius), though the mean annual temperature near the South Pole is about -70 degrees Fahrenheit.
—Shackleton's Way[2]

The vista looked like the wreck of a shattered world.
—Farther Than Any Man[3]

S.O.S. I NEED YOUR HELP. I AM INJURED, NEAR DEATH, AND TOO WEAK TO HIKE OUT OF HERE. I AM ALL ALONE, THIS IS NO JOKE, IN THE NAME OF GOD, PLEASE REMAIN TO SAVE ME. I AM OUT COLLECTING BERRIES CLOSE BY AND SHALL RETURN THIS EVENING. THANK YOU, CHRIS MCCANDLESS. AUGUST?
—Into the Wild[4]

...for all have sinned and fall short of the glory of God....
—Romans 3:23

PADDLING OUT

All expeditions face obstacles—some appear too great to overcome. For Edmund Hillary the moment of uncertainty came while on the 26,070 foot-high (7,900 meters) South Col of Mount Everest. Harsh reality flooded into his mind as he listened to the menacing, roaring wind. It flowed in a mighty, unrelenting stream over the inhospitable wastes in the "death zone" of the tallest mountain in the world. Hillary's tent was flapping in a tormented fury. He could feel the icy breath outside penetrating into his tent, through his sleeping bag, right through his down clothing and into his bones.[5] Near the top of Everest, he questioned "the sense of it all."

Ernest Shackleton and James Cook also spoke of the incredible obstacles they faced on their expeditions: freezing temperatures, fierce winds, fear, and loneliness. For most people, however, the biggest obstacle to embarking on an expedition is just getting started. They don't know there is an expedition to embark upon, they don't know where to start, or the entrapments of life grip them and keep them from moving beyond where they are.

I (Linus Jr.) remember my first try at surfing bigger waves than I had previously ridden. Professional surfing friends introduced me to "Todos Santos," a premier 20-foot (6 meters) wave in Mexico. They took me out in a boat to get closer to the wave and then encouraged me to "paddle out and drop in." I sat on my board frozen by the thought of getting thrashed by attempting to ride one of the giant waves relentlessly rolling in. The moment came when I had to choose to go for it or turn back to the safety of the boat. Fear gave way to challenge, and I went for it. Even though I got "worked," excitement, exhilaration, and a sense of accomplishment followed.

To embark upon the Divine Expedition takes a similar choice to either paddle out and drop in on the risk-ridden adventure of following Jesus, or turn back to the comfort and conformity of following culture. To use another metaphor, we can fight our way upstream with a Divine sense of mission and purpose, or we can drift downstream with the current of cultural conformity, unaware of the danger of the rapids and waterfalls of life that lay ahead that will plunge us downward.

PARADISE LOST

Beginning in Romans 1:18 and continuing until the middle of Romans chapter three, Paul paddles through the roiling rapids and plunging waterfalls of defective approaches to life. Cultural, philosophical, and religious worldviews pound against us, sweep us along, and keep us from knowing and following Jesus. Defective worldviews inhibit the adventure God designs for us.

> Paul paddles through the roiling rapids and plunging waterfalls of defective approaches to life.

The first of these thunderous waves is the worldview that God is irrelevant, or what you believe about Him doesn't matter. It is a kind of indifference or disdain toward God. Surprisingly, Paul follows by examining two more battering waves: morality and religion. Each of these approaches to life, indifference to God, morality, and religion, is similar in that they depend upon self-reliance, numbing and leading us to a false sense of satisfaction and security. Each of these worldviews obscures what it really means to be connected to God.

Thus, Paul begins unpacking the message of the Divine Expedition by addressing why we need to be rescued. Indifference toward God results in the loss of God's design for humankind. Man (male and female) was gloriously created in the image of God, but this image or design became marred and damaged as man drifted from God. We as individuals, and mankind as a whole, are not what we were created to be. Murder, war, brutality, holocaust, ethnic cleansing, environmental disaster, exploitation, greed, and much more are evidence that something is terribly wrong in our world.

Eastern religion addresses the brokenness of our world by denying the reality of evil and suffering, asserting this world and all that is in it isn't real. Not dissimilar, self-reliant overly optimistic people diminish the gravity of evil and suffering around them, thinking somehow things are getting better or will get better. Try as we might to deny evil or hope that mankind will find a way to correct the destructive course of our world, the reality is that the world isn't what it was designed to be—and mankind seems to be at the center of the problem.

Thumbing through history, we are faced with the unpleasant reality that something is broken. The universal history of mankind points to the reality that God's design for humanity has been lost. Paul pulls back the curtain and exposes the problem of man's brokenness, as well as the inadequacy of both non-religious and religious attempts to fix things. Restoring the Divine Design begins with an exposé of the damaged condition of mankind and the inadequacy of human solutions. All humankind is infected with a viral condition that distorts God's image and design.

> Restoring the Divine Design begins with exposing the damaged condition of mankind....

"THE BIG S"

My wife, Sharon, and I (Linus Sr.) were having dinner with a friend who solemnly recounted that several of her close friends were stricken with cancer—what she called "the Big C." She went on to say that all of her other friends were afraid of contracting the same thing. Her comment led me to reflect upon the sad reality that all of us, at some point or another, will be stricken with the Big

C or something just as fatal. The ratio of deaths to births is still one-to-one. Good health is just the slowest way to die.

However, Paul points to another kind of death, also with a one-death-to-one-person ratio. It is an inner spiritual malady that could be called "the Big S"—*Separation*—separation from God and His design. Our greatest malady is that we suffer from a spiritual and relational deformity that disconnects us from God and what He created us to be. Our lives, relationships, and the world around us are damaged by this separation. None of these functions the way they were designed or the way that deep down inside we wish they did.

Many people resign themselves in skepticism and cynicism to the prevailing disorder and dysfunction of our world. Others comfort themselves that things will get better if we apply the right moral action, political system, economic policy, or religious belief. Still others escape into sex, drugs, video games, the Internet, music, mystical religion, or a myriad of other escapes and pursuits.

THREE FUTILITIES

Romans 1:18-3:21 outlines three futilities; that is, three futile attempts or approaches to navigate the brokenness of our world and give life meaning. The first of these futilities is covered in this chapter and the next two are addressed in the following chapter. At first glance, this section of Romans appears to be judgmental or condemning. Paul, however, is merely shining the spotlight on the way things are. Like a good doctor diagnosing a disease, a treatment cannot be prescribed until the true nature of the malady is identified. Paul probes and exposes three non-effective and futile approaches to dealing with the problem caused by separation from God. He does so in order to direct us to the only real cure, which he presents in the middle part of Romans chapter three.

THE FIRST FUTILITY: INDIFFERENCE

The first futile approach to our separation from God and the brokenness of our world is *indifference*, indifference to God and His revelation (1:18-32). We marginalize God, suppress and rationalize away the evidence of His existence, and ignore our need to be in a dependent, intimate relationship with Him. We absorb ourselves with our own interests, ideas, and pursuits. We displace God from the center and push Him out to the margins of our lives. We replace a relationship with God with our own self-interest and reliance. We live day-to-day without acknowledging our need for Him, or only doing so minimally.

One of the ways that we justify indifference to God is to play the blame game. We shift the blame for our world's dysfunction to God. We magnify the apparent inconsistency between the existence of evil and a good and all-powerful God. How could a good God allow suffering or evil? Why doesn't an all-powerful God do something about it? Thus, we blame God for the broken state of our world, suggesting that whatever is wrong is His fault because He allows evil to exist. We rationalize that God is impotent, indifferent, doesn't exist, or doesn't matter. We become so locked into our logic that no other explanation is allowed, however reasonable it might actually be. By blaming God, we feel better about ourselves, and suppress the fact that the existence of evil is an evidence of our own dysfunction and separation from God and His goodness.

> We replace a relationship with God with our own self-reliance.

The problem with indifference to God and blaming Him for the problem of evil is that it plays out negatively in how we live. It leads to further dysfunction, brokenness, and evil. Without God's intervention, empowerment, and guidance in our lives, we are left to our inner drives, wants, and compulsions. These lead us even farther from God's design.

An example of this is my (Linus Sr.) own life. During my university days, I professed atheism, reasoning that if I needed religion, I would invent my own. I loved to argue against God's existence on the basis of the existence of evil. I further adopted an argument that if God could do anything and if God could make anything, why couldn't He make a rock so heavy that He couldn't lift it? I formulated a lose-lose argument about God. He either can't do everything or He can't make everything. He is inadequate either way. I thought my logical word play was quite clever, but in reality it was arrogantly reductionistic.

My argument made as much sense as reasoning that someone with a PhD is someone who knows more and more about less and less until he (or she) knows everything about nothing. While logically clever, it was really just an illogical-logical word game. In my argument against God, I set up a logical impossibility (God creating something so heavy He couldn't lift it), and used it to deny His existence. My argument allowed me to replace *Him* with *Me*. I elevated myself as the All-Wise center of the universe. But my arrogance had consequences, as my Self-centeredness led to the disintegration of my marriage, an increasing alienation from others, and a vain search for affirmation and meaning.

DUMBING DOWN

When we ignore God, negate His revelation with speculative concepts and rationalistic word games, or displace Him with other ideas, religions, philosophies, or self-centered pursuits, life doesn't work, as it should. The farther we move from God, or distort who He is, the farther we move from His Divine Design. There is truth to the saying, "Life is difficult! If you're stupid, it's really difficult." Life is indeed difficult, and when we turn away from God and His revelation, it becomes even more difficult. The Psalmist agrees saying, "The sorrows of those will increase who run after other gods" (Psalm 16:4). Paul describes the outcome of turning from God in the verses that follow (1:24-32).

> "Life is difficult! If you're stupid, it's really difficult."

It is easy to make a wrong turn in life, thinking we are on the right path when we are not. Chris McCandless perished due to that kind of thinking. McCandless grew up in Annandale, Virginia, and died at age twenty-four in a wilderness area in the state of Alaska. After graduating in 1990 from Emory University, he ceased communicating with his family, gave away his savings of $25,000 and began traveling, later abandoning his car and burning all the money in his wallet.

McCandless traveled to Alaska and headed down a snow-covered trail to begin a wilderness odyssey with only ten pounds of rice, a .22 caliber rifle, several boxes of rifle rounds, a camera, and a small selection of reading material—including a field guide to the region's edible plants. He became isolated and apparently died due to eating wild potato root, which had a poisonous fungus on it, thus leading to starvation.[6] A Biblical proverb warns, "There is a way that seems right to a man, but in the end it leads to death" (Proverbs 14:12). So it was with Chris McCandless.

When we turn from God and His revelation, we head down a wrong path. The Psalmist states, "The fool says in his heart there is no God."[7] Paul warns in Romans that turning from God is foolish because it leads to darkness and futility (1:20-22). Without God we are left with only a partial view of the universe and reality. We miss the spiritual core of the universe or have a distorted view of what that core is.

Without Biblical revelation, we are left to speculate about the nature of God and reality. What is God really like? What does He require of us? What is really real? How can I know the difference between good and evil? Ignoring the message of Scripture leads to a speculative futility, including blaming God for evil in the universe. Those who blame God for evil do not allow for the alternative Biblical explanation. It is like missing a critical piece to a puzzle. While our logic in blaming God may seem tenable, we are unable to complete the picture.

WHO'S REALLY TO BLAME?

One of the characteristics of drug or alcohol dependency is denial. I (Linus Sr.) once sought to help an alcoholic friend whose wife asked me to intervene as she told me his alcoholism, under control for a season, had flared up again. Responding to her request, I spoke to her husband and later with a pastor whom I thought could help (I had moved thousands of miles/kilometers away, while the pastor lived near my friend).

When my alcoholic friend learned (I told him) that I had discussed his situation with his pastor, he threatened to take me to the World Court in The Hague (Den Hague) for "a breach of confidentiality." He professed he was cured of alcoholism and that it was okay for him to drink again. Because of his denial, my hands were tied and I was unable to help him further. Sadly, he continued to drink himself to death, ending up on his living room floor in a pool of his own blood, the outcome of his alcohol abuse.

My alcoholic friend blamed me rather than face his life-threatening dependency and my effort and the effort of others to help. We do the same with God. We blame Him for the ills of our world instead of turning to Him for the help we need to navigate life. The real issue of who is really to blame is captured in the following dialogue:

"Sometimes I would like to ask God why he allows poverty, suffering, and injustice when He could do something about it."

"Well, why don't you ask Him?"

"Because I'm afraid He would ask me the same question."[8]

Incredibly, God does takes the blame, but not in the way we expect. This is the unfolding meta-story of the Bible that culminates in the Good News of the death of Jesus in our place, as we shall see.

HOW LIFE WORKS [AND DOESN'T]

There is a direct relationship between what we believe and the way life works. If we get the belief part right, then there is a greater chance we will get the way-life-works part right. By owning the blame of our separation (it's something within us) and turning to Jesus as Messiah-Son-King-Lord (for the something He did for us), we become connected to God and His Divine Design for us. In turning from our self-reliance to reliance upon Him, we diminish many of the difficulties of our lives, at least the ones created by our defective and distorted views of the world and ourselves, causing our lives, relationships, and society to malfunction.

Paul calls the consequences resulting from our distorted view of life "the wrath of God" (1:18). The term "wrath of God" in Romans chapter one points to the reality that God created the universe to work in accord with His design. We are wired to be in relationship with God and live in alignment with His Divine Design. Without this we cannot comprehend our true make up or successfully navigate relationships with others or the world around us. Life doesn't work the way it is meant to work. The wrath of God is the breakdown of ignoring God's design. It is like driving a car without oil in the engine. An engine melts down without oil—and so do we when we try to circumvent our design.

The wrath of God is evidenced on a macro-scale by the failed "isms" of the twentieth century: Communism, National Socialism (Nazism), Nihilism, Existentialism, Fascism, Secularism, and unbridled Capitalism. Each of these "isms" ignored, denied, distorted, or domesticated God, with the result that they wrought havoc upon humanity. Ignoring, denying, marginalizing, domesticating, or distorting God and His revelation plays out, not only in our missing the Divine Design, but also in national and international man-made catastrophes. Turning from God on a macro scale leads down a path of horror and destruction. The wrath of God doesn't mean that God is waiting to smite us. It means when we ignore the way He designed us, society breaks down.

> The "wrath of God" points to the reality that God created the universe to work in accord with His design.

"God's wrath" is experienced on a micro-scale in a thousand ways when we ignore the wisdom God makes available to us for daily living. Counselor and author Larry Crabb notes that we erroneously tweak our understanding of the meaning of life to accommodate our felt desires. We change the plot of life that God designed into a drama that prioritizes the longings of our own hearts—for intimacy, respect, fullness, and comfort. But the effect is disastrous.[9]

Our friend Rocky is a financial advisor who has long counseled his clients to stay out of debt. Many of those affected by the current economic downturn ignored his advice and were overly leveraged. One of them exclaimed, "This is God's judgment!" to which Rocky replied, "This is not God's judgment; this is God's consequence!" This is what Paul has in view in Romans 1:18: the wrath of God is the consequence of ignoring God and His guidance.

SLIP SLIDING AWAY ["GIVEN OVER"]

The wrath of God is more than an impersonal cause-and-effect mechanism built into the universe. There is an unseen Person who interacts with His creation, expressed in Paul's phrase, "God gave them over" (1:24, 26, 28). Behind God's wrath is the commitment of the Creator to restore the world to His design, to put right what is distorted and disfigured. The words 'justice,' 'justify,' 'right,' and 'righteousness' used by Paul all come from the same root and express the theme that God is moving to restore and put right His creation (including us) once again.

God *gives us over* in order to *put us right*. The statement, "God gave them over," is used three times in Romans chapter one. Each usage expresses a progressive state of dysfunction of our lives and society and our drift from God and His design. The farther we move from God and an intimate relationship with Him, the more His design for us and our world is diminished. Any person or culture that turns from God begins to "slip slide" away from God's design of the universe.

> God gives us over in order to put us right.

Too often, things have to get worse before we acknowledge a problem and take the steps necessary to address it in our lives. Unfortunately, my alcoholic friend's life ended without his acknowledging he had a problem and getting the help he so desperately needed. The purpose of God "giving us over" is that we would recognize our need for help.

CRAZY-MAKING

In my (Linus Sr.) leadership role, I have observed many times the tendency of people to deny issues that negatively affect theirs' and others' well-being. I have mused over and over again at how often we blame others and engage in what is called "crazy making," that is, turning a criticism back on others, thus denying any responsibility for the problem being addressed.

Not long ago, I received an email from a friend who walked away from our leaderships' attempt to address an issue that would have helped him resolve an escalating conflict with others. Instead of embracing the input with humility and appreciation, he resisted, faulting first the message being given, then the messengers giving it, and finally the way the message was delivered. Our feedback contradicted the image he had of himself and his assessment of the situation, even though there was a consensus on the part of many others that the primary problem lay with his actions and attitudes.

My fellow-worker's combative responses to repeated attempts to address the issues reached the point when it became clear that he was not going to accept our input and give up his defensiveness, so we encouraged him to find an organization whose leadership he could embrace. He moved on, but the next path he chose didn't work out either. He wrote a letter explaining his decision to abandon the new work and, upon reading his explanation, another of our leaders replied: "It is interesting that this is all catching up with him. I don't wish him harm, as I know you don't, but that God could break down his pride and self-sufficiency. I always mistrust people who are never wrong, and he is one of them." Yet another of our leaders close to the situation wrote, "Most interesting. No remorse or self-reflection—only a sense of being a victim. Sad, I think."

As much as it pained me to see my friend and fellow worker turn away from the help we were offering, I know that God is still at work in his life and will use the "reproofs of life" to soften him somewhere down the road. I "know" this because too often, I too have had to "learn the hard way," the result of which has made me (hopefully) more humble, teachable, and dependent upon God than I would otherwise be. I am still on this journey, trying to keep in view the Proverb, "A man's pride brings him low, but a man of lowly spirit gains honor" applies to me (Proverbs 29:23).

Paul notes that our indifference and denial is actually a willful suppression of God's revealed truth. God's invisible qualities— His eternal power and divine nature—are sufficiently in view so that we are without excuse to turn away or ignore Him (1:18-23). Suppression of the truth is not uncommon. When younger, my (Linus Sr.) mother knew for some time that something was not right in her abdomen. She experienced increasing pain but was afraid of what her doctor might find, so she carried on, ignoring the symptoms.

She suppressed the truth of something abnormal growing within her, hoping the problem would go away. Her pain finally became so unbearable that she was persuaded to see a physician, who removed a grapefruit-sized tumor from her stomach. Fortunately for her and for us it was not malignant. Left unattended, it would have killed her. The same is true with God.

IDEA-OLATRY

Once we turn onto the path of indifference to God, we move toward idolatry and farther from His design and purpose. What starts out as indifference or suppression of the truth about God leads to an elevation and preoccupation with other ideologies, often expressed in the worship of unseen forces or inanimate objects. The Biblical term for this is "idolatry." Another term that could be used is "idea-olatry." Idolatry or idea-olatry is the elevation of any idea, philosophy, value, passion, obsession, or any other thing above God and His purpose for us. Indifference to God leads to idolatry/idea-olatry. If God is not at the center of our lives, then something else will be.

IMMORALITY

Turning from God is not static. Indifference leads to idolatry, which in turn leads to additional stages of slip sliding away from God and His Design. These additional stages are revealed in Paul's use of the phrase, "God gave them over." The first of these is "God gave them over to *sexual impurity*" (1:24-25). Without prioritizing a relationship with God, we are vulnerable to preoccupation or obsession with our sexual impulses. Lust for sexual pleasure displaces God. Replacing God with lust creates an insatiable drive for sexual stimulation.

Western culture is oversexed but under-satisfied.

Unfortunately, the more we give ourselves over to sexual stimulation, the more it yields diminishing results. Western culture is oversexed but under-satisfied. We seek intimacy and identity through sexual passion and pleasure, and that which God designed as a gift to enhance us becomes an obsession that enslaves us. We actually become slaves to our own sexual desires. Obsession with sexual pleasure becomes exploitive and hurtful to others, ultimately leaving us unfulfilled and unsatisfied.

When pursued within the boundary and safeguard of God's design in monogamous marriage, sex is wonderful and fulfilling. When pursued with disregard to God's design, our sexual drive pushes us toward exploitation, fantasy, disappointment, disillusionment, destruction, and pain. The same sexual drive God designed to serve us, elevated as lust, becomes a tyrannical master. The Playboy philosophy may lead to lots of sex, but it also leads to exploitation and a lack of meaning and fulfillment. In the words of Indian author Vishal Mangalwadi, the Playboy philosophy turns "men into (Play) boys and women into 'Desperate Housewives.'"[10] This too is "a way that seems right but the end is death."

IDENTITY CONFUSION

Sexual immorality morphs to a second "given over"—*confusion of sexual identity* (1:26-27). This is expressed by the phrase "God gave them over to shameful lusts." When other-gender sex becomes unfulfilling or disappointing, lust turns toward those of the same sex.[11]

When the tyranny of the sexual drive is intensified, the Divine Design is further diminished. A further drift from God's Design is that men and women abandon natural relations with the opposite sex and are inflamed with lust for those of the same gender. Men lust after other men and women lust after other women. Given-over-to-lust-stage-two

> As we move farther and farther away from God and His design, society becomes increasingly fragmented....

leads us away from what it means to be human as male and female, as gender is at the core of God's Design for us. Same-gender sex rationalized, legitimized, and normalized leads to a further slip sliding away from our true humanity. This too leaves us unfulfilled and unsatisfied, and is exploitive and hurtful.

INSANITY

Russian author Fyodor Dostoevsky wrote, "If there is no God, everything is permitted."[12] The next stage of being "given over" and drifting from God's Design is *cultural insanity*. Paul comments, "God gave them over to a depraved mind." As we move farther and farther away from God and His Design, society becomes increasingly fragmented and driven by self-centered pursuits. This leads to a breakdown of societal restraint and cultural insanity ensues. The futility of finding fulfillment through sexual relationships gives way to increased self-centered drives and compulsions, regardless of how they affect others.

Romans chapter one concludes with Paul's listing of wickedness, greed, depravity, envy, murder, strife, deceit, malice, gossip, slander, hatred of God, insolence, arrogance, boastfulness, senselessness, faithlessness, heartlessness, ruthlessness, and callousness as indicators that show how far a culture has moved away from the Divine Design (1:28-32). No one evidences all these behaviors— many abhor them. Nevertheless, the farther society moves away from the Divine Design, the more these behaviors proliferate in society.

One of the places that an eroding cultural insanity is evidenced historically is in the Biblical book of Judges. The theme that runs through the book is "everyone did that which was right in his or her own eyes." At first glance it is difficult to understand why the book of Judges is in the Bible. The stories are increasingly sordid. If it were a movie, Judges would get an R-rating, as it is filled with stories of conflict, unfaithfulness, brutal assaults, immorality, civil war, brash vows, and slaughter. Some of the characters highlighted in Judges connect their violent and immoral acts to their belief in God (just like today).

One of the most troubling stories in Judges is about a Levite who retrieves his runaway concubine, who is then sexually abused by some of the citizens of Gibeah, a town in the tribal region of Benjamin. The Levite subsequently cuts his dead concubine's body into pieces (we told you this was R-rated) and sends them to the other eleven Israeli tribes to get their attention and mobilize them to take action against the perpetrators of the crime.

Judges shows the increasing insanity of a culture that turns from God in which "everyone does that which was right in his or her own eyes." Like Western culture today, Israel at the time of the Judges had a fading memory of God. Although there was still a measure of belief in God, that belief became distorted, leading to cultural decay and craziness. Both Judges and Romans chapter one describe what happens when people turn from God and His design.

A daily dose of the morning or nightly news convinces us that something is wrong with our culture. It is as if our world has embarked on a suicidal journey. We are "slip sliding" away from God's design. Much like Chris McCandless, stranded in the Alaska wilderness, or Ernest Shackelton, trapped in the frigid Antarctic, people are in dire need of rescue. Blown against by the icy winds of "idea-olatry," shivering because of the cold frost of lust and self-gratification, or just bruised and beaten by life's insanity and brokenness, we have slipped from the warmth of connected-ness to God and become trapped, as if in a desolate wilderness bus or on a freezing Antarctic shelf.

> It is as if our world has embarked on a suicidal journey.

Where do we turn? Where do we go? What do we do? Paul pursues this further in Romans chapter two.

CHAPTER 6

ROMANS 2:1-3:20
THE FUTILITY OF
MORALITY AND RELIGION

...tragedy struck.

—Into Thin Air[1]

The expedition was lauded in Europe and North America for exploits seen as heroic. On his return to England Captain Stairs was named a Fellow of the Royal Geographical Society and the Royal Scottish Geographical Society in 1890. Then details emerged of the many Africans killed by the expedition.

—"The Stairs Expedition to Katanga"[2]

What shall we conclude then? Are we any better? Not at all!
—Romans 3:9

FAILED EXPEDITIONS

Not all expeditions are successful. Not all are noble. In 1996 dozens of teams of climbers made their way to Nepal, seeking the greatest trophy in the world of mountaineering—summiting

Mt. Everest. Unexpectedly, a snowstorm swept down on two teams as they made their way down from the mountain, and tragedy struck. Eight members of the two expeditions died from exposure, including the team leaders.

This incident illustrates the many things that can go wrong on expeditions, especially when self-preservation overrides concern for others. As Jon Krakauer, a participant in the fateful 1996 Everest expedition, writes, "We were a team in name only, I'd sadly come to realize. Although in a few hours we would leave camp as a group, we would ascend as individuals, linked to one another by neither rope nor any deep sense of loyalty. Each client was in it for himself or herself, pretty much. And I was no different."[3]

Even more damning was the Emin Pasha Relief Expedition of 1887 to 1890, led by famous journalist Henry Morton Stanley, at the time the most celebrated living explorer of Africa. Emin Pasha was a German doctor and naturalist who had been appointed Governor of Equatoria (today located in the extreme south of present-day Sudan along the upper reaches of the White Nile and most Northern part of present day Uganda including Lake Albert). The Mahdi Rebellion that began in 1881 cut off Equatoria and Emin Pasha from the outside world, leading Stanley to set off in a rescue effort.

The first man Stanley hired was Lieutenant William Stairs, a twenty-nine-year-old officer in the Royal Engineers. Stairs sailed from London on January 20, 1887 and met Stanley in Suez on February 6. Their expedition started from Banana at the mouth of the Congo River on March 19, 1887 and ended in Bagamoyo, Tanzania on December 5, 1889. During the 3,100-mile (close to 5000 kilometers) journey across Africa through some of its most difficult country consisting of almost impenetrable rainforest and swamps, Stanley, Stairs, and their colleagues suffered frequently from malaria and dysentery. After immense hardships and great loss of life, Stanley discovered the Ruwenzori Range and Lake Edward and emerged from the interior with Pasha and his surviving followers at the end of 1890.

Another acclaimed achievement of the rescue mission, was that Stairs discovered one source of the Nile, the Semliki River.

He also became the first non-African to climb in the Ruwenzoris, reaching 10,677 feet (3,048 meters) before having to turn around. But a darker side of the mission occurred when Stairs was seriously wounded in the chest by a poisonous arrow (from which he recovered) during an attack by natives who assumed they were an Arab slave-raiding party. The Stanley-Stairs expedition retaliated by killing hundreds of their attackers in return.[4]

The expedition was lauded in Europe and North America for exploits seen as heroic, but details emerged of the many Africans killed along the way. The expedition also used brutality against its own porters. Stanley's own accounts revealed how he shot Africans who impeded the expedition's progress. As a result, Stanley spent his remaining years defending himself and the expedition from criticism of excessive force and mismanagement of the expedition's Rear Column. Unfortunately, the brutality of the expedition tarnished the success of Stanley's achievements.[5]

The Emin Pasha rescue mission led by Stanley and Stairs shows what can happen when noble ends are pursued by ignoble means. A mission can be well intentioned but end up in failure. The same is true in the way we live out our lives. In Romans chapter one, Paul shows that indifference to God leads to the loss of the Divine Design and a defective view of self, our world, and our relationship to others. Indifference to God opens the way for something other than God to absorb our thoughts and affections, ultimately leading to disillusionment, harm to ourselves and others, and cultural insanity. The farther we drift from God and His Design, the more human degradation and societal breakdown occur. We need to be rescued from our slavery to self-absorption, compulsion, and lust. We need to be restored to God's Design.

Moving on from the futility of indifference, Paul presses forward in Romans chapter two to examine the defectiveness of both morality and religion as avenues to rescue us from the fallout of our separation from God and His Design.

A mission can be well intentioned but end up in failure.

THE SECOND FUTILITY: MORALITY

The second futile approach to navigating life is relying upon morality (2:1-16). The moral person may or may not believe in God, but has a sense that certain things are right and certain things are wrong. His or her approach to life is based upon a pragmatic sense that life works better if we adhere to some standard of morals. For the moral person who believes in God, there is an assumption that God credits us for the good deeds we do and the sincerity we have. For the moral person who doesn't believe in God, there is a still a sense that morality is beneficial.

> Life works better if
> we adhere to some
> standard of morals.
> _____

Those who rely upon morality follow a path of being or doing "good," seeking to rise above the immorality and cultural insanity they detect around them. They view lust, violence, dishonesty, greed, and other immoral behavior as destructive and repulsive. Many moral people strive to be generous and kind and are often advocates and participants in good social and moral or philanthropic causes. While involvement in such causes is a good thing, the deficiency of the morality approach to life is that it falls short of the even higher morality and spirituality needed to truly transform society. The highest morality of all is to love God with all our hearts, minds, souls, and strength, and to love our neighbors as ourselves (Matthew 22:37-40). No one measures up to this standard, so all of us fall short of the greater good. Only the transforming love of God can reverse the downward slide of society and the self-centered destructive tendency of humanity.

Morality falls short of an intimate relationship with God and the fullness of a life of love, joy, peace, grace, mercy, and compassion for others that God alone can impart. Morality falls short of a life-giving relationship with God and the life-transforming flow of His power to reverse the downward slide of the world around us. God's Design is not for us to live out of moral "duty," but to live out of His passionate love and empowerment. Jesus is the One who restores to us an intimate relationship with God and releases in us the flow of God's love. Jesus promises that rivers of living water will flow from those who receive and believe in Him (John 7:38).

Morality is certainly preferable to immorality in that it brings us a step closer to God's design of the universe (though morality can also be harsh and judgmental and move us farther from that design). The problem with the reliance-upon-morality approach to life, however, is that it doesn't lift us high enough or align us close enough to that design. It also fails to answer the question of how good is good enough?

HOW HIGH IS HIGH ENOUGH?

How good do you have to be to gain God's acceptance (or avoid being recycled to a lesser form, if you believe in Karma)? What about those times we don't measure up to our standard of morality? What about the times we fall short or mess up? Does it matter? Do we only count our positive achievements and not our shortcomings? Is being sincere and trying hard good enough? How sincere do we need to be and how hard do we have to try? Who decides? If God's acceptance depends upon my goodness, sincerity, and effort, how do I know when or whether I am good enough, sincere enough, or am trying hard enough? Paul says, "If I give all my possessions to the poor and surrender my body to the flames, but have not love, I gain nothing" (1 Corinthians 13:3).

Most who follow the rely-upon-morality approach to life base their sense of how well they are doing by comparing themselves to others. A friend of mine recently asked me (Linus Jr.) "Did you hear about Dave (not his real name)?" He then went on to talk about how Dave had messed up morally. My friend's comment was in part because it made him feel better about his own level of morality. I must admit I have done the same thing. As long as someone I am comparing myself to is doing worse than I am, I feel I'm okay. I'm afraid both my moralistic friend and I are like the person who says, "I look down on people who look down on people." We are often oblivious to the fact that we are guilty of the same faults we point out in others, even if to a lesser degree.

> The justification of our morality is almost always made on the basis of a downward comparison.

The justification of our morality is almost always made on the basis of a downward comparison with those farther down the morality scale than are we. The moral person gauges his or her goodness to the less moral person, and the less moral person compares him or herself to the person who is even farther down the morality scale. Thus, you hear statements like, "At least I have never killed anyone." Or, "At least I've never stolen an old lady's purse." Or. "At least I didn't embezzle a billion dollars," and so on.

HYPOCRISY

In addition to comparing ourselves with those lower down the morality scale, we are also prone to focus on the flaws of those whose morality is perceived as greater than ours. Our culture loves a scandal and especially likes to highlight the failure of religious leaders who don't "walk the talk." It makes for good media coverage, but it also gives us a sense of moral justification. Truth be told, it is not just those who profess to be religious who fail to "walk the talk." None of us does. We all fall short. We may feel morally better by pointing out the shortcomings and hypocrisy of others, but this doesn't absolve us of *our own failure* to live up to our own standard of morality. Moral or not, "good" or not, religious or not, all of us are hypocrites. None of us lives up to our own standards or ideals however low or high they might be.

> It is not just those who profess to be religious who fail to "walk the talk." None of us does.

The less-moral person might find comfort in pointing out the hypocrisy of the supposed more-moral person, but this doesn't diminish the culpability of the less-moral person. Likewise, the non-religious person may find solace in pointing out the hypocrisy of the religious person, but this doesn't negate the non-religious person's own moral shortcoming. The rub is this—none of us lives up to our own standard of morality, let alone the even higher standard God revealed in the Ten Commandments. This is the point Paul makes when he says,

> Paul alerts us that there will be a final moral examination.

"You, therefore, have no excuse, you who pass judgment on someone else, for at whatever point you judge the other, you are condemning yourself, because you who pass judgment do the same things" (2:1-3).

Paul alerts us that there will be a final moral examination. At this exam the completely righteous judgment of God will be revealed and our moral shortcomings will be exposed. The futility of our morality is akin to the futility of attempting to climb a thousand-foot wall with a six-foot ladder. The focus of God's examination will not be on how far up the six-foot ladder we've climbed, on how many people are lower down the ladder than we are, or on how the people two rungs above us are still far short of the top of the wall, but on how far short we are from the top and how foolish we were to think we could ever reach it with a six foot ladder. The comparison of our moral accomplishment will be upward toward God rather than downward toward others when the moral examination occurs. It will embarrassingly be made clear that we fell short of the moral standards we professed (2:5).

The divine examination will be based on our own professed standard of morality with a rendered verdict: "you who pass judgment did the same things" (2:1). To fall a little short of one's own morality is more serious than it seems.

> The gap between God's goodness and ours is far greater than we might realize....

Falling short of our own moral standard actually means we fall a long, long way short of God's rightness (righteousness). The gap between God's rightness and goodness and ours is far greater than we might realize or want to acknowledge. Trying to be "good enough" is like trying to jump across the Atlantic Ocean. A great athlete can jump farther than a couch potato but neither the athlete nor the couch potato comes anywhere close to making it from Europe to America (or the reverse). Even more than a vessel to carry us across the Atlantic, we need a vessel to carry us over the even greater ocean of righteousness separating us from God.

No amount of moral achievement can bridge the gap. The moral person might come a little closer to God's design than the immoral person, but neither person reaches the mark of "good enough." Relying upon our own morality is not the solution for our separation from God. It still leaves us disconnected from God and His design.

DO MORAL PEOPLE NEED RESCUING?

Recently, I (Linus Sr.) attended a dinner party in Portugal hosted by my daughter Laina and son-in law Phil. Present was a successful and accomplished group of people. Although each person there considered his or her self as moral, most had no belief in God. For those who did, God was impersonal and distant. Though each was accomplished, there was brokenness in their lives that leaked out. Upon my request, Laina later wrote to me the following thumbnail sketch of those in attendance:

American L. is just discovering genuine faith for the first time. Pretty famous concert pianist, she was married to a top conductor/violinist who was not a well man and left her a few years ago. It was a scandalous divorce. One of their sons is just sober one year and trying to figure faith out. L. is now coming to our Alpha group every week, and my Bible study. Her son is struggling to be satisfied with anything, as he has not yet dealt with the years of pain that he covered up with drugs. L. has never had a real sense of community or friends she can trust. She has had no understanding of a healthy faith.

Portuguese T. grew up Catholic. Her parents were European royalty. She has had much pain and is guarded; however, she seems quite interested in us, and our faith, and may come to the relationship retreat.

Portuguese P., T.'s brother, married, divorced and then married a French woman (scandalous situation). You can tell that they have a miserable marriage. She is ignored among his family, as she is perceived to be the brunt of the scandal. My heart really breaks for her.

Portuguese S. is a singer, quite famous apparently. He went to an English boarding school. He too is interested in what we believe and in coming to Alpha in the near future. He is Catholic, but not a believer.

British N. is a wealthy land developer. He divorced the mother of his children and remarried someone much younger. He is quite opinionated about everything, but curious.

Russian S. left home to dance at the age of 9. Her life was the Russian ballet. Raised in an atheistic country, she found religion taboo and scary. Her mother became involved in yoga and a cult. Her aunt became Orthodox and rigid. S. now feels lonely and a bit lost. We are getting together for coffee this week. I really like her.

English T. married a Portuguese man who died 10 years ago. She says she doesn't know a thing about the Bible, nor does anyone else she knows. She is sweet, and alone. She is my neighbor and wants to get together.

American H. is a concert cellist. His older brothers are disabled in some way. His mother was Jewish, his father nothing, but both converted to Christianity. H. says that he doesn't want any of it, but secretly I think he is open.

Swedish M. is a violinist, married to H. She is Lutheran, as she says are all Swedes. She has no faith right now, but her heart seems soft and she wants a friendship with us.

South African P. was raised in the Dutch Reformed church, but hated it. He has had lots of hardships in life, but is quite an overcomer. He has lots of anger, but is coming to everything we invite him to and seems to love what he is discovering. He has a solid spirit, only needing an understanding of God's grace and a relationship with God for himself. I just love him.

Half-English, half-Danish P. is a writer and a sculptor. He went to a Catholic boarding school in England, which really damaged his understanding of faith and God. He is a faithful Alpha member...very questioning with a soft heart. He has become a dear friend. He argues with us, but we never argue back, as we usually are agreeing with him. His argument is with religion, not Jesus. He has yet to understand

Jesus, however, and give his life to him. But, I know God is pursuing him.

Portuguese Z. is coming to our Alpha group tonight (though she didn't come when you were here). She is dating a guy who is controlling and all about power. She called me and wants to spend more time with us. I am hoping to see her mature and grow.

German S. was raised as a Jehovah's Witness. She has lots of baggage with that and she has just ordered a Bible. She is in a healing and growth place, and soon will make a commitment to Christ. We have talked at length about it. She is scared but has said she wants that.

Zimbabwean C. is a teacher. She had a harsh legalistic upbringing. She doesn't get grace but is hungry for it. She thinks being in the Bible study is 'a dream come true.'

When you get to know people close up, you see that there is something, even in the lives of successful, accomplished, and moral people, that is broken and incomplete. People are grasping for meaning, floundering in their relationships, and searching for identity. Left on their own, like all of us, they have little remedy for the state they find themselves in. It is only through a relationship with God that wholeness in their understanding of themselves and health in their relationship with others can be found. Moral people, like those indifferent to God, need rescuing.

THE THIRD FUTILITY: RELIGION

The third futile approach to life and the problem of our separation from God is religion (2:17-3:20). Paul specifically singles out Judaism because this was his background, plus there were many Jewish believers in the Christ-following community in Rome still trying to work through the connection between Judaism and what it meant to follow Jesus. Paul points out that the religious approach to life is similar to the morality one. It too is based upon a standard we must strive to live up to. For Judaism the standard was the Mosaic Law.

The futility of religion, albeit Judaism, Islam, or pseudo forms of Christianity, is that no matter how religious we are or how close we come to meeting our religious standard, we fall short of God's righteousness and fail to tap into His love and spiritual power. In the particular case of Judaism, both individually and collectively, its adherents failed to live up to God's revealed standard in the Ten Commandments. But the same is true of all religions and all religious approaches to life. Just as the moral person falls short of his or her chosen moral standard, so the religious person fails to measure up to his or her religious standard. No one, however moral or religious, comes close to attaining to the level of the even higher standard of God's righteousness.

Religion is based upon human effort to gain God's approval or achieve oneness with Him or His will. It is based upon the assumption that by my religious actions I can somehow merit God's favor and that my sincerity and effort will negate my failures. Religion focuses on *my* effort, *my* actions, and *my* behavior to observe certain "do's and don'ts" or follow religious rules and practices. Religion says that by these means I can justify myself before God.

But how can we gain God's acceptance if we fall short of the rules, standards, and practices we profess? This is the problem of religion. It is not just the problem of Judaism. In Islam, God is perceived as Most Gracious and Most Merciful

> But how can we gain God's acceptance if we fall short?

(every *surah* or chapter in the Qur'an or Koran except the ninth starts with this declaration), believing that God will be gracious and merciful to those who practice Islam. Unfortunately, much of Islam is ungracious and unmerciful toward others—even toward other Muslims. Religious profession and even strict adherence to that religion does not negate the culpability of being unforgiving and merciless, however religiously it is justified.

Islam is not alone in this. Many Christians likewise rely upon religious profession and self-effort, thinking this is what God requires. An example of this is my (Linus Jr.) friend Joe (not his real name). Joe is adamant about staying away from what he calls "the line" or "grey areas." Joe and I attended a school that was steeped in religiosity, where the emphasis was on external behaviors, rooted in the religious subculture and tradition of the religious denomination of which the university is affiliated.

On one occasion, while traveling in Europe, Joe began yelling at me because I was drinking a beer, which, according to him and the cultural tradition of our university, "crossed the line." Drinking anything with alcohol content was a "grey area" to be avoided at all times. If I had been drinking in excess, Joe would have had a point. But I wasn't and I don't. What amazed me is that Joe's focus on "grey areas" kept him from seeing his own explosiveness, critical-ness, and judgmentalness (which was evident on many occasions). To me, this was a greater issue than drinking a beer.

EXTERNAL OR INTERNAL TRANSFORMATION

Morality and religion are like the failed expeditions of Krakauer and Stanley. The ignoble in us taints and distorts the noble. The damage and dysfunction in our inner selves is only whitewashed by trying to live up to some external moral or religious standard. Jesus highlighted this when He said that it is not what goes into a man that defiles him; rather it is what comes out of a man that makes him unclean.[6] Something is distorted inside us, resulting in our separation from God, the loss of the Divine Design, and the brokenness of our world.

> Something is damaged and distorted inside us.
> _____

The inner damage or dysfunction is called 'sin' (a greater problem than 'sins'). It is this sin-within that alienates us from God who is without sin. It is sin-within that distorts who we are cre-ated to be. No amount of human self-effort will fix this defect, pro-duce the intimacy we were created to have with God, or give us the strength to overcome our weaknesses and brokenness. Morality and religion will not eradicate the deeper effects of our contamina-tion by sin. Only an inner transformation at the deepest level of our human hearts can restore us to God's Divine Design.

Jesus puts the spotlight on the heart of the matter saying that the two greatest commandments are to love the Lord our God with all our heart, soul, mind, and strength, and to love our neighbor as ourselves (Mark 12:30-31; Deuteronomy 6:4, 5; Leviticus 19:18). These two commands are the ultimate standard by which we are to measure ourselves and by which we will be measured. They are the ultimate expression of spiritual health and inner wellbeing. Love for God and others is the thermometer that tells us if we are healthy or unhealthy. Do we love God with all our heart, soul, mind, and strength, and do we love our neighbor as ourselves? All else pales in comparison with these two simple statements. To rise to this standard requires a radical inner transformation and empowerment that only God can affect within us.

I (Linus Sr.) know that when I am inordinately angry or I feel shut down toward my wife, children, or others my heart attitude needs realigning. The realignment I need takes place when I open my life to God's transforming power through Jesus. My inner disposition is refreshed and rekindled by my responsiveness to God's love, grace, and presence (and sometimes His discipline as seen in Hebrews 12).

Abraham was out of alignment with God when he went to Egypt and lied about Sarai being his sister (she was his wife). As the story unfolds, Abraham's deceit was discovered and he returned somewhat chagrined to Canaan. The first place he revisited is where he first "called on the name of the Lord" (Genesis 12:8-13:4). It was a place of heart alignment with God. The story of Abraham in Genesis is a journey of progressive transformation through connecting with God over and over again, and thereby being transformed by His presence and power. It is the same with story after story in the Old Testament and New. Abraham's growing faith can be traced by observing the unfolding names and titles for God he uses from Genesis 12-22 (LORD or Yahweh, God Most High, Creator of heaven and earth, shield and great reward, Sovereign Lord, God Almighty, and The LORD Will Provide).

The need for inner transformation and divine empowerment is highlighted in Jesus' sermon on the mountainside found in Matthew's Gospel. In His "be-attitudes" message, Jesus emphasized being poor in spirit, mourning for the brokenness around us, being meek, hungering and thirsting for righteousness, being merciful, being peacemakers, and enduring persecution for doing what is right (Matthew 5:3-10). These qualities are all part of the Divine

Design. When we measure ourselves against them, we are aware that they are sorely lacking in us and in the world around us. They can only be imparted to us through a relationship with Jesus and attained by His transforming power.

God's acceptance is not a reward for our religious behavior or observance; it is a gift that results in a transformed heart. No moral or religious effort can produce the inner God-like character of love, unselfishness, humility, mercy, and righteousness (rightness) needed to be accepted by God and restored to His Divine Design. God alone produces these characteristics in us through Jesus' transforming indwelling presence.

> God's acceptance... is a gift.

THE GREAT DELIVERANCE

One friend referred to the transforming power of Jesus in her life as "the GREAT DELIVERANCE," writing of having come back "from the edge." Finding transformation and strength in Jesus, she expressed,

> He will not let me be tempted above what I am able. I have never come back so fast from having gone so far. It was a miracle. The day after I wrote, my mind came back, and even though I broke down again and was stranded in the pouring rain with no coat, He helped me to let go of the bar and raise my hands like on a roller coaster drop, and just scream with terror and delight in seeing what God will do in all this craziness. I am beginning to understand that the dismantling and loss in my life has been allowed by God to get me to let go of my huge control issues and just let Him be God. It is all becoming a bit clearer, and I can honestly say that I have stopped wrestling. Thank you for praying and caring for me. Your prayers and labor of love made all the difference.

No moral or religious approach to life can remove the barrier of sin-within that separates us from God. No moral or religious approach can impart the transforming power we need at the heart level. Thus, Paul divides the world into three kinds of people: indifferent (1:18-32), moral (2:1-16), and religious (2:17-3:20). Each is a futile approach to navigate the brokenness of our world and remove the root problem of our separation from God and the loss of His Divine Design. The indifferent approach ignores God and drifts toward idea-olatry, immorality, confusion of identity, and cultural insanity. The morality approach keeps God at arms-length, relying upon self-effort and human goodness. The religious approach domesticates God and relies upon self-righteous religious belief and practice.

Paul concludes his diagnosis of these three approaches and groups by saying: "All have sinned and fall short of the glory of God" (3:23). The expression "fall short" is an athletic term that refers to an archer who shoots his arrow but misses the mark (or a long jumper who falls short, or a basketball player who "bricks" a free throw). Indifference, morality, and religion alike miss the mark of God's righteousness, goodness, and holiness. Paul states it even stronger, concluding: "There is no one righteous, not even one" (3:10). Whether indifferent, moral, or religious, we all fall short of the Divine Design and "miss the mark" of the Divine Design and the adventure of the Divine Expedition.

Fortunately, God has taken the initiative to remove our separation, draw us back to an intimate and loving relationship with Him, and bring about the inner transformation that restores us to His intended Design. We shall see this more clearly in the next chapter.

CHAPTER 7

ROMANS 3:21-4:24
THE RENEWAL OF THE DIVINE DESIGN

This event set his life on an entirely new course. He saw the potential and anticipated the popularity of Antarctic exploration and set out to acquire a new set of skills. In 1899, he joined the Royal Geographic Society (RGS), where he was exposed to the culture of exploration.

—Shackleton's Way[1]

The expedition has been authorized but is still confidential; I have chosen Captain Lewis to lead it; Lewis needs advice and instruction.

—Thomas Jefferson[2]

But in my heart, I knew that the only way to attempt this mountain was to modify the old standards of safety and justifiable risk and to meet the dangers as they came: to drive through regardless. Care and caution would never make a route through the icefall. If we didn't attack it that May, someone else would.

—Sir Edmund Hillary[3]

But now God has shown us a different way of being right in his sight...we are made right in God's sight when we trust in Jesus Christ to take away our sins.

—Romans 3:21-22[4]

CRITICAL DECISIONS

When the three-masted ship *Endurance* became trapped in the polar pack ice of the Weddell Sea, it left explorer Earnest Shackleton and his crew stranded in the Antarctic. After nine months, the ship hull succumbed to the ice pack's relentless pressure, and the *Endurance* sank. Shackleton and his men spent an additional four-and-one-half months on an ice floe before escaping in three lifeboats through turbulent, ice-filled seas, landing on the deserted and frigid Elephant Island.

Leaving most of his exhausted crew behind, Shackleton forged on in one of the sturdiest lifeboats an additional 800-miles (1,280 kilometers) through Antarctic waters with several of his men to seek help from the nearest whaling station on South Georgia Island. Landing on the west side of the island, Shackleton and mates, Worsley and Crean, traversed the treacherous snow covered mountains and glaciers separating them from the whaling stations on the east side of the island. Shackleton, Worsley, and Crean overcame unimaginable obstacles in his efforts to rescue the rest of their crew.

The expedition of Meriwether Lewis and William Clark likewise overcame incredible challenges and obstacles. On June 2, 1805, they arrived at a major fork in the Missouri River, the confluence of the Maria's and Missouri Rivers in north-central Montana. This was unexpected, as no Indian informant had mentioned it. Which of these rivers was the Missouri? They knew that both paths did not lead to their destination. The issue was fraught with danger, as they needed to reach the Rockies, find the Shoshoni Indians, obtain horses, portage to the head of the Columbia River, and reach the Pacific Ocean before winter closed in. To choose the wrong route "would probably so dishearten the party that it might defeat the expedition altogether."[5]

Accordingly, the two army co-captains sent search parties up both rivers. When the results proved inconclusive, they set out to see for themselves. Clark went forty-five miles up the Missouri, found that it ran swift and true to the west of south, and returned persuaded. Lewis went nearly eighty miles up the Maria's and confirmed that it headed from too much to the north to be their route to the Pacific Ocean. The captains' findings represented the triumph of field observation over hypothetical image; they corrected their maps and, sure of themselves, chose the true Missouri.[6]

> Morality and religion block our path to God and, inhibit the flow of His love and grace to us.

Choosing the wrong course would mean failure for Shackleton to save his stranded crew as it would for Lewis and Clark to complete their expedition. The same is true for us in navigating the brokenness of our world. Choosing the right course to rescue us from our separation from God is crucial. Relying upon morality or religion are wrong paths. They block us from truly knowing God and inhibit the flow of His love and grace to us. Morality and religion do not remove the defect of sin residing at the core of every person. Instead, they distort our view of God and life and leave us stranded and separated from God and His Divine Design. Worse, insisting upon self-reliance through indifference toward God or through morality or religion entrenches a trajectory that leaves us facing the possibility of separation from God forever. Akin to Edmund Hillary's quote above, we must "modify the old standards"-that is, of trying to reach God through morality and religion.

GOD'S LIFELINE

Happily, Paul begins Romans 3:21 with the words "But now."

> There is a way to connect with God, renew His Design for us, and reverse the insanity of our culture.

The "but now" contrasts with the previous section of Romans (1:18-3:20), describing the futility of human effort to connect with God and His Design for us. We are like Shackleton's men on the frigid arctic deserted island, stranded and in need of rescuing—and like Lewis and Clark, we face a critical choice of which route to take. The "but now" of Paul points to the way.

The "but now" is the incredible news that God has initiated a rescue operation, providing us with all we need to reach Him. The "but now" is that God provides an anecdote for the infection of sin-within. The "but now" is the pathway God makes for us to connect with Him. The "but now" is God's doorway into our lives to renew His Design in us. The "but now" is the way God transforms us and reverses the insanity of our culture.

That "but now" is Jesus. He is God's lifeline. He does for us what we cannot do for ourselves. He does for us what morality and religion cannot do. He provides us with what we need to be accepted by God and transformed by Him. The "but now" is that Jesus makes "a righteousness from God" available to us (3:21-22).

The medieval church taught that God is righteous and that we cannot enter His presence without our also being righteous. This was a correct assessment of what it takes to be right with God. Unfortunately, the medieval church also taught that we must provide the righteousness God requires through our own effort (albeit, as prescribed by the church). To take this approach leaves us in a perpetual state of guilt, as we can never attain sufficient righteousness to bridge our separation from God. In contrast, Paul's "but now" announces that God rescues us from our plight by supplying the righteousness we need. This righteousness is *from God* (1:17; and twice in 3:21) and is imparted *by faith in Jesus Christ* (3:22).

The good news of Romans and the entire New Testament is that the seemingly insurmountable problem of our separation from God and loss of His Divine Design is solved. Indifference, morality, and religion leave us hopeless because they do not produce the inner transformation and righteousness to be right with God. Through Messiah-Son-King-Lord Jesus, God entered the human scene in a powerful act of rescue. He came as our sin-bearer, righteousness-provider, and life-giver. When we place our trust in Jesus, God removes the barrier of our unrighteousness and graces us with the righteousness to be in relationship with Him. He activates the Divine Design in us and releases God's power within us.

DIVINE INTERVENTION

Some years ago I (Linus Sr.) came down with a case of walking pneumonia. It sapped my energy and paralyzed my left recurrent laryngeal nerve, the one controlling my left vocal chord. No amount of rest, exercise, or proper diet on my part overcame the pneumonia. The infection remained until I took a stout dose of antibiotics, which attacked the bacteria and restored my health.

Even though the antibiotics cleared up the pneumonia, my left vocal chord remained paralyzed. Over the next few months my undamaged right vocal chord also began to be problematic. Like a pulled muscle, my right vocal chord fatigued upon taking the full load of my vocal use. When the right vocal chord stressed, I would completely lose my voice for days at a time. Needless to say, it was frustrating to me—more so to my family, as they got tired of the whistling signals I made to communicate (one whistle means "yes," two whistles means "no," up and down whistle means "please come here").

The problem appeared to be insurmountable, as the paralysis of my left vocal chord was permanent. One day, after losing my voice (right vocal chord fatigue) for the umpteenth time, I walked home in frustration following a lunch appointment. When I finally arrived at our house several hours later, Sharon met me at the door and asked if anything happened on my way home? I whispered, "What did you expect?"

She replied, "I prayed for you. I prayed before, but this time I *really prayed* and I just knew that God was going to do something."

I shrugged my shoulders in doubt—but that evening my voice came back. Although still weak at times, I have not lost it since.

> When all seemed lost, God rescued us in the only way possible, by sending Jesus....

Years afterward, I visited a voice specialist, who examined me and announced that my left vocal chord was vibrating. He told me that once paralyzed, a vocal chord seldom comes back. Was it coincidence that my recovery coincided with the day Sharon "really prayed" for me? I am convinced that my vocal paralysis was overcome through Sharon's prayers and God's supernatural intervention.

God did and can do what is humanly impossible. Far more incredible than answering Sharon's prayer and healing my paralyzed vocal chord, however, was God's supernatural divine act to overcome our alienation and separation from Him. Jesus accomplished this by taking the blame and bearing the guilt and judgment we deserve for falling short of God's holiness and righteousness (3:25). When all seemed lost, God rescued us in the only way possible, by sending Jesus, thus providing a breathtaking solution to an insurmountable problem. By turning to Jesus as Messiah-Son-King-Lord and placing ourselves in His hands, our guilt is removed, and we receive the complete righteousness we need to connect to God.

TWO TRANSACTIONS

Paul's says when we trust in Jesus Christ, "We are made right in God's sight" (3:21). There are two parts to this redeeming transaction. The first is that God transfers our sin and guilt to Jesus. Our sin is no longer counted against us because it is transferred to Jesus, who was separated from God in our place. He takes our blame. At the point Jesus screamed out during His violent crucifixion, "My God, my God, why have you forsaken me?" (Matthew 27:45-46), He bore our guilt and was separated from God. God in His perfect righteousness pulled away from Jesus who was carrying our unrighteousness. At that moment, our debt and penalty for sin was paid. The resurrection of Jesus three days later is the proof that God accepted the death and separation payment of Jesus for our unrighteousness.

The second part of this transaction is that God transfers or credits to us the righteousness of Christ. The exchange of our debt for His righteousness is outrageous grace. He takes our debt and provides us with His righteousness as a gift that is neither deserved nor merited by us. God credits to us the righteousness we need to be in His favor and good standing. God credits us with the perfect righteousness of Jesus, faultlessly manifested throughout His life. This credit of His righteousness is transferred to us, making a new relationship with God and a whole new way of living possible. It is, so to speak, the biggest bailout in history.

Many people think that a relationship with God depends on their own effort to earn a good standing with Him. Unaware of the enormity of the debt separating us from God, they intend to make small, steady installments of goodness, morality, or religious observance to pay off what is owed. Others ignore the debt, hoping it will be overlooked. Those who take the work-off-the-debt or hope-it-will-be-overlooked approaches to God typically view Jesus as a religious teacher who showed us the way to live a better life so that we can earn the credit we need. What these approaches fail to realize is that Jesus' death and resurrection was God's bailout of a debt that otherwise could never be satisfied nor overlooked.

SCHOLARSHIPPED

The credit of the righteousness Jesus provides us is like a scholarship. A scholarship is a payment someone else (in this case, Jesus) provides on our behalf. I (Linus Jr.) was not able to earn the amount of money I needed to attend the university I did. The cost of tuition, books, and room and board far exceeded my ability to pay. The amount I earned during summers and part-time during the school year met some of my minor expenses but was insignificant compared to the total amount needed. Had I taken out loans, I would likely be paying them back for the rest of my life.

Fortunately, between the help I received from my parents and school scholarships (provided by others), I was able to go through school debt free. Even more fortunately, I received the scholarship of Jesus' righteousness. I did so by realizing that attaining the righteousness I needed to be accepted by God by my own miniscule payments was impossible, and that my only hope was to be credited with a righteousness I could never earn.

A friend of ours, Chris, discovered this as well during his student days at the University of California at Los Angeles (UCLA). Chris thought he was in good standing with God because he attended church and reasoned that he had earned sufficient merit with God by being a 'good person.' His sense of self-assurance, however, came crashing down after a series of encounters with a college roommate who thought it was his duty to mercilessly tease and belittle Chris.

Chris became so enraged toward this person that one evening he hid at the bottom of the stairs where they lived, lying in wait with a knife to stab his tormenter who he knew was about to descend and pass by where Chris was hiding. His roommate started but suddenly turned back when someone upstairs called to him. Shaken by the violent deed he was about to commit, Chris awakened to the darkness in his life and started attending meetings at the training center near U.C.L.A. that we helped start. Chris soon embraced Jesus and received the forgiveness, righteousness, and new life that come through Him. Today Chris is the Chancellor of Eastern University.

When we turn to the risen and living Jesus and receive him as Messiah-Son-King-Lord, we are scholarshipped with an unlimited credit of righteousness. We are no longer separated from

> When we turn to Jesus, we are scholarshipped....

God, but instead are in good standing with Him. By His power, an inner transformation begins to occur, leading to the restoration of the Divine Design and a new spiritual journey. This is the thrust of the second half of Romans chapter three.

MERCY SEAT

After reiterating the hopelessness of our plight in Romans 3:1-20, he points us to the "but now" righteousness from God of Romans 3:21-23. He then goes on to speak further of the impact of the sacrifice of Jesus saying, "we are justified freely by his grace through the redemption that came by Jesus Christ. God presented him as a sacrifice of atonement, through faith in his blood" (3:24-25). The word *atonement* in Greek (*hilasteœrion*) is the same word translated by the Hebrew word *ki'pur* from which *Yom Kippur* is derived. *Yom Kippur,* known as the Day of Atonement, is the holiest day of the year in the Jewish calendar. Its central themes are atonement and repentance. The highlight of the Day of Atonement was the act of the high priest entering the Jewish Tabernacle (and later Temple) to sprinkle sacrificial blood on the "atonement cover" or "mercy seat" that rested on top of the Ark of the Covenant (Exodus 25).

Inside the Ark were three items: a pot of manna, Aaron's rod or shepherd's staff, and a copy of the 10 Commandments. Each symbolized the sin of Israel in rejecting God. The pot of manna symbolized Israel's rejection of God's provision in the Wilderness. Aaron's rod (used by Moses) represented Israel's rejection of God's leadership through Moses. The two tablets with the 10 Commandments given at Sinai symbolized Israel's rejection of God's word. Looming over the mercy seat were two gold angels symbolizing the righteousness and holiness of God. The angels looked down at the mercy seat (atonement cover), which separated the angels from the Ark itself underneath, inside of which were the symbols of Israel's sin and rebellion (Exodus 37).

Without going into all the details in the symbolism involved, the sprinkling of the blood over the atonement cover or mercy seat each year assured the Israelites that their sins were temporarily covered, atoned for, and not counted against them. The entire Old Testament sacrificial system and the Day of Kippur was a picture of the ultimate sacrifice that was to come through Messiah Jesus. Jesus is our *hilasterion*, our *kippur*, our atonement, and our mercy seat. The shed blood and sacrifice of Jesus provides forgiveness, not just temporarily, as in the annual Day of Atonement, but once and for all. The sacrifice of Jesus was the payment that provides us the scholarship of righteousness we desperately need to be in right standing with God.

TWO ROUTES?

Paul presses the theme of credited righteousness further in Romans chapter four, addressing the faulty supposition that people in the Old Testament gained God's acceptance by human effort. Paul points out that the Jewish heroes such as Abraham and David understood, as did Paul, that the righteousness they needed to be justified and in right standing before God only came as a credit or scholarship, and not through their own merit. The key word in Romans chapter four is the word "credit." It is used 10 times in Romans chapter four.[7]

The key word in Romans chapter four is "credit," used 10 times.

Paul reiterates over and over again that Abraham and David understood they had to be credited with righteousness to gain a right standing with God. Quoting from Genesis 15:6 Paul says, "Abraham believed God and it was credited to him as righteousness" (4:3). Pointing to Psalm 32:1-2, Paul notes that David speaks of the blessedness of the man to whom God "credits righteousness apart from works" (4:6). Paul states clearly that righteousness was credited to Abraham and David apart from their works (4:6). It came by faith (4:11, 13) and God's grace (4:16).

Righteousness, then as now, is not something we earn or produce; it is something we receive. It is not something we do for God; it is something God does for us. This rubs against the cynical perspective of "Nothing is free," as well as the presumptuous idea, "If I do thus and so, then God owes me." It is incredible to think that all we have to do is receive the gift of God's righteousness through Jesus, especially in spite of all the wrong things we have done.

All of Shackleton's efforts to save his crew would have been futile had he sailed the wrong course, more so if they had not found someone willing and able (Norwegian whalers) to rescue them. Shackleton's and his two mates incredible journey across icy seas and snow-covered mountains led them to the only location possible where they could get help. So it is with Jesus. He is the only one who can rescue us and impart to us righteousness and new life. Our rescue and the renewal of the Divine Design are made possible because Jesus was "delivered over to death for our sins and was raised for our justification" (4:25).

CHAPTER 8

ROMANS 5:1-8
DIVINE RESOURCES

"MEN WANTED: FOR HAZARDOUS JOURNEY. SMALL WAGES, BITTER COLD, LONG MONTHS OF COMPLETE DARKNESS, CONSTANT DANGER, SAFE RETURN DOUBTFUL. HONOUR AND RECOGNITION IN CASE OF SUCCESS."
—Sir Ernest Shackleton[1]

He (Lewis) had all the authority he needed, including the specific permission from the commander in chief to make his judgments in the field. Jefferson realized that, when Lewis reached the Pacific, 'You will be without money, clothes or provisions.' To deal with that situation, Jefferson provided a letter of credit for Lewis, authorizing him to draw on any agency of the U.S. government anywhere in the world, anything he wanted.
—*Undaunted Courage*[2]

We had been instructed to meet Shipton and his party at the railhead of Jogbani on the Indian-Nepalese border, but first we had to purchase stocks of food and fuel…. We loaded all of this and our equipment….
—Sir Edmund Hillary[3]

Therefore, since we have been justified through faith we have peace with God through our Lord Jesus Christ, through whom we have gained access by faith into this grace in which we now stand. And we now rejoice in the hope of the glory of God.

—Romans 5:1-2

EXPEDITION RESOURCES

Whether sailing across a sea, leading a trek cross-country, ascending a mountain, or traveling into outer space, expeditions require the right preparations and the right resources. Ernest Shackleton not only sought a good crew but also invested in the finest quality tools and equipment before sailing the *Endurance* to Antarctica. He gave personal and detailed attention to the supplies his crew would need.[4] Similarly, Meriwether Lewis spent several months acquiring the right tools and supplies for the journey across the North American continent. Edmund Hillary and his climbing team also purchased critical stocks of food and fuel, not to mention procuring the right equipment to summit the world's tallest mountain. The Hillary expedition totaled over 400 people, including 362 porters, twenty Sherpa guides and 10,000 pounds of baggage and supplies.[5]

Expeditions require resources. Their leaders frequently solicit investors and benefactors in order to procure the resources needed. In Lewis' case, Thomas Jefferson provided him with a letter of credit giving him access to unlimited resources. Lewis could draw on any agency of the U.S. government anywhere in the world for anything he wanted.

> Expeditions require resources.

SPIRITUAL RESOURCES

When we embrace Jesus, we are given a treasure chest of spiritual resources to draw upon for the expedition ahead of us. The Divine Expedition begins when Jesus puts us right with God who welcomes us into His family. The moment we place our trust in Messiah-Son-King-Lord Jesus, the defect of sin-within no longer alienates us from God. We are credited with righteousness and are completely accepted and made right with God.

Divine resources are available to us, enabling us to navigate the brokenness of our world. They are as critical to our survival as the resources used by Bear Gryll in his exploits. The Discovery television series *Man Vs Wild*[6] centers on former British Special Air Service member, Bear, parachuting in to some of the most inhospitable deserts, jungles, and mountains on earth. To survive and find his way back to civilization, he depends upon three tools he always takes with him: a knife, a flint, and a water bottle.

In the same way, God provides us with the essential tools we need to navigate our way forward in life successfully. This is the focus of Romans chapters five through eight. In these chapters, ten resources are revealed as part of the Divine Design, equipping us for the Divine Expedition. Having been put right with God by receiving the credited righteousness of Romans 3:21-4:25, God now makes the resources of the Divine Design in Romans 5:1-8:39 accessible to us.

The first eight of these resources are spelled out in Romans chapter five, a ninth resource is revealed in Romans chapter six, and a tenth is unveiled in Romans chapter eight. The first four resources are found in Romans chapter five verses 1-8 and relate to our upward relationship with God. The next four are laid out in the same chapter in verses 9-21. Each of these eight resources (as are resources nine and ten to follow in Romans chapters six and eight) is essential to transform us and strengthen, sustain, and equip us to carry out our mission to rescue and restore others.

PEACE WITH GOD

The eight resources in Romans chapter five can be thought of as the "4x4," as they fall into two groups of four each. The first of these is *peace with God* (5:1). Jesus removed the barrier separating us from God; thus, we no longer are alienated from Him. God accepts us as we declare our allegiance to Jesus as Messiah-Son-King-Lord. When we embrace Jesus, we lay down our weapons of resistance such as indifference, skepticism, resentment, anger, and hostility toward God. Our alienation is replaced with a loving relationship with Him. We are granted amnesty and are no longer in revolt. When we surrender to the love of God poured out in Jesus, to our surprise we discover that God is a loving Father whose rule is one of grace and goodness. He loves us and is at peace with us and we with Him.

> ...to our surprise we discover that God is a loving Father whose rule is one of grace and goodness.

I (Linus Sr.) remember in my younger years trying to pray from time to time. Frustratingly, I sensed my prayers weren't getting through and eventually concluded that there was no one there to hear me so I became an atheist. Thereupon, I relished arguing against God's existence, blaming Him for the ills of the world (if perchance He did exist). It wasn't until I opened my life to Jesus that I knew God heard and cared about me. The turning point was when I prayed, "Jesus, I know that my sin and self-centeredness separated me from God. Thank you for paying the debt that I owe. I receive you as my sin-bearer and righteousness-provider." For the first time ever, I had a deep sense that the barrier separating me from God gave way and that God was for me. My hostility toward God (and my antagonism toward my wife) ceased, and I experienced an incredible sense of peace.

Peace with God is not a static, cognitive concept or belief; it is a dynamic, spiritual reality meant for us to draw upon and guide us through the jungle of life. We can access the supernatural peace we now have with God in the midst of turmoil and uncertainty. Jesus said, "I have told you these things, so that in me you may have peace. In this world you will have trouble. But take heart! I have overcome the world" (John 16:33). Peace with God is more than the absence of hostility; it is His dynamic presence. It is the assurance of Jesus' promise, "I am with you always, to the very end of the age" (Matthew 28:20).

The Greek word Paul uses for peace has as its background the Hebrew word *shalom*. *Shalom* includes completeness, wholeness, soundness, welfare, wellbeing, and peace. Because of Jesus we have *shalom* or peace with God. Consequently, God moves to bring about completeness, wholeness, soundness, welfare, and wellbeing. It is somewhat like an old wrecked ship being restored to its original design, and able to set sail again. We are aligned with the creator and sustainer of the universe who works in and through us in *shalom* or peace.

The more we grasp and then draw upon *shalom* with God, the more our inner anxieties and fears subside. Peace with God is not a tuning-out of the world (as in Buddhism), but a tuning-in to our relationship with God and His purpose for us. This is part of the Divine Design, God working in and through us to become "shalom-makers" or "peacemakers" in the midst of the turbulent world around us. We become *shalom*-makers by drawing upon the peace we have with God. The more we draw upon this peace, the more it permeates and fills our hearts and minds, and the more it flows out from us to others.

STANDING IN GRACE

The second 4x4 resource is perpetual *access by faith into this grace in which we now stand* (5:2). We not only have peace with God, but we have access to a continual flow of God's grace and favor toward us. When we grasp this, it results in a whole new way of thinking and living. As we embrace Messiah-Son-King-Lord Jesus, God's grace flows to us.

The lyrics to the song, "How He Loves," by John Mark McMillan point to power of God's love and grace toward us:

He is jealous for me
Love's like a hurricane, I am a tree
Bending beneath the weight of His wind and mercy
When all of a sudden, I am unaware of these afflictions eclipsed by glory
and I realize just how beautiful You are and how great your affections are for me.
Oh, how He loves us so
Oh, how He loves us
How He loves us so.

Yeah, He loves us
Woah, how He loves us

Woah, how He loves us
Woah, how He loves.

So we are His portion and He is our prize,
Drawn to redemption by the grace in His eyes
If grace is an ocean we're all sinking
So heaven meets earth like a sloppy wet kiss and my heart
turns violently inside of my chest
I don't have time to maintain these regrets when I think
about the way

That he loves us,
Woah, how He loves us
Woah, how He loves us
Woah, how He loves

Whereas before we were uncertain about our standing with God, ever striving to gain some measure of good standing with Him, we now have the assurance that we are in His favor. Whereas before we were bound by religious rules, attempting to measure up to some unobtainable standard of behavior, we now are assured of unlimited access to His grace. Whereas before we perceived God was distant from us, we now are certain that He is for us and loves us, no matter the circumstances. We are "bending beneath the weight of His mercy and grace", and His grace is "an ocean in which we are sinking."

Like peace with God, our new standing of grace is not meant to be a static cognitive belief. It is a dynamic spiritual resource we are to consciously draw upon in our day-to-day lives. We access and unleash His grace by depending upon and trusting Jesus. It is *...an incremental inner transformation.* this day-to-day conscious dependence and trust in Jesus that results in an incremental inner transformation. God's peace and our access to His grace are meant to be increasingly and ever more deeply experienced and embedded in us.

HOPE IN THE GLORY OF GOD

The third 4x4 resource is *hope in the glory of God* (5:2-4). Now that we are in relationship of peace with God, He begins to manifest the glory or splendor of His design in us and through us. The downward spiral described in Romans chapter one reverses. Romans 3:23 stated that we all miss the mark of God's design and fall short of His glory. The farther we drifted from God and His revelation, the less we radiated the splendor and glory of His design. But now the barrier between God and us is removed, and we have a new hope that God is again restoring to us the glory of His design.

Paul gives us insight into how the splendor of God's design is released in us saying, "we also rejoice in our sufferings, because we know that suffering produces perseverance; persevance, character; and char-

> Even when circumstances are frustrating or painful, we remain hopeful....

acter, hope. And hope does not disappoint us...." (5:3-5). *The glory of God* is released as we rely upon Jesus and persevere in the midst of trying circumstances, struggles, and suffering.

Perseverance is the inner attitude that sees beyond immediate circumstances to the work God is doing in the midst of what is taking place around us, however painful or difficult it may be. When things seem to be falling apart, we can have the confidence that God is working to ensure that things are really falling into place. No matter how trapped or disoriented we might feel, God has a counter move that furthers His work in us. Thus, even when circumstances are frustrating or painful, we remain hopeful, knowing that God is at work to shape us, guide us, strengthen us, and restore to us His glorious Design. This hope is what leads us to persevere.

As perseverance develops within us, strength of character forms (again, taking place incrementally). Strength of character occurs as we turn from trusting in ourselves to relying upon God in the midst of our circumstances. This in turn leads to more hope.

THE DIVINE DESIGN FLYWHEEL

This is like a spiritual flywheel, gaining momentum as it turns. The first thrust of the flywheel is *hope in the glory of God*; that is, hope that God's splendor is being restored to us. This hope *produces perseverance* in the midst of trying circumstances, which is like the next turn of the flywheel. Each time the Divine Design flywheel turns it picks up momentum. So hope turns to perseverance, which then leads to *character*—strength of character, so the flywheel turns yet again. Character then leads to more *hope,* so the Divine Design flywheel turns faster. Each turn of the hope-perseverance-character-hope flywheel builds more and more momentum, leading to the splendor and glory of God's Divine Design increasingly formed in us.

One of the affects of drawing upon the *hope in the glory of God* resource is that we shift from thinking of ourselves as victims to viewing ourselves as those who can overcome and cope with whatever comes our way. For many years of my life, my (Linus Sr.) mother habitually injected disappointment and guilt into our relationship. Any time I did or said something that displeased my mother she would lay on me a sense of guilt. When my dad was alive, he would jump in and come to my mom's defense when I took issue with whatever she was displeased about. It was impossible to interact with my parents in a rational way, particularly my mom, once she began down the disappointment trail. Whenever I tried to explain my position, she would jump to another grievance, and then another and another and another. The smorgasbord of offenses became so expansive that it was impossible to continue reasonably.

After my father's death, an occasion arose when I was able to press upon my mom the unhealthiness of her pattern of relating to others. Upon landing in Portland on our way to visit her, I called to say we planned to make a stop at the store before arriving at her house. When I phoned, she wanted to know why I was late (she had our arrival time wrong). When I tried to explain that we had just landed, she protested that she had made lunch for us and now it was going to be cold. She continued to fume and express disappointment. When we finally arrived, she didn't answer the door for five minutes. We were about to leave when she slowly opened the door. As she did her body language communicated the disapproval and disappointment that I experienced many times.

Entering the breezeway of my mom's house, I explained that I didn't want to relate to her out of guilt and disapproval. As usual, she responded defensively, then followed with more blame and accusations. The issue quickly escalated from her emoting, "You told me you were going to be here in time for lunch!" to, "You stopped loving your father and me when you went to college!"

As the discussion continued, I stated, "Mom, you seem to think of yourself as a victim."

She yelled back, "I AM A VICTIM!" and continued to excuse her pattern of communication.

I pressed further and said, "Mom, it is your blaming and disapproval of perceived offenses that cause people to withdraw from you."

After several hours of tense discussion, my mother paused, gave a sigh, and, following moments of silence, admitted, "I know I have been like that for a long time. I am sorry and apologize."

Years of frustration in our relationship dissolved in an instant. Gratefully, our relationship has vastly improved since. My mom's victim mentality has disappeared. For years this kept her from the loving relationships she could have had with our family and I am sure many others. Holding on to a victim mentality, for whatever reason, prevents us from accessing the peace, grace and hope resources intended to restore God's Divine Design in us. The hope I have led to perseverance in my relationship with my parents and kept me from giving up on relating to them. I'm glad I persevered.

HOLY SPIRIT LOVE

The fourth 4x4 resource is that *God has poured his love into our hearts by the Holy Spirit, whom he has given us* (5:5). This love is the love of Christ who died for us when we were ungodly and powerless (5:6). His love extends itself to us in spite of our sinfulness (5:7-8).

Paul writes elsewhere, "because of God's great love for us, God who is rich in mercy, made us alive with Christ, even though we were dead in transgressions" (Ephesians 2:4-5). He goes on to pray that we might be "rooted and established in love" and "have power, together with all the saints, to grasp how wide and long and high and deep is the love of Christ, and to know this love that surpasses knowledge" (Ephesians 3:17-19). In his first letter to the Corinthians, Paul tells us this love is patient, kind, does not envy, does not boast, is not proud, is not rude, is not self-seeking, is not easily angered, keeps no record of wrongs, does not delight in evil, but rejoices in truth. This love always protects, always trusts, always hopes, always perseveres and never fails (1 Corinthians 13:4-8).

This is the kind of love that the Holy Spirit produces in us (Galatians 5:22). When we embrace Christ, God's Spirit comes to indwell us and pour His love into our hearts. This too is both a Divine resource and part of the restoration of the Divine Design. As we grasp and experience this love, we are compelled to look upward in gratitude to God and to focus outward in compassion toward others. The Holy Spirit imparts to us a deep sense of God's love for us and for others.

> When we embrace Christ, God's Spirit comes to indwell us and pour His love into our hearts.

Accessing the Holy Spirit's love breaks down resentment and hurt and transforms our self-centeredness. As we open ourselves to the Holy Spirit's presence, love, and empowerment, His love becomes an increasing reality in us. He transforms us within and empowers us to love God with our whole heart, soul, mind, and strength, and our neighbor as ourselves. Like the other Divine resources, we must draw upon the Spirit's love on a daily basis.

TRADING PLACES

The 1983 classic movie, *Trading Places,* gives us a glimpse of how by apprehending the first four resources in this chapter (peace with God, standing in grace, hope in God's glory, and the Holy Spirit's pouring God's love into our hearts) we are transformed. *Trading Places* depicts a wily street con, Billy Ray Valentine (played by Eddie Murphy), who is transformed into a sophisticated commodity trader. Two wealthy Duke brothers (played by Don Ameche and Ralph Bellamy) make a bet that Billy Ray would become a successful business person if given the wealth, status, and position belonging to Louis Winthorpe III, a snobbish, privileged commodities investor (played by Dan Aykroyd). Through a series of humorous but devious events orchestrated by the Duke brothers, Billy Ray and Louis trade places.

Early in the movie, there is a scene that illustrates the transformation that takes place in our lives when Christ "trades places" with us and activated the Divine Design in our lives. When Billy Ray takes possession of Louis Winthorpe's house, wealth, and possessions, Billy Ray finds it hard to believe that they are really his—so he continues to operate from his street-person survival mentality. At a party at the mansion that he now owns, when he thinks no one is looking, Billy Ray sneaks things into his pockets. As the evening goes on, it sinks in to Billy Ray that the things he is stealing already belong to him. Billy Ray's whole mentality changes as he grasps that he has a new identity of wealth and status, and he begins operating from the reality of who he now is.

A similar shift occurs in us when we grasp our new status with God and appropriate the 4x4 resources now ours. As we draw upon the resources of peace or *shalom* with God, perpetual access to His grace, hope in God's glory being restored in us, and the love of God through the Holy Spirit, a transformation occurs in the way we think and live. By turning to Jesus, we have access to the resources of the Divine Design. These are the tools that enable us to carry out the Divine Expedition and chart a path through the jungle of life. Drawing upon these resources, we are incrementally and increasingly transformed. Living from the divine resources empowers us to extend to others the peace, grace, hope, and love that are now ours.

I (Linus Jr.) am impressed with the statement, "you can't give away what you yourself don't have." People can be "religious" or "good" but not able to exhibit or extend to others the kind of peace, grace, hope, or love this chapter talks about. You must first live from these Divine resources yourself. Without possessing these resources, there will be a lack of "weightiness" to our lives. The peace, grace, hope, and love we conjure up will only rest upon our own human strength. The strength we "manufacture" will still be just that, only human strength. We need Divine strength to rise above the defect of our sin, and truly make a positive difference in the midst of the craziness of our world. Divine strength is not something we manufacture; it comes when we "receive" Jesus and draw upon the Divine resources of Romans chapter five. Once received and accessed, supernatural peace, grace, hope and love well up in our hearts, then flow out to others.

Just as Hillary and Norgay needed ice axes to climb Mount Everest, Shackleton and his companions relied upon adzes to traverse South Georgia Island, and Roosevelt and Rondon trusted themselves to dugout canoes to explore the River of Doubt, so the 4x4 resources of Romans chapter five are critical for the expedition God invites us into. God doesn't abandon us to our own strengths and abilities; He empowers us with supernatural peace, grace, hope, and love, the tools we need to live fully and pursue the greatest adventure of all—following Jesus to rescue and restore others.

But there's more, much more.

CHAPTER 9

ROMANS 5:9-21
MORE RESOURCES...MUCH MORE

It seemed unlikely that one nation could govern an entire continent. The distances were just too great. To the west, beyond the mountains, there were no roads at all, only trails. People took it for granted that it would always be this way. The idea of progress based on technological improvements or mechanics, the notion of a power source, other than muscle, falling water, or wind, was utterly alien to virtually every American. Henry Adams observed that as "great as were the material obstacles in the path of the United States, the greatest obstacle of all was in the human mind. Down to the close of the eighteenth century no change had occurred in the world, which warranted practical men in assuming that great change was to come.

—Undaunted Courage[1]

Captain Lewis is brave, prudent, habituated to the woods and familiar with Indian manners and character. He is not regularly educated, but he possesses a great mass of accurate observation on all subjects....

—Thomas Jefferson[2]

Hillary finished primary school two years early, but struggled at high school, achieving only average marks. He was initially smaller than his peers there and very shy so he took refuge in his books and daydreams of a life filled with adventure. Though gangly at 6 foot 5 inch (195 centimeters) and uncoordinated, he found that he was physically strong and had greater endurance than many of his tramping companions.

—Philippe Naughton[3]

How much more... How much more... How much more... How much more...

—Romans 5:9, 10, 15, & 17

ADAPTING SKILLS AND RESOURCES

Vision for a desired outcome, skilled use of knowledge, and wise use of resources are essential to any expedition. Thomas Jefferson envisioned something grand when he commissioned Meriwether Lewis to chart a course to the Pacific Ocean. Lewis embraced Jefferson's vision and possessed wilderness skills, as well as an understanding about such matters as surveying, politics, natural history, and geography. His family background, formal education, and hunting and farming experiences all prepared him for the leadership role he would play—but these would not be enough. His curious and inquisitive nature[4] predisposed him to develop new skills and adapt new information needed for the expedition's success.[5]

Edmund Hillary's ascent up Mt. Everest depended upon more than just a desire to climb the mountain. It even required more than a fundamental understanding of mountain climbing, basic climbing skills, and a good level of fitness. Hillary too had to learn to apply and adapt the skills and resources he possessed to changing conditions. It took sixteen days for Hillary, thirteen other climbers, and three hundred and fifty porters just to reach the Tengpoche Monastery and set up a rear camp. To reach the monastery, the team trekked one hundred and seventy miles (272 km) up the hot and humid Kathmandu Valley. From their monastery rear camp, there were still thirteen miles (twenty-one kilometers) distance and 10,900 feet (3,322 meters) elevation to arrive at Base Camp.[6]

Leaving the Tengpoche Monastery behind, Hillary led some of the team on a rigorous climb up the Khumbu Icefall to the Base Camp. Climbing the icefall was hard work, and the bare landscape and jagged ice made it difficult to pitch tents once they arrived at Base Camp. This served as the expedition's home for the next seven weeks, during which time the team carved a route through the ice and set up eight relay camps with food and shelter leading toward Everest's summit. The team moved back and forth between these camps as they prepared for the final assault to the summit.[7] All the while Hillary had to learn as he went and adapt to the rigors he encountered.

God uses our past experiences and acquired skills as we embark upon the Divine Expedition, but these are not sufficient to complete the expedition and reach the summit God beckons us toward. We must continue to grow, develop new skills, and learn to adapt the resources available to us to the challenges ahead.

> We must continue to grow, develop new skills, and learn to adapt....

When friends Ralph and John Drollinger, along with my dad, my sister Laina, and I (Linus Jr.) set out to climb Mount Whitney, the tallest mountain in the contiguous United States, we set up our base camp at 7,000 feet (over 2,000 meters). All that was needed up to that point was a reliable vehicle to drive us to the Mt. Whitney Ranger Station campsite, warm sleeping bags, and food to snack on. To ascend the remaining 7,000 feet elevation up the Mountaineers Trail (the more rugged, less marked route) to Whitney's summit, however, we needed much more.

The subsequent climb required sturdy shoes, warm socks and clothes, hydration packs, headlamps, lightweight but nourishing food, as well as a keen sense of where the trail was and an under-standing of some technical climbing maneuvers. Even with the right equipment, as inexperienced as the rest of us were (my dad and sister, that is), we could not have navigated the challenges ahead of us without guidance. Fortunately, Ralph was an experienced mountain climber and had ascended and descended the Mountaineers Trail on a number of previous occasions, so he possessed the technical expertise we needed.

Beginning our climb while still dark we picked our way up the trail with the use of headlamps with Ralph leading the way. As we moved upward, Laina began to fatigue and vomit due to altitude sickness. Our progress was slow, as we had to repeatedly stop and wait for her. Ralph hoped she would feel better after her stomach emptied but she continued to grow weaker. At 11,000 feet elevation we stopped to rest, and Ralph made the decision that Laina, my dad and he would make their way back to the Ranger Station, while John and I continued on to the Mt. Whitney summit.

My dad volunteered to return alone with Laina, but Ralph insisted he accompany and guide them. Their route over the 12,000 feet high Wooton Ridge turned out to be harrowing. Without Ralph's skill and ability to adapt and make critical course adjustments, my dad and Laina would have been at great risk. We learned later that four climbers died the week before while descending that very same Mountaineers Trail my dad and sister planned to take. Without Ralph to guide them safely back down the mountain, my dad and sister might have experienced the same fate.

THE "MUCH MORE" RESOURCES

We cannot navigate the Divine Expedition landscape without a guide and without drawing upon all of the resources God provides for us. Jesus is the guide. Figuratively speaking, the first set of 4x4 resources (peace, grace, hope, and love) is what we need to reach the Tengpoche Monastery rear camp, and the second set of 4x4 resources in Romans chapter five is what it takes to ascend higher and reach Base Camp. To proceed all the way to the summit of the Divine Expedition we need to access the additional resources described in Romans chapters six and eight.

Paul outlines a second 4x4 set of resources in Romans 5:9-21, introducing each of them with the expression "much more" (5:9, 10, 15, & 17). The four "much mores" can be viewed as two couplets. The first couplet pertains to Christ's work "in us," while the second couplet refers to Christ's work "through us." Each of the four much mores is an essential part of the renewal of the Divine Design and are resources that propel us forward on the Divine Expedition.

FIRST MUCH MORE: SAVED FROM GOD'S WRATH

The first "much more" (5th4x4 resource) is that we are *saved from God's wrath* (5:9). Paul declares, "since we have now been justified by his (Christ's) blood, *how much more* shall we be saved from God's wrath through him!" *Saved from God's wrath* is "much more" than peace with God. It is the reversal of the destructive outcomes that accumulated from ignoring God or living apart from a right standing with Him (as in the repeated use of the phrase *God gave them over* of Romans chapter one). Living indifferently to God and relying upon our own moral and religious efforts resulted in the distortion of God's design for relationships and social order. Being "saved from God's wrath" reverses this.

> Saved from God's wrath is... the reversal of the destructive outcomes.

The renewal of the Divine Design does not negate the effects of past mistakes—but it does diminish them and supplant them with God's grace. As we draw from the trove of 4x4 resources available to us, the damage inflicted by past actions (ours and others) gives way to the outworking of God's transforming power and grace. The more we draw upon these divine resources, the more we experience the increase of God's redemptive work and the diminishing of the negative effects of the past. We are no longer defined or trapped by sin-within and the selfish, dark, and hurtful things that shaped us before. God's grace increasingly works its way into our lives, restoring His design and glory to us.

SECOND MUCH MORE: SAVED THROUGH CHRIST'S LIFE

The second "much more" (6th4x4 resource) is that *we shall be saved through Christ's life*. Paul says, "How much more, having been reconciled, shall we be saved through his life!" The first "much more" is what we are saved from; the second "much more" is what we are saved through—Christ's life. Jesus works within us, not only to save us from the wrath of God, but also to restore to us the life we are meant to live.

A new friend, Tom, is an example of this. Tom contacted me (Linus Jr.) about my surfing Stand Up Paddle (SUP) Board business, wanting to try out one of my "demo boards." I wasn't sure what to think of him over the phone. He sounded a bit odd, so I scheduled a time for us to meet in person. Face-to-face with Tom, I was impressed by his huge smile, and even more by his story. Tom spent years addicted to alcohol and drugs before opening his life to Jesus. The drugs and alcohol took their toll, but Jesus freed Tom from the entrapments of his past. He has been sober for the past twenty years, is active in a church, owns his own business, and is an encouragement to others. He is also an accomplished surfer and recently sent me a picture of himself on a surfboard paddling up to a whale.

The second "much more" is that we are saved through Christ's life.

No matter how dire the circumstances and difficulties of our lives, past or present, we can turn to Jesus to work in and through us. The Gospel of John speaks of abiding in Christ and allowing His words and love to abide in us. As we do, we are assured that we will "bear much fruit" (John 15:1-8). Tom's life is a testimony to this—and so is Pierre's.

Our friend Pierre testifies to what it means to be saved through Christ's life. Both Pierre's father and Pierre's sister committed suicide, deeply affecting him. His father shot himself in front of his mother while Pierre was in another room in their family home. Hearing the shotgun blast, Pierre ran into the living room to find his mother cradling his dying father. While serving in the South African army, Pierre got word that his sister had taken her life.

After his stint in the army, Pierre became despondent and decided to travel the world as a surf bum. Windsurfing off the coast of Spain, Pierre decided that, like his father and sister, he too would end his life. He set sail out to sea, vowing not to turn back. He would keep going until he perished. With the Spanish coastline a faint thin line behind him, the wind suddenly died, Pierre's windsurf sail fell flat, and unexpectedly he encountered God. Lying flat on his board for two hours, he experienced God's presence and care. As he did, Pierre opened his life to Jesus. The wind then picked back up, and Pierre turned his windsurf board around and returned to the coast of Spain. Running up and down the beach he shouted, "I've met God! I've met God!"

Pierre continued his travels until he reached Hawaii and began surfing with one of the pastors of Hope Chapel Maui. Pierre began to grow in his newly found faith, understand more about the message of the Bible, and experience the divine resources in the book of Romans. During the recent economic crisis, when many lost heart and sunk into depression, Pierre expressed confidence in Jesus saying, "I am not under the world's economy; I am under Christ's economy."

CHRIST "FOR US"

God's work in Tom and Pierre, and others like them who turn to Jesus, points to what Paul calls "salvation" (5:10). Salvation is Jesus' work as Messiah-Son-King-Lord-Savior *for us* to bring us to God and restore us to the fullness of His design.

Salvation is God's rescue and restoration process with past, present, and future dimensions, each of which is a sequential dimension of the Divine Design.

We were saved...we are being saved...we will be saved.

_____

The *past* dimension of salvation is that we "were saved." Salvation is provided for us because of what Jesus accomplished by His life, death, resurrection, and ascension into heaven. When we place our trust in Jesus, we are credited with His righteousness and brought into a right standing and relationship of intimacy with God. Once we embrace Jesus as Messiah-Son-King-Lord-Savior, we have been and are saved. Salvation is an accomplished fact. God saved us based upon what Jesus did for us, not on the basis of what we could do for Him. This is the past aspect of salvation and the starting point of the renewal of the Divine Design and the adventure of the Divine Expedition.

But salvation is more than a past event; it is an ongoing process. The *present* dimension of God's rescue and restoration is that we "are being saved." Jesus progressively and incrementally works in us as we access the resources of the Divine Expedition. The result of this interactive process is the increasing restoration of God's Divine Design in us. This is what is meant by the second "much more"—*we shall be (and are actually being) saved through Christ's life*. As we keep accessing the divine resources available to us, the Holy Spirit works in us to transform us to be more and more Christ-like. He repairs the broken pieces of our lives, creates new life-giving attitudes and patterns, and transforms and empowers us.

However, there is also a *future* dimension of salvation. The future dimension is that we "will be saved." This is the part yet to come. It is the complete and ultimate fullness of salvation that occurs when Christ returns to establish His final kingdom. The Divine Expedition culminates when the past, present, and future dimensions of salvation intersect. Together they make up God's overarching salvation plan to rescue and restore us.

THIRD MUCH MORE: OVERFLOW OF GOD'S GRACE

The third "much more" (7^{th}4x4 resource) is the *overflowing of God's grace*. Here Paul says, "how much more did God's grace and the gift that came by the grace of the one man, Jesus Christ, overflow to the many." This shifts our focus from what God is doing *in us* and *for us* to what He is going to do *through us* in the lives of others. God's grace and the gift that came from Christ are meant to overflow through us to others—to *many others* (5:15).

> The third "much more" is the overflowing of God's grace.

As we draw upon God's grace and the gracious gift that comes through Jesus Christ, His grace flows out through us to others. God's grace is not just meant to trickle out from us, but overflow through us. He intends for us to flood our world with His grace, love, goodness, mercy, and salvation. We are His agents to do so. This is what the Divine Expedition is about: extending to others what we ourselves received. God's gift of grace is greater than any human failure, sin, and dysfunction—but it is up to us to access, activate, and extend it (5:16).

FOURTH MUCH MORE: REIGN IN LIFE THROUGH CHRIST

The fourth "much more" (8th4x4 resource) is that we will *reign in life through Jesus Christ*. Paul writes, "how much more will those who receive God's abundant provision of grace and the gift of righteousness reign in life through the one man, Jesus Christ." When we draw upon God's abundant provision of grace and His gift of righteousness, we enter a new dimension of influence. We "reign in life" through Jesus, who is Messiah-Son-King-Lord-Savior. Jesus now lives in us and empowers us (5:17). No matter how small or great our position, Christ extends His sphere of influence or "reign of life" through us.

> The fourth "much more" is that we will reign in life through Jesus Christ.

I (Linus Sr.) recently received the following email, exemplifying how, by God's grace, Jesus extends His influence though us:

> Dear Linus,
>
> It has been many years (almost 40) since I saw or talked to you last. We met when you were in student ministry at Northwestern University in Evanston, Illinois. I was a football player. If you don't remember me I wouldn't be surprised but on the other hand you are very memorable to me. You were a great influence and friend during my freshman year.
>
> My life has been quite blessed. I have been healthy, married a wonderful woman, had a job (I am now retired) I enjoyed, and live in a great community (Holland, Michigan). Most importantly, my faith has grown and God's forgiveness and blessings are more meaningful today than ever. A lot of that I owe to people like you who were great to be around. Thank you.
>
> You may also remember Jack C. from Northwestern. He was a 'rounder' as they say up until he was about 40. He has become a believer and in fact preaches and plays gospel music with his wife. They were both small town Michigan physicians but now are doing their preaching and music exclusively.

I remember you having to sneak onto campus to meet. It was quite memorable. As an aside, my freshmen year roommate (who became a believer) and I keep in touch. He is still strong in his faith and is thankful you took time to meet with us.

I looked you up on Google because your name came to me last night and I was curious where you were and how you are doing. I recognized you immediately from your picture; so although you look great, you are no better looking than you were in the '60's. (Do you still have a sense of humor?).

Best wishes,

Ken

The "sneaking on to campus" Ken (I called him Kenny) referred to was due to the disfavor of the Northwestern University Board of Religion toward the student Christian ministry with which I served. The university embraced a rationalistic view of Jesus and the Bible, while we did not. They disdained such things as miracles and the literal bodily resurrection of Jesus from the dead. We were convinced, however, that these things were real and that we could know Jesus in a personal real way, not just as wishful thinking of people past or present. What especially annoyed the religious officials was that we had a vibrant work and a large student following.

I was called in to meet with the Board of Religion, made up of the university chaplain and other rationalistic religious leaders and was told that I was no longer allowed on campus. The reason given was that I "didn't have a seminary degree." When students involved in our work found out the Board of Religion's decision to kick me off the campus, they circulated a protest petition objecting to the Board's decision. At least 500 university students signed the petition (only 6,500 students attended the university at that time). In addition, parents of students and alumni of the school added their voices of protest because there was nothing in the Northwestern by-laws that said a seminary degree was required to work with students. It was an arbitrary decision based on philosophical/theological prejudice.

Because of the pressure put on them, the Board of Religion rescinded their decision, allowing me to return as a campus minister. During the following summer, however, the Board added the requirement of a seminary degree to the university's by-laws and kicked me off the campus again. This time, our organization brought in a seminary graduate whom I trained as a replacement—though I had to sneak onto the campus and sit in the bushes outside the meeting to do so. I was then transferred to U.C.L.A.

It was during this turbulent time that I met and got to know Ken. It is exciting to think back to how God extended the sphere of His influence through what happened and the relationships that were formed at that time. Since I was not officially allowed on campus, students like Ken passed a chair to me out of the campus meeting place so I could listen and later give input to the person I was training—fortunately, it was not yet winter in Chicago. It is exciting to know how God has worked through the years to spread His kingdom through Ken and other students who I met during that time.

The influence of Christ *in us* spreads to others *through us* as we draw upon our Divine resources in pursuit of the Divine Expedition. Through Jesus we move from impotence to influence. God extends His reign to the world through us. Our impotence and brokenness (Genesis 1-3 and Romans 1:1-18), is replaced by "God's abundant provision of grace and the gift of righteousness" through Jesus Christ. No longer bound by our weaknesses or inability to measure up to God's righteous standards, we are empowered to "reign in life." "Jesus Christ our Lord" working *through us* results in lasting positive effects in time and eternity (5:17, 21).

TREASURE CHEST OF RESOURCES

When we embrace Jesus as Messiah-Son-King-Lord-Savior, we are given a treasure chest of spiritual resources to draw upon for the Divine Expedition. We have a new *peace*, a new *standing in grace*, a new *hope in the glory of God*, and a new *love that is poured into our hearts* through the Holy Spirit. But we are given "much more."

We are *saved from God's wrath*; we are *saved through Christ's life*; God's *grace overflows through us* to others; and we *reign in life through Jesus Christ*.

As we look at the early years of men like Meriwether Lewis and Edmund Hillary, it is hard to detect that they would eventually become leaders of great expeditions. Lewis was not regularly educated, and Hillary struggled in high school, achieving only average marks. Yet something stirred within them, and they learned to utilize skills and adapt resources to seemingly insurmountable challenges that led to great accomplishments. Correspondingly, the greatest expedition of all is entrusted to us, unspectacular people who press in to take hold of the 4x4 Divine resources God provides—and allow the life of Christ to pulsate through us, as we see in the next chapter.

CHAPTER 10

ROMANS 6:1-23
DIVINE LIFE

In this nurturing environment, so conducive to reflection, Cook began to see his true potential. In his mind he became more than a cartographer and a ship's captain, he became a singular figure for the ages: a discoverer.
—Farther Than Any Man[1]

He (Magellan) emerged from the ordeal a very different man from the one who had begun the voyage.
—Over the Edge of the World[2]

Now world famous, Sir Edmund Hillary turned to Antarctic exploration and led the New Zealand section of the Trans-Antarctic expedition from 1955 to 1958. In 1958 he participated in the first mechanized expedition to the South Pole. Hillary went on to organize further mountain-climbing expeditions but, as the years passed, he became more and more concerned with the welfare of the Nepalese people.
—"Sir Edmund Hillary Biography"[3]

And just as Christ was raised from the dead by the glorious power of the Father, now we also may live new lives.
—Romans 6:4[4]

CHANGED LIVES

Leaders of expeditions for better or worse influence those who travel with them, those they meet along the way, and even those they report to. But more than their impact on others, expeditions especially effect and even change the leader. This is reflected in the statements above about English Captain James Cook,[5] Portuguese (though he sailed for Spain) explorer Ferdinand Magellan, and New Zealander mountaineer Sir[6] Edmund Hillary.

Expeditions bring out the best or the worst in us. In Hillary's case, ascending Mt. Everest brought out the best. His success led not only to personal acclaim, but also to humanitarian effort. He became concerned about the wellbeing of the Nepalese and the degradation of the environment of the Himalayas. He subsequently persuaded the Nepalese government to pass laws protecting the forest and used his great prestige to persuade the government of New Zealand to provide aid for the Nepalese. He continued to occupy himself with environmental causes and humanitarian work on behalf of the Nepalese people for the rest of his life.

In Magellan's case, the challenges he faced brought about mixed changes. A crucial evolution in Magellan's life occurred over a period of nine trying months from February to October in the year 1520. The Magellan of February was on the brink of being murdered by the men under his command. Most of the Spanish officers and even the Portuguese pilots on the expedition were convinced that their rigid Captain General was leading them to their deaths. The severe challenge to Magellan's leadership forced him to show more restraint than he might have otherwise, though unfortunately he continued to be authoritarian, harsh, and brutal in his leadership. In discovering the straight of Magellan, navigating uncharted reaches of the Pacific Ocean, and claiming the Philippines for Spain, his behavior was sometimes beneficent, sometimes menacing, and occasionally both, suggesting that his accomplishments had gone to his head.[7]

Both the best and worst were true of Cook. On the one hand, Cook is heralded for "His indomitable perseverance and courage, his disdain of comfort, his calmness and capacity in danger, and his singleness of purpose. These qualities, along with his stupendous achievements, marked him as one of the greatest of Englishmen."[8] Unfortunately, success appears to have gone to Cook's head. When the native Hawaiians mistook him for their great god Lono, offering divine honors to him, Cook strangely accepted them. Soon thereafter, trouble began, ending in Cook's violent death at the hands of the Hawaiians.

Expeditions change our self-perception, and we begin to see ourselves differently. They reveal our good qualities and expose our bad ones. They stretch us and require the development of greater inner strength. For those who embark upon the Divine Expedition, positive new characteristics, perspectives, and strengths emerge as we access the spiritual resources God designs for us. When drawn upon, these resources soften the rough edges of our character, implant new attitudes, draw out our unseen potential, enhance our leadership capabilities, and expand our influence. Drawing upon the supernatural 4x4 resources of the Divine Design changes us, as well as others around us.

> Expeditions change our self-perception.

THE 9TH RESOURCE: UNION WITH CHRIST

Romans chapter six plunges us further into the bevy of resources of the Divine Design and the transforming work of God in our lives. This chapter elaborates the ninth divine resource provided for us: an inseparable union with Messiah-Son-King-Lord-Savior Jesus. We enter this incredible union with Jesus when we put our faith in Him, resulting in new life in Christ.

Paul asserts that we are united with Christ Jesus (6:5), saying we are *baptized* into His death, burial, and resurrection (6:3-6). The word "baptized" means to immerse one thing into another. Baptism was a rite and symbol of initiation whereby a person became part of a new community. By placing our trust in Jesus as Messiah-Son-King-Lord-Savior, we are supernaturally and spiritually immersed into Jesus and the community of those who follow Him. Writing to the Corinthians, Paul says, "The body (new community of Christ's followers) is a unit; and though all its parts are many, they form one body. So it is with Christ. For we were all *baptized* into one body (Christ's body)—whether Jews or non-Jews, slave or free—and were given the one Spirit (the Holy Spirit) to drink."[9]

We are united with Christ by the supernatural action of the Holy Spirit. When we entrust our lives to Jesus, the Holy Spirit comes to indwell us, immersing us into the death, burial, and resurrection of Jesus (6:3-4), thus, rescuing us and making us a part of the community of His followers. The Holy Spirit is imparted to us when we open our lives to Jesus. Paul says in Romans 8, "And if anyone does not have the Spirit of Christ, he does not belong to Christ. But Christ is in you...."[10]

It could be said of the thirty-three miners, trapped for sixty-nine days 2,300 feet (700 meters) below earth in Chile that on October 13, 2010, they were baptized (immersed) into the rescue capsule that then carried each miner up through a shaft to the earth's surface. Without entering this twenty-four inch (sixty-one centimeter) capsule, none would have been saved.

The same is true of us. The moment we received Jesus as Messiah, Son, King, Lord, and Savior, the Holy Spirit baptizes us into Christ and supernaturally connects us to Jesus and the events that occurred 2000 years ago. These were real historical events, but their effect transcends time. Jesus lived in real time space and history but now dwells in a realm not limited by time or space—yet one that connects to all time and space. United with Christ, the historical death and resurrection of Jesus is efficacious to us.

> Because we are baptized into Jesus, just as He was raised from the dead, so we too may live a new life.

Because we are baptized into Jesus, just as He was raised from the dead, so *we too may live a new life* (6:4). Because we are immersed into Christ, *we will also live with him* (6:8). Through Jesus, the Messiah-Son-King-Lord-Savior, we are united with the infinite, eternal, creator God of the universe, who stands outside the time and space limitations of our universe. Thus, we have a new identity and a new life rooted in our connection to Jesus. When we grasp this, our lives are changed.

IT'S NOT ALL ABOUT ME

It took me (Linus Jr.) some time to grasp the unbelievable resources available to me through the Divine Expedition. When younger, I developed a belief that living as a Christ-follower relied on how much I did—how much I read scripture or other books on the Christian faith, how much I prayed, and how much I spent time helping others. The fuzziness of my thinking was the word "I." I mistakenly thought, "I must do it." I surmised, "It is up to me." I reasoned, "It's all about me." I felt it was on me to please God and ensure a right standing with Him. The things I was doing were good, but I came to realize that I could never earn what God had already provided me as a gift. My efforts were as futile as it would have been for a Chilean miner to try to dig his way out of his entrapment, rather than just get in the capsule.

My life began to change as I began grasped that my acceptance with God is based simply placing my trust in God's gracious gift of rescue in Jesus. I stepped into the rescue capsule of Christ as I realized He is the life-giver I needed and that the Christian life is based on His indwelling presence in my life. The only way to effectively follow Jesus was for me to rely upon His living in me. The more I realized this, the more I experienced God's transforming power and a new identity in Christ.

Being a Christ-follower is not about sin management; it is about being connected to Jesus and walking with Him. In this way, God empowers us to carry out the Divine Expedition. It is really that simple. Following Jesus is about opening our hearts to Him, letting Him indwell and work through us. It is about relying upon Him and allowing Him to express Himself through us. This leads us through a shaft of transformation and new life so that we reflect God's Divine Design.

Second century church father and apologist Irenaeus of Lyon said, "The glory of God is man fully alive." Because Jesus is at work in me, I experience "aliveness;" that is, an intimate relationship with God. I speak to Him through prayer, and He speaks to me through Scripture and the Holy Spirit. Comprehending this, I now enjoy reading, studying, praying, and have a passion to help others. I don't do these things to merit anything; I do them because they enhance my sense of God working in me and through me. This is what it means to be a follower of Jesus and a participant in His mission to rescue and restore others.

NEW LIFE IN CHRIST

Because of our new spiritual reality of union with Christ, we "count" ourselves "dead to sin but alive to God in Christ Jesus" (6:11). This activates our new life in Christ. The word *offer* (other translations use the words *present* or *yield*)[12] is another word that Paul uses in this chapter to communicate how we activate new life in Jesus (6:13, 16, 19). To *count*, to *offer,* to *present,* to *yield* is the action step we take that releases Christ's life within us, restores the Divine Design in us, and outfits us for the mission of the Divine Expedition. As we offer ourselves to God over and over again, we increasingly experience the transformation, love, and good that God purposes for us.

> To count, to offer, to present, to yield is the action step we take that releases Christ's life within us.

To offer ourselves means we follow Jesus, so to speak, off the diving board. He jumped into the loving and good hands of God by His sacrificial life, doing so to rescue us. Though he disappeared briefly in His death (three days), He was lifted up by God's resurrection power. Now it is time for us to follow His example. Offering ourselves daily as followers of Jesus releases the supernatural resurrection power of God through us (6:10-14). The incremental changes accumulate in us and become visible in wholeness, holiness, empowerment, fruitfulness, and effective participation in the Divine Expedition. Thus, the real purpose of our lives unfolds (6:19-23).

> Eternal life does not begin at the end of our physical existence.

Although we were previously marked by death (separation from God), we are now connected to God and have the free "gift of eternal life in Christ Jesus our Lord" (6:23). Eternal life does not begin at the end of our physical existence; it is the life of a transcending union with Christ we now possess. This new life commences when we receive Jesus, empowering us to live to God (6:10).

Being united with Christ and new life in Him transforms our outlook, even when facing difficulties and death. One of my (Linus Sr.) mentors was Ian Rennie, my church history professor at Regent College in Vancouver, BC, Canada. Ian influenced me greatly, not only by what he taught me in class, but also by the kind of person he was outside the classroom. He was a great teacher, had an enormous love for Christ and for people, and was a constant learner. While at Regent, he took special interest in my studies and directed my Master's of Christian Studies' dissertation.

On one occasion, Ian and his wife, Lee, invited Sharon and me to join them at a conference he was leading in Fort Saint John in north east British Columbia. Sharon and I stopped by their hotel room prior to one of our meetings and discovered Ian reading a phone book. Now I had never seen someone read a phone book before so I asked what he was doing. He replied he was learning about the ethnic origins of the city by reading the names of people listed in the phone book. I would never have thought of doing that.

Ian was more than a professor, he was also a pastor, friend, and example of what it means to live from the indwelling life of Christ. When I heard about the terminal cancer of Ian's life-long wife and friend, Lee, as well as his own failing health, I called to express my deep appreciation for the influence he had upon me. As always, he exhibited his usual kindness and other-centeredness, asking me about my family and me. He later wrote a note to me that said, "Our days in this world are limited with Lee having a recurrence of chemotherapy. I am not able to do much writing, and cannot drive or speak in public—yet there is endless joy in our Lord."

Knowing we are united with Jesus brings joy. We are so intimately connected with Jesus that we are in Him and He is in us. Jesus said, "I am the true vine...abide in me and I will abide in you. No branch can bear fruit by itself; it must remain in the vine."[11] The abiding presence of Jesus in us is what empowers us to live for God and engage in the Divine Expedition. We receive Him when we believe in His name (Jesus: Messiah-Son-King-Lord-Savior) and trust Him for all He did on our behalf. When we open the door of our lives to Him (John 1:12; Romans 6:1-4; Revelation 3:20), we are infused with His supernatural, resurrected life. The very life of Jesus pulses within us, energizing and transforming us, thus enabling us to live a new life (6:4).

This realization is explosive. The message of the Gospel is not "God left us the Bible, so we'll see Him when we die." It is, rather, an exciting journey of intimacy, adventure, and union with Him. It is a relationship of empowerment. A relationship with God through Jesus is not like tuning up an old car engine so that it can run better for a while. It is rather like replacing the car engine with one from a jet airplane. The jet engine is much more powerful—powerful enough to propel us forward on the Divine Expedition with Messiah-Son-King-Lord-Savior Jesus as the pilot.

"BUT GOD"

With Jesus residing in us, life is no longer a matter of what we can do in our own strength. Prior to moving to France to start a new church, I (Linus Sr.) met with some of the leaders (deacons) of the church we were members of to seek their support for our missional endeavor. When I told them that Sharon and I sensed God leading us to start a new church in France, they discouraged us from going. They reasoned we were too old (I was thirty-eight), we had too many children (six), it wouldn't be cost effective, and the cultural adjustment would be too difficult for a family with children ranging in ages from newborn to eighteen. I made a list of their objections and left the meeting a bit discouraged, thinking that when I recited them to Sharon, she would conclude we shouldn't go.

> Living life is no longer a matter of what we can do in our own strength.

Sitting down together with Sharon, to my surprise she began her reply to each of deacon's points with the words, "*But God.*" She exclaimed, "*But God* could use the experience of an 'older couple'." "*But God* could provide the resources we need." "*But God* could use a larger family to connect with others." "*But God* could get us

119

through the cultural adjustment." Buoyed by the sense that God was guiding us, we decided to move to France, trusting in "But God" to provide for us, and work through us. We believed that Jesus would lead us, meet our needs, and provide for us—and He did.

The Divine Expedition is based upon the *"But God"* factor. It is based upon the life transforming, resurrected power of "But Jesus living in me." As we draw upon His life, we are not only freed from sin, (6:5-7; Hebrews 12:1-2); we are empowered to live a new life. God strengthens and guide us in the midst of life's challenges, and our new life in Jesus catapults us into the mission of rescuing and restoring others.

To carry out the mission God calls us to requires accessing His provision of empowerment. Our connection to Jesus imparts to us new life, replacing the spiritual deadness previously infecting us (6:8-9 with 5:21). We release this new life by "counting" ourselves "dead to sin but alive to God in Christ Jesus" (6:11). Each time we do, the bondage of old sin-influenced patterns is diminished, and the new reality of being brought from death into life emerges (6:13).

Another way Paul expresses how we activate our new life in Christ is the call to "wholeheartedly obey the teaching (the good news about Jesus and the resources and new life we have in Him) to which we have been entrusted" (6:17). To obey means to 'come under,' that is to embrace, accept, and trust Jesus and the grace and strength He imparts to us.

JUMP WITH JESUS

I (Linus Jr.) know many men and women who feel disconnected to God. Underneath, they are fearful of surrendering to God because they are unsure that He is good and really loves them. Jesus, however, is the proof of God's goodness and love. His own submission to God led to His death, but also to His resurrection to new life.

Jesus' resurrection assures us that we can trust God. Following Jesus is like following someone off a diving board. Jesus trusted God's love, goodness, and power, jumped into the arms of God in His death, and came back up, paving the way for us to take the plunge of trusting God with our lives. The lasting fulfillment and joy each of us seeks in life only comes by "jumping with Jesus;" that is, in trusting, surrendering, and coming under God's goodness, love, and power as Jesus did.

Each time we offer ourselves to God and use our bodies as instruments to carry out His will, we tap into new life in Jesus and find that like Him we are in the care of a loving and good God. When we embark upon following Jesus, like Hillary, we find that the expedition changes us...for the good.

CHAPTER 11

ROMANS 7:1-25
WHY ISN'T IT WORKING?

After his (Captain James Cook) departure from Botany Bay he continued northwards, and a mishap occurred when Endeavour ran aground on a shoal of the Great Barrier Reef.
— *The Captain Cook Encyclopædia* [1]

Just as they had dropped off to sleep, a crack in the ice tore through their camp and they had to scramble to another spot for safety. It was suddenly clear they were going to face an extraordinary challenge just to stay alive. The men had expected to be working in relative comfort in a base camp, or to be doing ship's work. Instead, they were stranded on a vast, unstable layer of ice that was their only refuge from the depths of the Weddell Sea, or even worse, the jaws of a killer whale or a sea leopard. And it was -16 degree Fahrenheit.
— *Shackleton's Way* [2]

For the next hour and more we were engaged in a struggle which none of us will ever forget. We were trying to put up just one of those two small tents, fighting with the wind, an invisible enemy, which pulled the canvas from our hands and made our task all but impos-

sible. Weak as we were after our climb, deprived now of oxygen, we were hopelessly inadequate for the job.
—John Hunt[3]

He was entering a heart of darkness.
—*Undaunted Courage*[4]

I do not understand what I do. For what I want to do I do not do, but what I hate I do.
—Romans 7:15

RUN AGROUND

Expeditions don't always go as planned; they often face moments of crisis. One such situation for Captain James Cook came as he nursed his broken ship, *Endeavour,* north between the eastern coast of Australia and (unknowingly) the Great Barrier Reef, which angled toward the coastline. Suddenly, *Endeavour* slammed hard into the coral reef and ground to a violent halt. The mighty surf pounded the beleaguered ship, wedging her wooden hull tightly on the reef. In desperation, Cook ordered everything expendable of great weight to be heaved overboard. Still the ship stuck fast. Cook admitted years later that, in spite of his outwardly cool demeanor, inwardly he feared being stuck forever on what came to be named "Endeavour Reef."[5]

Romans chapter seven points to the fact that the bearers of the Divine Expedition can run aground as well. The voyage so far—the renewal of the Divine Design, including our credit of righteousness (3:20-4:25), access to the 4x4 Divine resources (5:1-21), and new life in Christ (6:1-23)—is off to a promising start. Now, however, we are introduced to a problem as threatening to the Divine Expedition as the crack in the Antarctic ice was for Shackleton, the fierce Himalaya wind was for the Hunt-Hillary Everest expedition, and the Great Barrier Reef was for Cook.

> The bearers of the Divine Expedition can run aground as well.

Paul tells us how the restoration of the Divine Design can be stifled and the Divine Expedition can run aground. Like a crack in the ice, there is a dynamic that hinders the activating of the Divine Design resources of Romans 5 and stymies the release of new life in Christ of Romans 6. This dynamic keeps us from doing what we want and causes us to do what we don't want (7:14). It is as though the vessel of the Divine Expedition is stuck in an ice floe with the resources of the Divine Design trapped inside.

More than a few times, my (Linus Sr.) expedition progress has been hampered, as I have had to address issues in my life that I was blind to. One such experience occurred during my student ministry days. My staff members asked me to meet with them. Since I was normally the one who scheduled our meetings, I knew there was a problem—and that it probably involved me. During the session that followed, my team complained that I spent more time with one of our teammates, the one who worked with athletes. The rest of my staff believed I gave them less support and felt slighted.

While painful to admit, I realized I was guilty as charged and apologized for my insensitivity. Because one of the disgruntled team members exaggerated what they felt I had done wrong, my dear wife Sharon came to my defense. I appreciated her support but I knew I had to acknowledge to the team that I slighted them and was sorry. Had I not done so, the issue would have festered, and our team's *esprit de corps* and ability to work together would have been derailed.

In leadership, the shoe is often on the other foot, as I have had to address issues with others that I felt could shipwreck the team, the work, or the individual. At times, the response is one of appreciation followed by an effort to correct whatever the issue may be and to try to grow through it. Unfortunately, at other times, the input is met with blame, denial, and resistance. The person resisting the input typically faults the message, the messenger, or the way the message was delivered—sometimes a combination of all three.

LIFE IS DIFFICULT

It is challenging to speak into peoples' lives. The difficulty is due to the frequency with which people become defensive. I am amazed at how fragile people are to input, and the lengths they will go to keep from facing substantive issues that hurt them or others. It is a universal human trait to fend off hurt and push away criticism, but it is important to learn to discern when it is merited and constructive. When it is merited, we need to embrace it, or at least the part of the input that is constructive. By pushing away constructive input, we accumulate more hurt and difficulty. Author and psychiatrist M. Scott Peck says something similar in *The Road Less Travelled*.[6] After opening his book with the statement "Life is difficult," he goes on to say,

> "What makes life difficult is that the process of confronting and solving problems is a painful one. Problems, depending upon their nature, evoke in us frustration or grief or sadness or loneliness or guilt or regret or anger or fear or anxiety or anguish or despair. These are uncomfortable feelings, often very uncomfortable, often as painful as any kind of physical pain, sometimes equaling the very worst kind of physical pain. Indeed, it is because of the pain that events or conflicts engender in us all that we call them problems. And since life poses an endless series of problems, life is always difficult and is full of pain as well as joy."

Fearing pain, most of us, to a greater or lesser degree, attempt to avoid facing problems [including critique]. We seek to skirt them rather than meet them head on. We attempt to get out of them rather than work through them. Unfortunately, according to Peck, the tendency to avoid facing problems and emotional suffering is the primary basis of all mental illness. When we avoid legitimate suffering that results from dealing with problems, we also avoid the growth that overcoming those problems demand from us.[7]

> The tendency to avoid problems and emotional suffering is the primary basis of all human mental illness.

THE FOUR SPIRITUAL LAWS

Romans chapter seven deals head on with a serious problem that all of us face. Left unaddressed, this problem will prevent us from accessing the fullness of God's design and purpose for us. Paul telescopes in on this issue by introducing 'four spiritual laws' or interactive dynamics that influence us, profoundly affecting our ability to activate the resources of the Divine Design and carry out the Divine Expedition. The first three laws are in Romans chapter seven, and the fourth is found in Romans chapter eight.

The *first law* or dynamic is the *law of God* (7:1-16). This is the Old Testament Mosaic Law containing the Ten Commandments given to Moses on Mount Sinai (Exodus 20). The Mosaic Law (called 'God's law' or the 'law of God,' and henceforth in this book capitalized as 'God's Law' or the 'Law of God' for clarity) expresses the moral character of God and the moral and spiritual structure He built into the fabric of creation. God's Law was given to bless and protect us as it reveals the design of the universe. When we ignore or violate the structure of God's Law, life doesn't work in the way it is meant. When we adhere to God's Law, we are in alignment with God Himself, the universe He created, and the way we are designed. Thus, we are told that God's Law is "holy, righteous and good" (7:12).

> The first law or dynamic is the law of God.

THE SECOND LAW

The *second law* or dynamic is what Paul calls *the law of my mind* (7:23). When we embrace Jesus as Messiah-Son-King-Lord-Savior, a spiritual sensitivity is birthed within us that recognizes and acknowledges the rightness of God's Law. There is a new inner desire to "do what is good" (7:18). This desire is the spark of the Divine Design (Romans 3:21-6:23) now kindled within us, and at play in our minds.

> The second law or dynamic is the law of my mind.

"The law of my mind" delights in God's law (the first law or dynamic) because we realize it was given for our wellbeing (7:22). We mentally consent to the fact that what God revealed in the Mosaic Law is holy, righteous, and good. We are relieved to know that chaos and relativism are not the ultimate reality of the universe, but that there is a grand design giving structure, order, and meaning to our lives.

THE THIRD LAW

Unfortunately, there is a *third law* at work within us. This is the *law of sin* (sin-within). It is this dynamic that inhibits us from living out *God's Law*, which *the law of our mind* desires to do. The defective dynamic of sin-within drags us down and produces death in us (7:13-20, 23-24). The force of the *law of sin* is as menacing to the Divine Expedition as the Great Barrier Reef was to Cook's ship *Endeavor.*

> Unfortunately, there is a third law or force at work within us.
> _____

THE SIN-WITHIN VIRUS

The *law of sin* is like an infection or virus weakening us and sapping our strength. Even though we have access to the Divine resources of Romans 5 and the new life in Christ of Romans 6, the virus of sin lurks within us, hindering us from fully activating the Divine Design resources in us and allowing Christ's life to shine through us.

I (Linus Sr.) at one stage of my life had recurring sore throats and bronchial infections, one of which resulted in pneumonia and the paralysis of my left vocal chord. Doctors finally discovered that the source of my illnesses was a permanent infection embedded in one my tonsils. It was so scarred over that it was not easily detectable. The only solution was a tonsillectomy, the removal of the infected tonsil. In a similar way, sin-within is embedded in us and wages war against both *the law of my* mind and *the Law of God* (7:21-23).

The dynamic of sin-within weakens us so that we end up doing what we don't want to do and aren't able to do what we want. This was the problem of Judaism. Sin-within weakened the followers of Judaism, preventing them from fulfilling their pledge to keep God's Law (Exodus 19:8). The same is true of all religions and all humanity. Sin-within traps us and holds us captive, resulting in destructive behavior and the breakdown of society. Unexpectedly, in the sequence of Romans, this is also true of those who have turned to Jesus and are embarking upon the Divine Expedition. In our journey to follow Jesus, we run into the reality that the dynamic of sin-within is still present in us.

I (Linus Jr.) was close with someone who said that he had been verbally abused growing up, but swore he would never do the same. Sadly, he confessed, "Now I am doing the same thing." Even though professing belief in Jesus, he was being dragged down by the woundedness of his past and the infection of sin-within. Because he did not understand the "four laws" or dynamics of Romans 7 and 8, he remained trapped in destructive patterns. The Divine Design was stunted in his life.

Without the transforming power of the *fourth law* or dynamic, found in Romans chapter eight, we are spiritually and relationally vulnerable to the impulses of sin-within, exhibited by a friend who at a recent high-school class reunion shared with me (Linus Sr.) that he was having marital problems. I did not know the extent of the difficulty until I received word a few weeks later that he shot his wife multiple times, killing her before turning himself in to the police. He now awaits trial for second-degree murder. He too professed to be a Christian but gave in to the dynamic of sin-within. While the push and pull of the destructive force of sin may not express itself as tragically as this in most people's lives, the dynamic of sin-within plays out in all of us in some way and to some degree.

> Without the transforming power of the fourth law or dynamic, we are vulnerable to the impulses of sin-within.

THE SIN-WITHIN DETECTOR

The infection of sin-within is not always easily detectable. Thus, God's Law was given as a "sin-detector." The dynamic of sin-within is actually aroused and intensified as it comes in contact with God's Law as Paul speaks of "the sinful passions aroused by the law" (7:5). The *law of God* (God's Law) is like an agitator that causes the dirt in a wash to come out. The Law of God not only reveals the character of God and His design of the universe, but it also detects embedded sin-within (7:7-13).

God's Law is like a motion sensor that warns of an intruder, or a barometer that indicates a rising storm. It alerts us to the influence and presence of that which is out of alignment with God's Law. This is consistent with Paul's earlier statement that the Law of God was given so that "the trespass might increase" (5:20). In other words, God's Law wasn't given to make us better; it was given to bring about awareness that something is defective within us.

> God's Law reveals that we are out of alignment with His design.

Many people mistakenly think that God's Law is like a ladder that morally or spiritually enables us to climb our way to God. The problem is that the ladder of self-effort (morality and religion) can't reach high enough; it doesn't even come close. God's Law, rather, is like a thermometer that shows us we are sick. A thermometer will never make us better; it merely alerts us that we have a fever. Only when we detect that we have a fever, revealed by the thermometer of God's Law, can we address the underlying infection weakening us (7:14-20). It is the dynamic of sin-within that prevents us from activating the 4x4 resources of the Divine Design and our new life in Christ. It is sin-within that hinders us from moving forward on the Divine Expedition. It is imperative to treat this in order to go forward.

REALITY CHECK

Remembering that the book of Romans is intentionally sequential ("Where are you in the Book of Romans?"), chapter seven serves as a reality check. Many who aspire to follow Christ get stuck and fail to go forward because they do not know how to deal with the downward pull of the ongoing presence of sin or the wounds and damage that sin-within effects in their lives. They deny, ignore, or are oblivious to the debilitating influence of sin-within upon their thinking, behavior, self-image, and the way they relate to others.

Surveys indicate there is very little difference in the morality and lifestyle of those who consider themselves "born-again" Christians and those who do not consider themselves religious.[8] This is due to the naïveté regarding the ongoing dynamic of sin-within and the failure to access the empowerment of the *fourth law* to counter the influence of sin-within.

The high numbers of Christian leaders involved in moral failure indicate that leaders, too, underestimate their vulnerability to the dynamic of sin-within. Sin-within often channels through festering wounds rooted in the past. Without recognizing or giving adequate weight to their vulnerability and woundedness, leaders easily become overconfident in their charisma and fail to develop the needed underpinning of inner integrity, character, spirituality, as well as accountability in community with others.

This same vulnerability to sin-within is seen in many (but fortunately not all) Biblical characters. A study of the forty-nine leaders mentioned in the Bible with information on how they finished their lives indicates that only thirteen finished well, a mere twenty-six percent. Those who did not finish well succumbed to things like pride, abuse of power, sexual temptation, mismanagement of money or other such issues.

All of us carry wounds from our past that predispose us to relational, emotional, and psychological dysfunction. These dysfunctions become magnified in later life if not addressed. A desire to do what is good may be present, but, as Paul recognizes, "we can't carry it out" (7:18-20). Unrecognized and unattended wounds and dysfunction become the springboard for the already present dynamic of sin-within, causing us to do what we don't want, and keeping us from doing what we want. Whatever the mix of causes, all of us are prone to run aground or be swept under by the infectious presence of sin-within.

> All of us are prone to run aground or be swept under by the infectious presence of sin-within.

SUCKED UNDER

I (Linus Jr.) love surfing big waves (not giant ones). One winter my friend Zac and I drove south of the U.S./Mexican border to one of our favorite surf spots where we found a large swell. We parked, put on our wetsuits, grabbed our surfboards, made our way down a pathway to the shore, and paddled out. We had done this many times before, but this day would be different. The sea was angry, and the waves were huge and wild. I caught a few good-sized waves and watched Zac ride some big ones as well.

We were having a great time until suddenly I looked up and saw looming above me a huge "clean up" wave roaring toward us like an enormous sea monster. A clean up wave is a wave that breaks too far out to paddle over and is so powerful that it wipes out everything and everyone in its path. As the dark (not jolly) green giant roared toward me, I frantically yelled to Zac, "What do we do?" Panicked, I irrationally wished Zac could wave a magic wand, signal a helicopter, or do some miraculous thing to rescue us.

The moment before the giant wave slammed me, I threw myself off my board and dove as deep as I could to escape the 20-foot mountain of water crashing on top of me. The wave's vibration rocked the sea around me and drove me downward. I held my breath, waiting for it to pass before popping back up as I normally did. The force of this wave, however, sucked me even deeper by its turbulent force, and I tumbled underwater like a rag-doll in a washing machine. I was close to losing consciousness before the wave finally released me from its grip and I bobbed back up to the ocean's surface, gasping for air. That ended my desire to surf that day! I was done and paddled in.

In Romans chapter seven, Paul is saying, "sin-within will suck you under." Its presence is like a dark forceful wave that will hold you down unless you know how to deal with it. Many who profess faith in Christ have a cognitive understanding of "justification by faith" and "peace with God" but are rendered powerless by the force of sin still resident within. They are held down and tossed around, unable to progress on the Divine Expedition.

The helplessness rendered us by sin-within is expressed by Paul's words, "Who will rescue me (us) from this body of death?" The only way to break loose from the death grip of sin-within, release the full resources of the Divine Design, and continue the rescue mission of the Divine Expedition is through the breakthrough power God makes available to us in the *fourth law*—found in the next chapter.

CHAPTER 12

ROMANS 8:1-39
DIVINE POWER

I was less dazed now, and the 'voice' had banished the mad thoughts from my mind. An urgency was creeping over me, and the 'voice' said: 'Go on, keep going ... faster. You've wasted too much time. Go on before you lose the tracks.'

Joe Simpson[1]

I know that during that long and racking march of thirty-six hours over the unnamed mountains and glaciers of South Georgia, it seemed to me often that we were four, not three.

Ernest Shackleton[2]

...through Christ Jesus the law of the Spirit of life set me free from the law of sin and death.

Romans 8:2

...but those who live in accordance with the Spirit....

Romans 8:5

SUPERNATURAL DELIVERANCE

Simon Yates had just reached the top of a 20,813-foot (6,444-meter) Siula Grand peak of the Peruvian Andes Mountains when disaster struck. As he and his climbing partner, Joe Simpson, began their descent, Simpson plunged off the vertical face of an ice-ledge, breaking his leg. In the hours that followed, darkness fell and a blizzard raged as Yates tried to lower his friend to safety. Moments before he would have been pulled to his own death, Yates was forced to cut the rope.[3]

The next three days were an impossibly grueling ordeal for both men. Yates, certain that Simpson was dead, returned to their base camp consumed with grief and guilt over abandoning his fellow climber. Miraculously, Joe Simpson survived the fall, but crippled, starving, and severely frostbitten, he was trapped in a deep crevasse. Summoning vast reserves of physical and spiritual strength, he made his way down the mountain and hopped and crawled over the cliffs and canyons of the Andes, reaching base camp hours before Yates planned to leave.[4]

Expeditions often exceed the abilities and wisdom of the participants. Success, even survival, requires summoning help beyond the strength and insight of those involved. Although in the movie version of *Touching the Void*, Joe Simpson claims not to believe in God, the book version speaks of a mysterious inner voice urging him to push forward in spite of his broken leg and rugged icy obstacles.

Explorer Ernest Shackelton sensed the presence of a "fourth person" when he and his two companions traversed the South Georgia Island mountains and glaciers separating them from the whaling station and the help they needed to rescue the remainder of the *Endurance* crew. In his book, *Escape from the Antarctic,* Shackelton writes, "I know that during that long and racking march of thirty-six hours over the unnamed mountains and glaciers of South Georgia it seemed to me often that we were four, not three. I said nothing to my companions on the point, but afterwards Worsley said to me, 'Boss, I had a curious feeling on the march that there was another person with us.' Crean confessed to the same idea."[5]

Even Captain James Cook and his crew were dependent upon influences surpassing their own cunning. In their case, they needed a specially high tide to lift their ship from the coral reef that held the *Endeavour* in its grasp. Cook's ship was perched atop that pile of coral like a statue on a pedestal, leaning on one side. Time was running out. Unless she could be navigated off, the coral and waves would rip and shatter into pieces the vessel's already weathered hull. The only hope was from the high tide at midnight. Cook and his crew nervously watched as the night fell and the tide rose. The high tide that morning had failed to float the ship free, but the evening tide was higher—just enough to gain *Endeavour's* freedom.[6]

THE FOURTH LAW

Perhaps the above deliverance stories can be attributed merely to natural causes such as the summoning of a personal inner strength or an unusually but natural high tide. Be that as it may, in order to break the grip of sin-within, crippling us from renewing in us the Divine Design and preventing us from continuing on the mission of the Divine Expedition, a supernatural power is needed. Romans chapter eight introduces us to that power in the form of a *fourth law* or dynamic. This one trumps the previous three and is *the law of the Spirit of life* (8:2). This is the supernatural transforming power of the Holy Spirit working within us. Only through the Holy Spirit can we overcome the bondage of sin-within and release the life of Christ in us. The Holy Spirit alone sets us free from the *law of sin and death* (8:2).

> Only through the power of the Holy Spirit can we overcome the bondage of sin-within and release the life of Christ in us.

At the end of Romans 7, Paul cries out despairingly, "Who will rescue me from this body of sin?" (7:24). He joyously follows with an anticipatory shout of victory: "Thanks be to God—through Jesus Christ our Lord" (25). The reason for his joyful thankfulness is based upon what immediately follows in Romans 8: "There is now no condemnation for those who are in Christ Jesus, because through Christ Jesus *the law of the Spirit of life* set me free from the law of sin and death" (8:2). Our victory over "this body of death," infected as it is by sin, occurs as we are empowered and live from God's Spirit.

The Holy Spirit's power is seen in the lives of Beth and Dave who began living together while both were in the midst of troubled marriages. Beth's Catholic faith was nominal, and Dave had no faith, and in fact mocked it. When Beth's sister died and Beth miscarried her pregnancy with Dave, she feared that God was punishing her for having an affair. A breakthrough came when Beth discovered that God was gracious and merciful, not harsh and punitive as she thought.

Through reading the Bible and the influence of some friends, Beth decided she wanted to follow Jesus. Today the Holy Spirit is releasing her from the sense of guilt and condemnation she struggled with for years. Beth says, "I cannot-not cry whenever I think about God's goodness." The fallout from sin-within is still evident in Beth's life and her relationship with Dave, but the Holy Spirit is beginning to change the harmful attitudes and behaviors that characterized her before she made the decision to embrace Jesus.

WITH YOU AND IN YOU

Jesus promised to send His Spirit, not only to be with us, but also to be in us (John 14:17). He called the Holy Spirit "another Helper" (John 14:15). The Greek word Jesus uses is *parakaleo*, which combines two smaller words *kaleo* meaning "called" and *para* meaning "alongside." In other words, the Holy Spirit is the One God calls to be alongside us.

Older versions of the New Testament translate *parakaleo* by the English word "comforter." Comforter is also the combination of two words: *com* meaning "with" and *fort is* meaning "strength." The Holy Spirit is the Divine Comforter who gives us strength. Jesus was the one "called alongside" to strengthen and fortify His disciples, during His three years of public ministry. Following His resurrection and ascension, He sent the Holy Spirit to "come alongside" His disciples to "with strength" empower them to counter the dynamic of sin-within.

> The Holy Spirit is the Divine Comforter who gives us strength.

Parakaleo is also translated by the English word "counselor" (John 14:16, 26; 15:26; 16:7). It is used of Jesus as our "advocate" or "defense attorney" (I John 2:1). Jesus is our defense counsel, representing us before God and presenting the legal argument that because He Himself paid our debt for sin we stand acquitted. The Holy Spirit too is our *parakaleo,* counselor, or advocate, continuing to remind us that we are acquitted based on Jesus' payment of our debt. The Greek, *parakaleo,* and the English words "comforter," "counselor," and "advocate," each capture nuances of the Holy Spirit's work in our lives. He comes alongside us to strengthen, counsel, and advocate on our behalves.

But the Holy Spirit not only comes alongside us, He also indwells us (John 14:17). He is the indwelling Spirit of Truth (John 14:17), whom the Father sent in Jesus' name to teach us and remind us of everything Jesus said (John 14:26; 15:26). The Holy Spirit is the One who indwelt and influenced the followers of Jesus to record the New Testament Gospels and Epistles,

> The Holy Spirit comes to indwell, strengthen, counsel, and advocate for us.

as He impressed upon them remembrance of Jesus' life and teaching. The Holy Spirit indwells us as well and testifies to Jesus through us (John 15:26). The Holy Spirit is also at work in the world convicting the world of its guilt, regarding sin, righteousness, and judgment (John 16:7-8).

UNLEASHING THE SPIRIT

How do we release Christ's life through us and counter the dynamic of sin-within? By living according to the Spirit. This involves a conscious and continuous focusing of our minds on what the Spirit desires (8:5), intentionally allowing the Holy Spirit to empower and control us (8:9). The mind set on what the Spirit desires is life and peace (8:6). Sin-within still infects us, but the Holy Spirit infuses Divine life into our mortal bodies as we live by the Spirit and allow Him to guide and empower us

> Living according to the Spirit means a conscious and continuous focusing on what the Spirit desires.

(8:11-13). Like the high tide that lifted Cook's ship *Endeavour,* the Holy Spirit lifts us and frees us from the grip of sin and death. Like the voice that urged Joe Simpson forward, or the "presence" Shackleton, Worseley, and Crean sensed, there is "another person with us." That Person is the Holy Spirit who prompts us, empowers us, and guides us forward.

By setting our minds on what the Spirit desires and inviting Him to empower us, we put to death harmful attitudes, habits, and actions prompted by sin-within. The Holy Spirit affirms and empowers us to show forth our new identity as sons of God (8:14), assuring us over and over again that we are children of God and that God is our "Dear Father" or "Daddy" (8:15).[7] The Holy Spirit reminds us that we have an inheritance with Jesus and will one day share in his glory (8:16-17).

Through the redemptive work of Jesus and the empowerment of the Holy Spirit, we are ransomed, rescued, and given new identities as sons and daughters in God's family. Grasping this generates a desire to follow God and press toward intimacy with Him. We realize that He is not the indifferent, distant, detached 'Old-Man-in-the-sky' or the 'Divine-Cop-waiting-to-bust-us' that many people perceive Him to be. He is not sitting back with a big book, writing down everything we do that is right or wrong. He is a caring, compassionate, engaged, merciful, loving Father, who sent His Son to rescue us and His Spirit to counsel, assure, help, strengthen, and guide us.

The Holy Spirit's advocacy is evidenced in my (Linus Sr.) friend Ken's life. Ken took a new position with a financial institution just before the current economic crisis, and worked hard to get his company through the downturn. Putting in seventy hours a week—not counting travel. Ken was exhausted and on the verge of burnout when we spoke by phone. He was extremely conscientious toward his work, family, and God, and felt pressure, as he said, to "glorify God and love people." In his struggle to do so, he fatigued and become numb toward both God and family.

> The Spirit helps us in our weakness.

I spoke with Ken about the fact that God doesn't need us to glorify Him. God is perfect in His glory and nothing we do can add or take away from it. Rather, God wants to share His glory with us. Ken wept as it sunk in that the Holy Spirit was at work to walk alongside, strengthen, and manifest His glory in him. God wasn't demanding "more, more, more." He was at work, instead, to encourage and guide Ken, and bring about a glorious outcome in his life even in the midst of the pressure he was under.

Although we face many struggles, the Holy Spirit helps us in our weaknesses (8:26). He intercedes for us, even when we don't know how to pray (8:26-27), and He gives us the assurance that God causes all things to work together for the good for those who love Him (8:28).

STRONG AT THE BROKEN PLACES

Living according to the Spirit does not exempt us from "present sufferings" (8:18). We groan in frustration as we await the ultimate liberation, restoration, and glory to come. In the midst of the struggles and frustrations of live, however, the Holy Spirit strengthens us and produces in us a glorious effect that surpasses our present struggles and sufferings (8:18-25).

After living in France for four years, our family and two other families successfully laid the groundwork for the Crossroads Church, just across the border from Geneva, Switzerland. Toward the end of our time, some tensions arose and I (Linus Sr.) concluded it best to move our family to the other side of Geneva to start a new church. This was met with resistance from one of the team members, who saw this as a threat to the existing work we founded. Although frustrated, disappointed, and a little hurt (ok, a lot hurt), I purposed not to do anything that would harm the new church or the rest of the team, so our family decided to leave and return home.

In the midst of this conflict, I began reading a little booklet entitled, *Finding Grace in the Dungeon*,[8] authored by Selwyn Hughes. As I worked through the daily readings, the statement, "Life breaks us all," struck me. I reflected upon the loss I felt in leaving the fledgling Christ-following community our family helped birth, as well as the helplessness I felt to resolve the tension on our team. I had no idea what I would do after I returned to the U.S. The way forward seemed bleak, and it was definitely a "life-breaks-us-all" experience for me, affecting the future of my whole family.

> Through the Holy Spirit we find strength in the broken places.

As I read farther in *Finding Grace in the Dungeon*, another phrase grabbed my attention. Following the phrase, "Life breaks us all...", Hughes added, "but some are made strong at the broken places." I locked on to this and asked the Holy Spirit to make me strong at the broken place in my life. I asked Him to strengthen me and guide me. While disappointed with the breakdown of the relationship with my co-worker and the loss of the opportunity to start another church, I, nevertheless, purposed to rely upon God's Spirit and find strength in the broken places within me.

Through the Holy Spirit's encouragement and empowerment in the months that followed, I experienced a supernatural strengthening and guidance in my life. Looking back upon the passing of years, I now see the bigger picture that God had for me, far greater than the plan I conceived before leaving Geneva. If my plan had succeeded, we might have started one or two additional churches. Instead, through the Holy Spirit's strength and guidance, God unfolded a far greater plan. To date, some 50 Christ-following communities have been established through our efforts in the cities of Europe and beyond.

INNER TRANSFORMATION

I (Linus Jr.) have been captivated by the Discovery Channel's coverage of recent efforts to summit Mount Everest. A critical part of such endeavors is the base-camp leader. The base-camp leader studies weather conditions and monitors the health, water, oxygen, and progress of the climbing teams. He knows when to encourage a group forward or call them back. His vantage point gives him a more complete view of climbing conditions than the climbers themselves. Thus, the climbers are dependent upon the base-camp commander and rely upon extremely close communication with him. Without this, they are blind to the conditions and risks around them. So it is with the Holy Spirit and us. God's Spirit has an infinite and eternal perspective to guide us.

As we depend upon the Holy Spirit, we move from confusion to clarity and from powerlessness to empowerment. Through the Holy Spirit we find strength in the broken and weak places of our lives. A friend recently confided that he was in the process of a divorce that left him devastated, confused, and wounded. Seeking the Holy Spirit's counsel, he felt God direct him to read Psalm 34, where the following words jumped out at him: "The LORD is close to the brokenhearted and saves those who are crushed in spirit" (Psalm 34:18). Though brokenhearted and crushed, he found strength to avoid the shame, guilt, anger, and bitterness stalking him.

Through the Holy Spirit, we experience strength when broken-hearted. Through the Holy Spirit we also experience inner transformation, as God unleashes our new life in Christ, strengthening us to carry out the Divine Expedition. We have a certainty that God will continue His work to produce a glorious outcome in us through Jesus (8:29-30). We are assured that God, who did not spare His own Son but gave Him up for us, intends to "graciously give us all things" (8:32). God had us in view before we knew anything about Him or His plan for us. He even pre-determines to conform us into the likeness of Jesus.

> Through the Holy Spirit, we experience inner transformation and begin to radiate Christ's life in us.

I AM CONVINCED!

Paul puts an exclamation mark on the Holy Spirit's work and God's love for us by asking five questions, the implied answers of which are all affirmative (8:31-35). Paraphrasing, these questions are: Who can be against us when God is for us? Because God did not spare His own Son, but gave Him up for us all, will He not also, along with Him, graciously give us all things? Since we have a new standing and identity before God, who can bring a negative charge against us? Inasmuch as Christ Jesus died for us, was raised to life, and is sitting at the right hand of God interceding for us, who can condemn us? Because we are "more than conquerors" regardless of trouble, hardships, persecution, famine, nakedness, danger, sword, and even death, who can separate us from the love of Christ? (8:31-35)

As affirmative statements these read: We know that God is for us, so we are confident that we can handle any criticisms or accusations. Since we know that God gave us the greatest gift of His Son, then we are assured that He will also graciously give us everything else we need. Because we are certain that God chose us, we don't worry about any charges others might bring against us. Convinced, as we are, that Jesus Christ has put us in right relationship with God, we don't sweat condemnation. And we are also absolutely confident that nothing can separate us from God's love.

The thrust of the affirmative answers to the questions is that God is and will always be for us. I (Linus Jr.) have interacted with many people who don't believe that God's disposition towards them is good. They distrust that God really wants to bring good things into their lives. The result is that they rely solely upon themselves, seeking to control all aspects of their lives (and others). My observation is that this plays out in drivenness, boredom, dissatisfaction, and passionlessness. Worse, I see that distrust of God expresses itself in self-contempt, harshness, criticalness, cynicism, unsatisfying relationships, selfishness, inability to forgive, and all kinds of compulsions and addictions. By expending their energies in centering the universe on themselves, they are thwarted from experiencing the love of God and the supernatural empowerment of the Holy Spirit. They are unable to live beyond themselves to love others and help rescue them from the entrapments of life.

GOD'S HEART

Romans chapter eight shouts out that God's heart towards us is good. He wants what is best for us and can be trusted. He wants to guide us though the rough and tumble of life in a way that leads to the satisfaction and fulfillment we seek. Intimacy with God and trust in Jesus as the Good Shepherd of our lives frees us to take risks. While we will experience adversities in life, none of them can defeat us and none of them can separate us from God's love because we are secure in Jesus. We possess a God-given assurance that neither the crisis of death, the traumas of life, demonic forces, anything past, anything present, anything future, anything in the highest or lowest places on earth, nor anything in all creation can separate us from the love of God that is ours in Christ Jesus our Lord. We can face all challenges through the empowerment of the Holy Spirit.

> Romans chapter eight shouts out that God's heart towards us is good.

141

With Paul we too can declare, "I AM CONVINCED" (8:39). I am convinced I am in right standing with God. I am convinced I have peace with God. I am convinced His grace is working in and through me. I am convinced He is my loving Father. I am convinced the Holy Spirit is pouring God's love into my heart. I am convinced I have new life in Christ. I am convinced I have a new identity in Christ. I am convinced; I am convinced; I am convinced!

Two of the most powerful statements that Paul makes related to Christ's work and the Holy Spirit's empowerment in Romans chapter eight are the phrases "there is now no condemnation for those who are in Christ Jesus" (8:1) and "I am convinced that neither death nor life, neither angels nor demons, neither the present nor the future, nor any powers, neither height nor depth, nor anything else in all creation, will be able to separate us from the love of God that is in Christ Jesus our Lord" (8:38-39). My (Linus Sr.) son-in-law Phil has a tattoo of a flaming cross that covers his entire back. It is a statement of his faith, as are the two smaller crosses tattooed on of my eldest daughter's forearms. Their tattoos have opened lots of conversations and are expressions of their convictions about Jesus as Messiah-Son-King-Lord-Savior. I don't have any tattoos, but if I did, I would have the words "No condemnation!' tattooed on one shoulder, and "I am convinced!" on the other.

GOD IS FOR US

The bottom line of Romans 8 and the whole of the Divine Expedition is this: GOD IS FOR US! (8:31), the greatest proof of which is the life, death, and resurrection of Jesus (5:8). Jesus gave Himself for our sins to rescue us (Galatians 1:6), and purposes to graciously give us all things (8:32). He chose and justified us (8:33). He now intercedes for us at the Father's right hand (8:34). Through Christ who loves us, we are more than conquerors (8:37). Nothing can separate us from God's love that is in Christ. He lives in us and will never leave us or forsake us (8:35-38). All of this is mediated and made real through the Holy Spirit's presence and empowerment in our lives.

> The Holy Spirit's action in us lives is the pinnacle of our spiritual resources.

The Holy Spirit's action in us is the pinnacle of our spiritual resources and the crescendo of the restoration of the Divine Design and the first-half of Romans (chapters 1-8). The Holy Spirit is the One who restores God's design to us, activates God's resources in us, and releases Christ's life through us. And yes, it is the Holy Spirit who empowers us to carry out the mission of the Divine Expedition.

WHAT ABOUT CREATION?

Romans chapter eight connects the Holy Spirit's work in us to the incredible creation around us. Paul says,

> "The creation waits in eager expectation for the sons of God to be revealed. For the creation was subjected to frustration, not by its own choice, but by the will of the one who subjected it, in hope that the creation itself will be liberated from its bondage to decay and brought into the glorious freedom of the children of God" (Romans 8:18-21).

God cares about the created order. As we experience His redemptive work in our lives we in turn have a redemptive role to play in all areas of life. Our relationship to creation is to be one of care giving and stewardship. The restoration of the Divine Design (the first fruits of the Holy Spirit) works its way out not only in a desire to rescue others, but also in a responsibility to care for the environment. God's purpose for our world, including all of creation, was frustrated because of our sin and excessive exploitation. God's plan includes the liberation of creation from its bondage to decay. We have a role to play in this as we live out our glorious freedom as the children of God (8:18-25). Just as Jesus is at work to redeem us, restore us, renew us, and breathe new life into our brokenness, so are we to be the redemptive stewards of the world around us.

In the first half of Romans (chapters 1-8), we followed the pathway of the loss and renewal of the Divine Design. In the second half of Romans, we journey on the road of the loss and restoration of the Divine Expedition (chapters 9-16).

PART III

THE LOSS
AND RESTORATION
OF THE DIVINE
EXPEDITION

CHAPTER 13

ROMANS 9:1-39
THE DIVINE EXPEDITION RELAUNCH

There was danger that the camp would become completely invisible from the sea, so that a rescue party might look for it in vain.

—Ernest Shackleton[1]

On Fiala's orders, the expedition's provisions were bundled together for safekeeping on the ice, which gave way one night as Fiala and his thirty-eight men slept. They awakened in horror to find half of their food supply, and all of their coal lost; only the discovery of supplies from another expedition kept the entire party from perishing.

—River of Doubt[2]

ARCTIC EXPLORERS SAVED BY RELIEF CREW; Steamer Terra Nova Rescues Fiala-Ziegler Expedition. ALL BUT ONE MAN ALIVE Seekers of North Pole Had Been Gone Two Years and Lost Ship in Ice Early in Trip.

—New York Times Archives[3]

Hey, we've got a problem here.

—Jack Swigert, Apollo 13 crewmember[4]

I have great sorrow and unceasing anguish in my heart...for the sake of my brothers....

—Romans 9:3

FAILED MISSION

Sometimes those embarking on an expedition are themselves in need of rescue. The Imperial Trans Antarctic Expedition of 1914-1917 led by Ernest Shackleton was such a case. Disaster struck when its ship, Endurance was trapped and slowly crushed in pack ice. There followed a sequence of exploits and an ultimate rescue without the loss of life, eventually assuring Shackleton of hero status, although this was not immediately evident.

Another example is the Fiala-Ziegler Arctic Expedition of 1903-1905. Anthony Fiala had been in a high-stakes race with an elite group of men for one of history's greatest geographical prizes: to reach the North Pole. Fiala was promoted from photographer to commander of the expedition, but the renamed Fiala-Ziegler Expedition never made it farther north than 82 degrees latitude. Its ship was crushed in the Arctic ice and sank without a trace. Fiala and his men were out of reach of rescue ships and were stranded north of the Arctic Circle for two excruciating years before being rescued by the *Steamer Terra Nova*.

The *Apollo 13* crew and spacecraft needed rescuing as well. America launched seven Apollo expeditions to land on the moon. Of these, six succeeded; *Apollo 13*, the third of these, failed. It suffered a major electrical failure, leaving the astronauts with a power loss in two of their three fuel cells. Without all three cells, *Apollo 13* would not generate enough power to fire the spacecraft's onboard engine to return back to Earth. This loss of power resulted in a diminishing amount of air, forcing the astronauts to abandon ship and make their way into the lunar module as a "lifeboat,' in hope that the problem could be fixed remotely.

The original launch of the Divine Expedition also ran into trouble.

The original launch of the Divine Expedition also ran into trouble and was in need of rescuing. Israel's purpose was to be a "light to the nations," bringing God's salvation to the ends of the earth (Isaiah 49:6). Unfortunately, the Israel rescue expedition failed, as she turned from dependence upon God, abandoned God's design, and aborted her mission. Paul chronicles in Romans 9 how the Jews turned from a loving trust in God to a dependence upon their own legalistic self-righteousness. Rather than rely upon God for His strength, righteousness, and goodness, they increasingly trusted in their own religious system. Instead of reaching out to others with compassion and mercy, they withdrew into an extreme form of religious and nationalistic separatism. The result was that Israel ceased to reflect God's glory and God's name became blasphemed among the very people Israel was commissioned to rescue (Romans 2:24).

Israel dropped out of the expedition for which she was chosen. On my (Linus Jr.) NOLLS wilderness expedition, our team set out to climb the highest peak in the Olympic Mountain Range. We spent sixteen days traveling through old growth rainforest, pushing upward to higher alpine snow and ice, and then traversing some of the largest glaciers in the contiguous United States. It was tough, requiring determination, stamina, and endurance. Increasingly one of our expedition members fatigued and dropped farther and farther behind. Ultimately, due to foot sores, our teammate was unable to complete the trek and had to be evacuated so that the rest of us could continue on. The same was true of Israel's participation in the Divine Expedition.

In spite of Israel's failure, God did not abort His purpose to rescue and restore the world. Instead, He set aside Israel, now in need of rescue herself, and sent Messiah-Son-King-Lord-Savior Jesus to set up a new missional community of those He called to follow Him. Romans 11 makes it clear that this made it possible for even more people to be rescued and become a part of God's family. It also became the means to rescue Israel. Now, all who embrace Jesus become part of God's family and His mission to reach, rescue, and restore others.

MISSIONAL MARKERS TO REACH OTHERS

From Romans 9 forward, the loss and restoration of the Divine Expedition unfolds. Though scorned and rebuffed by his fellow Jew, Paul doesn't give up seeking to reach and rescue them along with those they failed to reach (non-Jews) in their aborted mission. Romans 9-11 reveal ten markers that underlie Paul's approach to reach and rescue others with the message of the Divine Expedition. These missional markers are instructive in how to go about reaching out to others, including those who initially might not be receptive to Jesus and the gospel message of rescue and restoration.

The first missional marker actually precedes Romans 9-11 and can be expressed by *inner-transformation*. This sums up the effect of the restoration of the Divine Design in our lives in the first eight chapters of Romans. The intentionally sequential flow of Romans makes clear that we ourselves first must be transformed within (Romans 1-8) to be able to carry out the mission of the Divine Expedition (Romans 9-16).

> The first missional marker is inner-transformation.

The mission of the Divine Expedition is to bring the Good News of Jesus to the maximum number of people in our world so that they too can be made right with God. When we embrace Jesus as our sin-bearer, righteousness-provider, and life-giver, and lean into the journey of transformation into His likeness, His life, character, and passion flow in us. Through the Holy Spirit's empowerment, we are restored to the Divine Design and receive strength and boldness to share with others the new life we have in Jesus.

Following the emphasis on *inner-transformation* in the first eight chapters of Romans, chapters nine through eleven exhibit nine more missional markers. Six of these are in Romans chapter nine, one in chapter ten, and two more in chapter eleven. All ten markers give us insight into what is required to effectively extend the lifeline of Christ to others. Paul's immediate application of these markers is toward his Jewish brethren, including his Jewish critics. But his concern does not stop with them. The mission of the Divine Expedition is to rescue the whole world. The ten missional markers are instructive in how to do so.

MISSIONAL MARKER #2: PROXIMITY

Building on our *inner-transformation*, the next missional marker is *proximity*. Proximity is about reaching those close to us. The whole of Romans chapter nine addresses those to whom Paul was in closest proximity: "my brothers, those of my own race, the people of Israel" (9:3). Paul later refers to himself as "an Israelite myself, a descendent of Abraham, from the tribe of Benjamin" (11:1), and further speaks of his desire to "arouse my own people to envy and save some of them" (11:14).

> The second missional marker is proximity.

Proximity means we must be in personal contact with those we want to reach. We must connect with them, understand them, and listen to them. Jesus exhibited proximity by coming as a flesh and blood Jewish person. He dwelt among us, so that we could see "his glory, the glory of the One and Only, who came from the Father, full of grace and truth" (John 1:14). His disciples heard Him speak, saw Him, and touched Him (1 John 1:1). Now that's proximity.

The word "dwell" in John's gospel means to set up a tent. Jesus set up His tent in our neighborhood and dwelt among us so that we could know Him close up. This is called the "incarnation," meaning "in the flesh." Jesus came in the flesh. In the same way, the Divine Expedition involves fleshing out our love and concern by being in proximity to others. God's plan of rescue and redemption depends upon our willingness to connect with those we desire to reach.

Normally, the first people we want to share the joy of our new life in Jesus are those with whom we are closest, such as family members, friends, neighbors, and close associates. Paul himself expresses a deep desire to proclaim the good news of Jesus with his fellow Jew. Knowing and experiencing Jesus as Messiah-Son-King-Lord-Savior, and being in right standing with God through Him, leads to a desire to be in the neighborhood and reach out to those we love.

Our eagerness to share Jesus with loved ones, however, isn't always welcomed. As a new follower of Christ (23 years-of-age), I (Linus Sr.) was eager to tell my parents what took place in my life. My attempt to do so was met with skepticism and resistance. My parents argued that I was already a Christian because I attended church with them when I was younger. They insisted that

I meet with a priest, who argued, as did my parents, that I was already a Christian. The priest eventually threw me out of his office for disagreeing with him, saying, "I have been to seminary for four years and you're telling me that you weren't a Christian until just recently?"

I hadn't been to seminary but one thing I knew was that I was separated from God and didn't know Him until I received Jesus into my life, something I had done only recently. I knew that going to church didn't make me a Christian any more than walking into an airport hangar made me an airplane (I walked into an airport hangar once and nothing happened). I was a Christian because I received Jesus as my sin-bearer, righteousness-provider, and life-giver. Although rebuffed by my family in my attempt to share my newfound relationship with Jesus, I did not lose my desire for them to know Him. I was encouraged to know that I was in good company in that both Jesus and Paul were rejected by many of their Jewish-brethren.

MISSIONAL MARKER #3: CONVICTION

The additional missional markers in Romans 9-11 instruct us in how to proceed when people are resistant and don't know they need rescuing. The next marker is *conviction*. Paul was convinced that those around him were in desperate need of the righteousness that only Jesus provides, whether they acknowledged it or not. This conviction is seen throughout Romans. In the opening chapter, Paul declares: "The gospel (good news) is the power of God for salvation for everyone who believes" (1:16). His conviction is seen further in his statements, "I am obligated" (1:14), "I am eager" (1:15), and "I am not ashamed" (1:16).

> The third missional marker is conviction.

Paul was convinced that salvation and redemption are only to be found in Christ. In Romans chapter eight he states, "I am convinced that...[nothing] will be able to separate us from the love of God that is in Christ Jesus our Lord" (8:38). This statement climaxes the first section of this book, the loss and restoration of the Divine Design. His "I am convinced" underlies Paul's desire to reach others for Christ in the second half of Romans (The loss and restoration of the Divine Expedition).

The depth of Paul's conviction comes out in the opening statement of the second half of Romans, where he exclaims,

"I speak the truth in Christ—I am not lying, my conscience confirms it in the Holy Spirit—I have great sorrow and unceasing anguish in my heart. For I could wish that I myself were cursed and cut off for Christ for the sake of my brothers" (9:1-2).

Paul's exclamation is based on his conviction that Israel lost its way and needs to be rescued. This conviction is further seen in the next chapter where he says, "My heart's desire and prayer to God for the Israelites is that they might be saved" (10:1). To reach others with the good news of the Divine Expedition, we must possess a deep conviction that others are in desperate need of God's power for salvation through Jesus. Such conviction is what moves us to press forward even when opposed.

MISSIONAL MARKER #4: COMPASSION

The fourth missional marker to reach others is *compassion*. Paul's statements of conviction are also statements of compassion. Conviction and compassion are fused together. Conviction that people need rescuing is not enough, as it can easily remain cognitive and not move us to action. It is not enough to know people need rescuing; we must be moved to do something about it. Compassion moves us to act, to do something. Paul's words evidence conviction and compassion, head coupled with heart.

> The fourth missional marker is compassion.

The depth of Paul's compassion is shocking as he declares: "For I could wish that I myself were cursed and cut off from Christ for the sake of my brothers" (9:3). Paul expresses a willingness to be separated from God forever himself if it would result in the rescue of his fellow-Jew. His compassion is unfathomable—a willingness to be eternally separated from God if his own people would be eternally saved! The more we understand the incredible message of the Divine Expedition (and the consequences of either embracing or turning from it) the deeper our conviction and compassion grow.

Although I (Linus Sr.) have grown in compassion for others over the years, I still fall far, far short of the depth of compassion Paul expresses, even more so the compassion of Jesus. The greatest act of compassion of all time was Jesus who submitting Himself to rejection and abuse, carrying our sin, and allowing Himself to be separated from God on our behalf. Each time I reflect upon the incredibly compassionate sacrifice of Jesus, deepening gratitude and compassion grow within me, compelling me to reach out to others so that they too might experience God's love, grace, and mercy. This is what compelled Paul to do the same.

MISSIONAL MARKER #5: CLEAR REASONING

This leads to a fifth missional marker—*clear reasoning*. Paul addresses the prejudices and arguments obscuring his fellow-Jew's understanding of the good news of God's grace through Jesus. The most erroneous notion Paul's critics held was that they merited God's favor because they were the people to whom God first chose to reveal Himself. The Jews of first century Israel assumed they deserved God's acceptance by right of birth and religious obser-vance (9:4-5). Many people today have a similar misunderstanding. We believe we are "in" with God or will have "good Karma" because we belong to a particular heritage, culture, religion, or because we do or don't do certain things.

> The fifth marker is clear reasoning.
> _____

Paul challenges this misconception with clear reasoning. He states, "not all who are descended from Israel are Israel" and points out that God's past dealings with Israel show that salvation, then as now, is based on grace not merit. In other words, you're not "in" with God because you belong to a particular nation or adhere to a certain religion.

Paul backs his argument up with the fact that Abraham's second son, Isaac, was the one through whom God's promise of salvation came. Normally, the first-born was the one through whom the family blessing was passed. (It should be noted that the descendants of Abraham's first born, Ishmael, can also be included in the promises given to Abraham, and can be made right with God, by putting their trust in Jesus as sin-bearer, righteousness-provider, and life-giver.)

Abraham's true offspring are those who, like him, embrace God's promise by faith and are credited with righteousness (9:6-9).[5] What is in view is not physical lineage or religious observance but God's rescue plan called "the promise" previewed in Abraham and culminating in Jesus. Those who embrace this promise and call upon and believe in Jesus as Messiah-Son-King-Lord-Savior, become the true descendants of Abraham, whether Jews or not. Jesus is the ultimate fulfillment of the promise to Abraham. He (Jesus) is the rock upon which we stand or the stone over which we stumble (9:32-33).

> Abraham's true offspring are those who embrace God's promise by faith.

Paul continues to reason clearly by undercuting his critics' misconception, referencing Isaac's two sons Esau and Jacob. Isaac's younger son (second born twin), Jacob, was accepted by God and included in the faith-lineage of those benefiting from God's promise, while the older son (first born twin), Esau, was not (9:10-13). Why? The story of Esau and Jacob in Genesis 25-35 indicates that Jacob valued God's promises but Esau did not. Esau disregarded God's promise and rescue plan and pursued a self-indulgent agenda. Even though Esau's brother, Jacob, was seriously flawed, he nevertheless valued and wanted in on God's promise. Because of this, God accepted Jacob's faith and credited him with righteousness. Because of Jacob's faith, God increasingly revealed Himself to him, resulting in Jacob's inner character transformation over time. Because of Jacob's faith, he inherited the promised blessings given to Abraham and passed on through Issac, and then to him. The promise was ultimately fulfilled in Jesus.

The contrast between Jacob and Esau shows that there were two approaches to God among the Jews. The one was acceptable and the other was not. The Jacob-approach pursued God by faith in His promise. The Esau-approach disregarded that promise. By the first century, Judaism degenerated into religious externalism and adherence. Only a remnant of Jews recognized that no amount of religious effort would be enough to gain God's acceptance and instead hoped in God's promise. This faith-in-the-promise-remnant was receptive to Jesus as Messiah. Similarly, humanity today approaches God in two ways. The Esau stream stubbornly relies upon self-merit through morality or religion. The Jacob stream recognizes the inadequacy of self-merit and relies instead upon God's promise of rescue through God's grace and loving provision of righteousness in Jesus.

A SECOND FAULTY NOTION

Paul further counters his detractors by addressing a second false notion with clear reasoning. Some who opposed the message of the Divine Expedition charged that it was unjust for God to accept some and not others (9:14). Paul challenges this by pointing out that God is generously merciful, evidenced by the fact that, even though people insist they can make themselves acceptable to God through their own merit, He somehow breaks through the barrier of self-reliance and skepticism and saves some of them anyway.

The fact that so many people do embrace the Good News of Jesus is evidence of God's mercy (9:15). God would be just even if He didn't save anyone because all fall short of His righteousness. God gives us genuine choice, which brings with it significant consequence—yet, He woos us, even sending His own Son to do so, and then mercifully saves those who turn to Him (9:16-18).

The reason the message of the Divine Expedition is such incredible good news is that God breaks through our willfulness and stubbornness and shows His undeserved mercy, transferring to Jesus the punishment we deserve. Jesus takes the blame that deservedly should fall on us. God's plan to send Jesus to bear the brunt of our failure preserves His justice yet demonstrates His incredible love and mercy.

THE BLAME GAME

Paul's critics go on to charge that it is God's fault if people don't respond to His rescue plan (9:19). They play the blame game claiming, "It's not our fault if we don't believe." They argue if some are lost, it's God's fault. It's unfair of God not to save all. By blaming God, they attempt to turn responsibility away from their own failure and culpability.

It's God's fault!

_____

156

Many in Western culture today hold a similar mentality, blaming God for the existence of evil in the world. We set up an either/or logical construct, reasoning that either God could do something about evil but won't, or He can't do anything about it. It's a no-win, either-or argument. God is either impotent or indifferent. Either way, He is a loser. He is not there or not worth trusting.

According to this line of reasoning, since evil exists (although Eastern forms of religion deny its existence or see it as the flip side of good) and God doesn't eradicate it, this must mean God can't or won't deal with it. The logical conclusion is that evil is God's fault and we are victims. But this line of reasoning leads to the illogical position that "God doesn't exist but evil is His fault." He gets all of the blame (for evil) and none of the credit (for good).

But, does the existence of evil preclude God being good? Might there be an alternative explanation to evil's existence, one that maintains God's goodness in spite of evil's existence? The unfolding Biblical story breaks the "either-or" (God can't or won't) construct, and presents us with a third option. Evil wasn't part of God's original design. Everything He created was good, including bestowing His created beings with significant choice. Without this, the Divine Design of love and freedom would have no meaning. "No-choice" means "no-love" and "no-freedom." Choice carries with it the risk of turning away from God and His goodness. Unfortunately, turning away led (and leads) to the willful distortion of God's design and the parasite of evil.

Evil commenced when a created angelic being, Satan, also endowed with significant choice, sought to elevate himself above God the Creator. Satan sought to be autonomous and make his own will the measure of all things. This scene repeated itself on earth as man (both man and woman) chose the same course, turning from a loving and trusting dependence upon God who was perfect in His goodness, rightness, and intention. Evil is a freely chosen deviation from good, the fault lying with the one turning away from the One who is perfect in His goodness. Evil entered both heaven and earth by the willful choice of the created turning from the infinitely good Creator and His perfectly good design.

INCREDIBLE MERCY

God's incredible mercy is that He restrains His justice while continuing to love and pursue us, even though we turned away and marred His Divine Design for us and the whole of creation. Paul undercuts his detractors by shifting the issue from their argument that "it's God's fault for not saving everyone," to the reality that "God is merciful to save anyone." The heart of Paul's assertion is "It does not, therefore, depend on man's effort, but on God's mercy" (9:16).

The question is not, "Why aren't all saved?" It is, "Why does God save anyone?" Isaiah says, "'we like sheep have gone astray' and Paul points out, 'All have sinned and fall short of God's glory?'"

> The question is not, "Why aren't all saved?"

The question the Bible asks is not, "How can a loving God let a poor sinful person go to hell?" but "How can a perfectly good, holy, righteous, and just God let a sinful person into His presence?"

The good news is that God in His mercy provided a way to pour out His love, grace, and mercy without compromising His goodness, holiness, righteousness, and justice. To be a beneficiary of God's love and mercy requires the relinquishing of a victim or blame mentality. It requires a humble acceptance of our culpability for turning from God and distorting His goodness, and a grateful acceptance of God's grace in Jesus.

WHY NOT?

Rather than insist that it is unfair for some to be saved and others not, why not give up that blame posture and embrace Jesus as sin-bearer, righteousness-provider, and life-giver and be saved? Why not give up the "I-am-a-victim" or "It's God's fault" postures and embrace God's merciful provision of Jesus as Messiah-Son-King-Lord-Savior?

Could it be that our man-centered rationalism, arrogance, willfulness, and pride imprison us and contribute further to the evil in our world? Might it be that our willfulness and self-reliance are evidence that "all we like sheep have gone astray?" Could it possibly be that our victim and blame game arguments are further confirmation that all have indeed sinned and fall short of the glory of God? Might it be that God would be perfectly just to let us remain separated from Him, if we refuse to give up our insistence on blaming Him or demand that He accept us on some other basis than embracing Jesus and the righteousness He alone can provide?

UNFATHOMABLE MERCY

God's mercy is unfathomable in that He sidesteps our pride, arrogance, willfulness, and self-justifying rationalism, graciously drawing some to the Divine Expedition, even while others around them reject it. God mysteriously and mercifully uses the rejection of those others to bring about the salvation of the some (9:16-18).

An example is Egypt's Pharaoh at the time of the Exodus. Pharaoh rejected God's instruction through Moses to release Israel from enslavement. Instead, Pharaoh "hardened his heart," intensified his resistance to God, and continued his persecution of the Jews (Exodus 7:13, 22; 8:15, 19; 9:7).[6] However, God delivered Israel in spite of Pharaoh's resistance. The Jews were freed, Egypt (and Pharaoh) was judged, and the surrounding world was awed, leading some of them to also be saved. In this one event, God displayed His mercy toward Israel, His justice toward oppressive Egypt, and His renown to the rest of the world (Exodus 1-14).

> God even mysteriously uses the rejection of some to bring about the salvation of others.

It is remarkable that God has mercy on anyone, given the fact that we have all turned away from Him, fall short of His righteousness, and egoistically ignore Him or insist He accept us on the basis of our human merit. Nevertheless, God mercifully saves all who turn from blaming Him and rejecting His grace, and instead respond with humble gratitude and thankfulness for His merciful provision of salvation—our friend Rita is someone who did.

Rita was born to Jewish parents who abandoned their religious faith for a secular way of life. God was not a part of their family discussions, but Rita remembers in middle and high school wanting to know if God existed, and how she could know Him if He did. Upon graduation from university, Rita was hired by TEEN Magazine. Over the next year her new boss, the first believing Christ-follower she ever met, talked with Rita about Jesus and His love for her.

Rita read the New Testament (a copy of "Good News For Modern Man") and began to see that Jesus was the God she had been searching for. This was not without some emotional and spiritual wrestling on her part, because she was raised to believe that Jews did not embrace Jesus in any way, shape, or form. Rita's parents were not thrilled with her pursuit to know God and Jesus, and suddenly their "Jewishness" became more important to them.

Eventually Rita prayed to embrace Jesus as her Savior. Telling her mother and father was one of the hardest days of her life. When she called her father to tell him she had become a Christian, he hung up on her, and it was two weeks before he would talk to her again. Rita loved her father and had always been very close to him, but she knew her first-day as a Jesus-follower that she had found an even more significant relationship than with her dad.

MISSIONAL MARKERS #6 & #7: PERSISTENCE AND PASSION

Rita's TEEN Magazine friend's proximity, conviction, compassion, and clear witness led to Rita's transformation. Throughout the whole of Romans chapter nine, two more markers are evident: *persistence* and *passion*. Paul's detractors hurl multiple criticisms at him, but he doesn't back off. He persistently and passionately pushes back against their criticisms.

> Markers 6 & 7 are persistence and passion.
> _____

Paul's critics charge that people can't resist God's will. This is similar to the theory presented in the movie *Jesus Christ Superstar*, in which Judas is portrayed as being "set up" to betray Jesus. If Jesus somehow forced or coerced Judas to do what he did, then Judas was not culpable—he was manipulated by Jesus to do it. Similarly, Paul's critics argue that we can't resist God's will to believe or not. If so, the logical conclusion is that it is God's fault if someone is not saved (9:19).

Paul persistently and passionately rebuts his critic's charge that we are helpless and can't resist God's will. He points out that those who become "objects of wrath" do so because of their unbelief, not God's will. That some don't believe actually highlights the riches of God's glory shown to the recipients of His mercy (9:20-29). God restrains His wrath in order to "make the riches of his glory known to the objects of his mercy" (9:23). Instead of executing judgment, as God would be perfectly just to do, He exercises patience so that some might turn and believe. This patience is exercised at great cost to Himself, sending Messiah-Son Jesus to bear the judgment for our guilt. In the words of Isaiah, "the Lord has laid on him (Jesus) the iniquity of us all" (Isaiah 53:6b).

Persistence and passion have been part of my (Linus Sr.) story in reaching out to my own family. In my passion for my sister to know Jesus, I invited her to have lunch with me a few months after I turned to Jesus as Savior. During the course of our meal together I shared with her my new faith in Jesus and encouraged her to receive Him into her life as well. I found out later, however, that she was offended by our conversation. My family (father, mother, sister) all believed they were already Christians because they attended church. Over lunch I discussed with my sister that only by receiving Jesus as our sin-bearer and righteousness-provider could we receive the new life we need to be accepted by God.

The next day, Christmas Eve, I arrived at my parent's home. When my father met me at the door, he furiously accused me of "button-holing" my sister. Before I could answer, he angrily blurted out, "I disown you! You are no longer my son! You are no longer welcome in this house!"

I don't know why I responded the way I did, but I replied, "I'm sorry, Dad, you can't disown me, I'm your son whether you like it or not."

I didn't mean to be disrespectful; I just had the assurance that I was still my father's son in the same way that I knew that I was now a child of God. Gratefully, my dad cooled down a day or two later and took back his vow to disown me. I refrained from overtly witnessing to my family for a while, but continued to look for opportunities to share the Good News of Jesus with them.

A few years later, I sent my sister a book that talked about the Second Coming of Christ. She called me after reading it and exclaimed, "Linus, I have eternity!" Somehow this book helped her open her life to Jesus in a way that she had not done before. We have had a close bond ever since.

Toward the end of my father's life I visited him in the hospital, and asked, "Dad, how are you doing?"

He whispered, "I'm at the end of the trail."

I asked, "Dad, you're at the end of one trail, but you're also at the beginning of another one. Do you know that if you died, you would be with Jesus?"

He replied, "I love the Lord; I gave my life to the Lord."

Over the next half-hour, I read various passages of Scripture to my dad, including the promise of Jesus:

> "Do not let your hearts be troubled. Trust in God; trust also in me. In my Father's house are many rooms; if it were not so, I would have told you. I am going there to prepare a place for you. And if I go and prepare a place for you, I will come back and take you to be with me that you also may be where I am" (John 14:1-3).

My times with my dad at the end of his life were precious, as he too affirmed his trust in Jesus. I thank God for the conviction I had about Jesus and the compassion He gave me for my family. I am glad I didn't back down from my persistence and passion to reach them with the Good News of Jesus and the clarity I had about my faith in Jesus.

MORE CLEAR REASONING, PERSISTENCE AND PASSION

Paul continues his clear reasoning, persistence and passion by noting that in spite of Israel's enormous effort to earn or merit God's acceptance through religious observance, she failed to obtain it (9:31). Israel erroneously substituted God's grace with religious practice. To use Paul's words, "But the Jews, who tried so hard to get right with God by keeping the law, never succeeded. Why? Because they were trying to get right with God by keeping the law and being good instead of depending on faith. They stumbled over the 'stumbling stone'" (9:32, NLV).

Paul concludes this chapter by driving home the point that non-Jews (Gentiles) who were not pursuing righteousness at all obtained it by faith. In contrast, Jews, who pursued righteousness through enormous legalistic self-effort and religion, failed to obtain it. The former embraced Messiah Jesus and were credited righteousness, while the latter stumbled over the only One who could provide them the righteousness they were seeking (9:30-35). Throughout this chapter, Paul persistently and passionately reasons with his critics about their need to embrace Jesus. If we back off from our conviction about Him when people question, challenge, or threaten us, we cut off the only hope they have of coming to know God and His purpose for their lives.

> God commissions those who trust in Jesus and receive righteousness by faith.

Israel failed in its mission to show forth God's mercy and grace, and rescue the world around them. In Israel's place, God commissions those who trust in Jesus and receive His righteousness by faith (including a remnant of believing Jews like Rita). These are the new heralds of the Divine Expedition (9:30-32).

Like the Shackleton, Fiala, and Apollo 13 expeditions, Israel too became in need of rescue. The grim reality is that the entire world is in need of rescue—and we are the rescue crew. We press forward on the mission of the Divine Expedition with compassion, conviction, clear thinking, perseverance, and passion. But even more is required, as we will see in the next chapters.

CHAPTER 14

ROMANS 10:1-21
THE DIVINE COMMISSION

I can regain control.

—Jim Lovell, commander of *Apollo 13*[1]

We now began to regard many things as treasures to which formerly we had paid little or no attention, such as axes, knives, awls, needles, thread, shoe twine, shoes, shirts, socks, sticks, strings, and similar things which in former days many of us would not have stooped to pick up.

—Georg Wilhelm Steller[2]

As John Hunt gathered his few personal articles, we talked. He told me of his deep belief that we had a duty to climb the mountain if we could, that so many thousands of people had pinned their faith and hope on us that we couldn't let them down.

—Sir Edmund Hillary[3]

Hear that? That's the sound of your rescue.

—Gary Moses, Glacier National Park ranger[4]

If you confess with your mouth, 'Jesus is Lord,' and believe in your heart that God raised him from the dead, you will be saved. For it is with your heart that you believe and are justified, and it is with your mouth that you confess and are saved. As the Scripture says, 'Anyone who trusts in him will never be put to shame.'

—Romans 10:9

How can they believe in the one of whom they have not heard?

—Romans 10:14

SALVAGED MISSIONS

The *Apollo 13* crew, made up of Jim Lovell, Fred Haise, and Jack Swigert, was close to 200,000 miles (320,000 kilometers) from home and five-sixths of the way to the moon when a mysterious explosion rocked the spacecraft, the cockpit dimmed, the air grew thin, and the instrument lights went out. The command module was soon without air or power, and the astronauts had to make their way into the lunar module. As a result, *Apollo 13* was unable to complete its mission of landing on the moon, and the mission shifted from a lunar landing to one of rescuing the crew from impending death. Incredibly, NASA's control center was able to repair the crippled vehicle remotely and bring it safely back to earth.

George Wilhelm Steller was part of a mission that had to be salvaged as well. Steller was born in Windsheim, Germany in 1709. After finishing university, he went to Russia, where he found work as a naturalist for the Academy of Sciences in Saint Petersburg. It was from there that he joined naturalist Vitus Bering in his last expedition into the ocean east of Siberia (now the Bering Sea). In 1741, Bering and Steller were on one of the two ships that set sail from Kamchatka, a peninsula in Russia, to explore the island of Bolshaya Zemlya. Steller became the first white man known to have stepped upon the land eventually called Alaska. Although he only spent three days there, he was the first European to provide descriptions of plants and animals in this land that was new to Europe.[5]

On the return trip to Russia, the Bering expedition ships *St. Paul* and *St. Peter* were separated in a storm. *St. Paul* stayed on course, but *St. Peter*, the ship carrying Bering and Steller, got lost and landed on an island now known as Bering Island. The storm had done too much damage for *St. Peter* to make it back to Kamchatka, so the vessel and its crew remained stranded while efforts were made to repair the ship. Soon food supplies began to run out, and the crew had to live off sea otters, seals, and all kinds of birds to subsist. In the year that it took to rebuild *St. Peter*, Bering the ship's captain died, and almost half of the crew perished from scurvy. With little food or water, only Steller and a few others barely managed to survive and sail back to Russia.[6]

Like the *Apollo 13* mission and the Bering-Steller expedition, the Israel mission to reach the world ran aground. Israel was commissioned to spread the message of the Divine Expedition to the rest of the world, but she too became stranded in need of rescuing.

MISSIONAL MARKER #8: PROCLAMATION

Romans chapter ten highlights God's plan to rescue both Israel and the rest of humanity. At the heart of this plan is the eighth missional marker of the Divine Expedition: *proclamation*. The proclamation of the Good News about Jesus is the major feature of Romans 10 and is the principal marker around which the others revolve. It is the lifeline thrown out from the rescue ship *Divine Expedition* to save Israel and the world.

> The eighth marker of the Divine Expedition is proclamation.

When *Apollo 13* ran into trouble, a flow of communication back and forth between NASA and the *Apollo* crew became the means of rescue. From the *Apollo* came the acknowledgment *"Hey, we've got a problem here."* From the NASA control center came instructions on how to correct the problem and save the spacecraft and its crewmembers. The salvation of Israel and the world involves a back and forth communication as well. It starts with the acknowledgement that there is a problem. Once the problem is acknowledged and identified, the solution can be communicated.

At the very center of the Divine Expedition is the proclamation that rescue and restoration are through Jesus. The essence of the Divine Expedition is that Jesus offers the lifeline of righteousness needed to rescue us. This conviction (Missional Marker #3) motivates us to proclaim the Good News of Jesus as our Rescuer. This proclamation is also motivated by an underlying compassion (Missional Marker #4) for those in need of rescue. "Christ's love compels us," Paul writes to the Corinthians.[7] It was compassion (evident throughout the Gospels) that compelled Jesus to give Himself for our sins in order to rescue us (Galatians 1:6). This same compassion moves us to proclaim the Good News of Jesus to others.

As seen in the last chapter, proclamation involves clear reasoning (Missional Marker #5), perseverance and passion (Missional Markers #6 & #7). How reprehensible it would have been if the NASA staff had been indifferent to the *Apollo 13* plight! Rather than indifference, the NASA Mission Operation Team sprang into action and worked passionately and tirelessly to bring *Apollo* and its crew safely back to earth.

DIVINE IMPERATIVE

Each of the preceding missional markers of Romans moves us to proclaim the Good News of Jesus. The Divine Expedition proclamation is this: take hold of Jesus, God's lifeline to rescue us. The entire book of Romans encompasses this proclamation. Romans chapter ten especially highlights the imperative to make known the Good News of Jesus' life, death, burial, resurrection, ascension, and appeal to others to embrace Jesus as Messiah-Son-King-Lord-Savior. It is a life and death matter that people receive Jesus as sin-bearer, righteousness-provider, and life-giver.

The message we proclaim is that Jesus provides the credit of righteousness that puts us right with God and empowers us to become His agents of grace and goodness in the world. The righteousness of Christ is imparted to us as a free gift when we place our trust in Him (10:1-4). All other approaches to gain right standing with God maroon or shipwreck us because they fail to produce the inner transformation that puts us right with God. Efforts to rescue ourselves through any set of laws, rules, practices, religion, or philosophy are futile because they leave us short of God's standard of perfect holiness (10:5). Reaching God through our own effort is like attempting to travel to the moon and back without a spacecraft (or a defective one). Jesus alone removes the otherwise insurmountable gap separating us from God. He alone is the only rescue vessel adequate enough to save us.

Our rescue requires that we grab on to the lifeline Jesus offers us. We do so by confessing our lack of rightness and receiving God's gift of righteousness through Messiah-Son-King-Lord-Savior Jesus. We are delivered from our failure to measure up to God's holiness/wholeness by gratefully and humbly confessing with our mouths that Jesus is Lord and believing in our hearts that God raised Him from the dead (10:6-11). That's it. That's all it takes. Every other approach leaves us adrift in the world without hope and without God (Ephesians 2:12).

> Our rescue requires that we grab on to the lifeline of Jesus offered us.

BLIND DAVE

I (Linus Sr.) observed the incredible impact of someone responding to the proclamation of new life in Jesus when I met "Blind Dave." Working with students at UCLA, I got to know Dave and found out that his blindness was caused by a self-inflicted gunshot wound. Even though friends and family assured Dave that they loved him, he grew up hating himself. He was filled with an inner self-loathing, as he felt he was unlovable, reasoning that others didn't really know his hidden flaws. So one night Dave broke into his father's locked gun case, took out a loaded pistol, put it to his temple, and pulled the trigger. The bullet passed into one side of his head and out through the other. Failing to kill himself as he hoped, the gunshot severed Dave's optic nerves, leaving him permanently blind.

Dave's self-hatred continued all the more, until one day a friend took him to a Christian meeting where the speaker made the statement, "God knows everything about you but still loves you." Dave was convinced that no one who *really* knew him could ever love him. But when he heard that God knew *everything* about him, still loved him, and sent Jesus to die for him, a light went on inside Dave's mind. Blind Dave took hold of the lifeline of Jesus and received His forgiveness and credit of righteousness. Dave was made right with God and delivered from his self-hatred. He became part of our campus ministry and subsequently graduated from UCLA. Blind Dave was one of the most cheerful and positive persons I ever met.

SINCERELY WRONG

Proclamation is crucial to keep people from heading in the wrong direction in life. In today's Western pluralistic world, it is assumed that all beliefs are equally valid (or to some, equally invalid). It is taken for granted that God will look kindly on us as long as we are sincere in our beliefs, the content of which really doesn't matter. Correspondingly, Western secu-

> The assumption that all beliefs are equally valid....is faulty.

larism holds that it is wrong to "proselytize" or attempt to "convert" others to our beliefs. If, by this, one means manipulating or using intimidation or force to cause conversion, we would agree. But the assumption that all beliefs are equally valid or that sincerity in itself is enough to gain God's acceptance is faulty.

It is faulty to say that all religions teach the same thing and that all roads lead to the same destination. There may be superficial similarities, but the core beliefs and worldviews of the "great" religions of the world are fundamentally different. It is as faulty to say

> Sincerity...does not make a direction headed or a belief held valid.

that all spiritual paths lead to the same destination as it is to say that it doesn't matter which direction you drive if traveling from Rome to Amsterdam. If you leave Rome and drive southeast you will end up in Naples, not Amsterdam. To get to your destination, you must turn around and drive northwest—toward the direction of Amsterdam.

Sincerity and zealousness do not make a direction headed or a belief held valid. If I drive north from Paris, I will never end up in Lisbon, however sincere and zealous I might be. To make it to Portugal from northern France, I have to drive south. If we can head in the wrong direction when driving, might it not also be possible to go in the wrong direction in the realm of religion and belief?

People hold many ideas sincerely and zealously that are false. For centuries, most people believed the world was flat, even persecuting those who thought it was round (more accurately, elliptical). Those holding the belief of a flat world were zealous and sincere, but they were sincerely wrong. More recently, the "isms" of the twentieth century (communism, fascism, national socialism, communism, existentialism) were sincerely and zealously believed but ended up proving false, destroying millions of lives in the process. These political, social, economic, and philosophical beliefs took their adherents in wrong directions. Their advocates were sincere—but sincerely wrong.

I (Linus Sr.) spent some weeks in Russia shortly after the fall of Communism, helping launch a new church in Moscow. One woman who embraced Jesus as her sin-bearer and became active in our ministry was the wife of a Russian military officer. She told me how she embraced Stalinism growing up. Along with her school classmates she sang songs of praise to Stalin, unaware of the mass atrocities he ordered. Now that the curtain was drawn back on Stalin's record and that of Soviet Communism, she realized she had been deceived. Another woman in our ministry was the daughter of Christian parents, both of whom died in insane asylums under Stalin's regime because of their faith in Christ. Under Communist rule, faith like theirs was treated as insanity. We can be sincere—but sincerely wrong—as were the followers of Lenin, Marx, and Stalin.

Might not the same also be true of sincerely and zealously held religious beliefs today? Cults and religions have sincere and zealous followers. Are all equally valid? Do all roads really lead to the top of the same mountain—or might they actually lead us away from where we want to go? Again, we can be sincere—but sincerely wrong.

Religious beliefs based on gaining acceptance with God through self-reliance and human-merit actually lead us away from God, and leave us without the love and grace He offers us in Jesus. Islam's emphasis on submission, Judaism's emphasis on keeping the Mosaic Law, and the do's and don'ts of all religions, including legalistic versions of Christianity, all rely upon human effort rather than God's grace. They fail to bring us into a relationship of intimacy with God or engage us in the true purpose and mission for which He created us. They fail to impart the resurrection life of Jesus and the empowering presence of the Holy Spirit that transforms us from within. Religion actually leads us away from God, not toward Him.

WHAT WE PROCLAIM

The message of the Divine Expedition is not valid just because it too is sincerely or zealously believed. Rather, its validity rests upon the large body of credible prophetic witness and historical testimony to the life, death, resurrection, and ascension of Jesus. These point to the reliability and trustworthiness of the Biblical message. Without this corpus of prophetic and historical testimony, as well as the work of the Holy Spirit changing lives throughout history, we have no way to know that we are headed in the right direction. Other religions lack this same foundation for belief.

When we proclaim the Good News of Jesus, we proclaim that the Old Testament prophets foretold in great detail the coming of Jesus, and that He explicitly fulfilled these prophecies (Matthew 1:22; 2:5, 15, 17, 23; 3:3; 4:14). We proclaim that the four Gospels originated in the first century and are eyewitness accounts of the life, death, burial, resurrection, and ascension of Jesus (Luke 1:1-4). We proclaim that because of the time and space resurrection of Jesus, we can have new life and hope in Him (Romans 6:13). We proclaim there is no other name than Jesus, given in heaven or earth, by which we can be saved (Acts 4:12). We proclaim that Jesus is the power of God for salvation to everyone who believes (Romans 1:16). We proclaim that Jesus is the way, the truth, and the life, and no one comes to the

> The message of the Divine Expedition is not valid just because it too is sincerely or zealously believed.

Father except through Him (John 14:6). We proclaim all this and much more.

POWER TO SAVE

The essence of what we proclaim is: "If you confess with your mouth, 'Jesus is Lord,' and believe in your heart that God raised him from the dead, you will be saved" (Romans 10:0). Our friend Diane was raised in a Conservative Jewish home. As a child and teen she regularly attended synagogue and even had a Bat Mitzvah ceremony at age thirteen. When she was sixteen, she moved to Israel with her family, settled in Ashkelon near her father's work, and attended a local Israeli high school. There, she became fairly proficient in Hebrew.

Part of Diane's high school course required national volunteerism, so her class chose to participate in an archaeological dig in Jerusalem. Subsequently, Diane was part of some fascinating discoveries from the Roman era, one of which led her to a sense that Jesus was real and that He was calling her to know Him. Diane and another student were chosen by the lead archaeologist to view something just uncovered. Using flashlights, the three of them crawled down a long ladder through a hole that had been dug. They emerged onto a roughly excavated, cobblestone street, and as they did, Diane felt "the cells in her body tingle." It was the Via Dolorosa, where Jesus struggled to bear His cross to the place where He was crucified. Diane didn't know how to process the feeling of awe and reverence she experienced, but it was the beginning of her quest to know Jesus.

Nothing became of that experience for many years. Diane was happily Jewish (and still is), but increasingly felt an overwhelming desire to connect with God and understand His purpose for her. She didn't know how to do this until she went on a date with a man who told her about Jesus in a way that, as a Jew, she could relate. Her date went through a number of Old Testament prophecies and showed Diane how Jesus fulfilled them. Grasping for the first time that Jesus was her Messiah, she began to cry. She felt God opened her eyes and she opened her heart to embrace Jesus.

The night Diane accepted Jesus as her Messiah she got the same "overwhelming tingle in every cell of my body" that she experienced years before on the Via Dolorosa archaeological dig. Diane says, "I can't express how grateful I am to be chosen by the Lord to know and love HIM (emphasis hers). My life has been transformed and my mind has been renewed. The Spirit of God has made His presence so clear."

Diane has faced lots of challenges since embracing Jesus, including the death of her brother with whom she was very close and who died in a tragic accident. Such challenges would have defeated and depressed her previously, but now she says, "I know Jesus saved me, and now He is my constant companion. I have been able to go through crises and difficulties with strength and hope because HE is there with me. Knowing Jesus has filled me with such love and peace. He is my Savior, my strength, and the greatest gift one could possibly receive."

SEARCHING FOR GREATER REALITY

Paul passionately proclaims that Jesus is God's lifeline and the way to find true spiritual significance. Our mission, like Paul's, is to make known the fact that God has come to us in Jesus. The life He imparts is more amazing than anything else we might hope for or seek.

All around us people are searching for a greater spiritual reality—and that reality is Jesus. Several years ago a friend invited me (Linus Jr.) to a beach house in Los Angeles to celebrate the birthday of an Oscar-winning actress. It sounded like a fun evening, so I agreed. A few hours into the birthday party I spoke with a well-known actor who described a recent trip he took to a proclaimed mystical location in Turkey in order to observe a much-anticipated solar eclipse. His goal was to experience some kind of enlightenment. Unfortunately, the day turned out to be cloudy, so his plan was thwarted.

My actor-friend went on to share with me another plan to travel to a special desert location, where he hoped to further his spiritual search. It was a fascinating evening, full of people like him, sharing their endeavors to connect with something transcendent to give more meaning to their lives. Unfortunately, there was an underlying futility to their stories of search for self-realization and greater significance. Listening to them deepened my desire to point them toward Jesus.

The Divine Expedition is the greatest news ever proclaimed. It is the good news that everyone who calls upon the name of the Lord Jesus Christ will be saved (10:12-13). It is that simple! It doesn't require a great search—it just takes a step of opening our lives to Jesus. To make it more complex reflects unbelief and pride, no matter how much we reason otherwise. All God requires is that we humbly and gratefully receive His grace, mercy, forgiveness, and new life in Jesus. By placing our faith in Jesus Christ, God imparts to us His love and His life-transforming Divine power to us, and gives us the longed for transcending meaning and purpose we seek.

> The Divine Expedition is the greatest news ever proclaimed... everyone who calls upon the name of the Lord Jesus Christ will be saved.

THE SOUND OF OUR RESCUE

To be embraced, the message of the Divine Expedition must first be heard, and for the message to be heard, a messenger is needed (10:17). People cannot call upon Jesus to rescue them if they've never heard about Him, and they can't hear about Him unless someone in proximity to them shares the Good News about Jesus with them (10:14-15). That's our job—to extend the lifeline of rescue to those we are in proximity to by telling them about the incredible new life available in Jesus. The Divine Expedition is a charge for us to be messengers of Jesus and proclaim the rescue and restoration found in Him.

Paul concludes Romans 10 by countering the claim that Israel cannot be held responsible if they did not hear the message. Underlying this, once again, is the argument, "It's God's fault!" Paul counters this by pointing out that Israel's failure was due to her obstinate refusal to respond to the message God communicated to her over and over again. The message was clearly accessible, but Israel turned a deaf ear. The Psalmist, Moses, and Isaiah all warned

Israel against this happening (Romans 10:16-21 with Psalm 19:4, Deuteronomy 32:21, and Isaiah 65:1-2).

Israel was God's first choice to proclaim the message of the Divine Expedition to the rest of the world. Sadly, she drifted into relying upon religious self-effort, thinking somehow that God's favor was a matter of self-merit. Like *Apollo 13* and Steller's ship, *St. Peter*, Israel became stranded. The result was that she ceased to be the messenger of God's grace. Fortunately, the story didn't end in hopelessness, as God sent a new messenger for the task—Jesus—and those who follow Him.

Park Ranger Gary Moses pointed to a helicopter coming to rescue Johan and Jenna Otter following a grizzly bear attack that left them seriously wounded in Montana's Glacier National Park. His words to the Otters, as he pointed to the arrival of the rescue copter, are applicable to the Good News of Jesus: "Hear that? That's the sound of your rescue." The name of Jesus is the sound of our rescue. Our role is like that of the ranger: to proclaim Jesus as God's vessel of rescue.

CHAPTER 15

ROMANS 11:1-36
THE DIVINE STRATEGY

No one's ever tried this kind of thing before. No one's even 'thought' of trying it.

—John Aaron[1]

As the slope steepened, I could feel the drag of altitude, which even the oxygen couldn't banish, and I set myself grimly to the task ahead. Soon the dreadful weakness disappeared from my legs, and I achieved a slow, laborious yet rhythmical pace that carried me steadily upwards. Work at these altitudes can rarely if ever be a pleasure—every step demands so much conscious physical and mental effort. And yet, when I could look back and see the South Col tents dwindling beneath us, I experienced a glow of achievement that made all this effort seem worthwhile.

—Sir Edmund Hillary[2]

Stephens flipped through the documents, appraising Cook's achievement, for better or worse. What lay before him, he soon realized, was a feat of navigation and discovery unparalleled in human history. He hastened to inform King George III.

—*Farther Than Any Man*[3]

...until the full number of the Gentiles has come in. And so all Israel will be saved....

—Romans 11:25-26

INNOVATIVE SOLUTIONS

Desperate times call for desperate measures. John Aaron[4] from NASA command center in Houston suggested that the crippled *Apollo 13* space-module be powered up without telemetry. Telemetry is a technology that allows data to be sent from a remote location to operate large complex systems such as the *Apollo 13* spacecraft. Powering up a spacecraft with readouts of temperature, power, and altitude, provided by telemetry, allows the equipment to be monitored as it goes on. Not to do so is like trying to paint a portrait of someone in a dark room.

The problem was *Apollo 13* could not afford to spare the power to use telemetry, so the decision was made to innovate and perform the power-up "blind." It was something that had never been tried; in fact, it was something that had never even been thought of before. But this incredible innovation resulted in the rescue of the *Apollo 13* crew and spacecraft.

Just as NASA saved the crippled *Apollo 13* and those aboard, so this chapter of Romans introduces us to an ingenious strategy to re-launch the Divine Expedition. God set aside His plan to use Israel to be His messenger to the rest of the world, at least for the time being. Because of Israel's failure, the Divine Expedition was at great risk. Instead of aborting the mission altogether, God accelerated the spread of the Divine Expedition throughout the world through Jesus and His followers. It was also the only possible means to bring about stranded Israel's rescue.

MISSIONAL MARKER #9: MASTER PLAN

Romans chapter eleven exhibits two more missional markers to spread the message of the Divine Expedition: *master plan* and *strategic action*. These two markers reveal God's revised plan to rescue the maximum number of people in history and draw them into His family.

Master plan refers to the unfolding story of God's plan to rescue humanity throughout history. Rather than indifferent to our human plight, as some surmise, God has always been at work to rescue and draw as many people as possible into a loving and redeeming relationship with Himself. Mysteriously, He does this without violating the dignity of choice He bestows upon us.

The master plan of the Bible is that God chose the Jews to reach the nations (Gentiles) that turned away from Him. Although Israel had some success, she too turned away. The arrival, life, death, resurrection, and ascension of Jesus is the greatest act of rescue in all history, resulting in a growing movement of Jesus-followers. Jesus' rescue operation began first with an offer to stranded Israel. The offer was then extended to non-Jews, and continues as an international movement, accelerating the rescue mission of God throughout the world.

> Master plan means to have in view the grand, unfolding story of God's plan to rescue humanity....

Looking toward the future, the current stage of the Divine Expedition will continue until "the full number of Gentiles (non-Jews) has come in" (11:25). Following this, the rescue mission of the Divine Expedition will be entrusted once more to Israel, and even more Gentiles will be rescued. In addition—"all Israel will be saved" (11:1-12, 26).

This master plan of the Bible enables us to see that God is at work throughout history to redeem humanity. When we see ourselves from this master plan perspective, we realize that God has called us and placed us at our own moment in history to participate in His meta-purpose. Understanding this master plan helps us see that God is at work to shape us for a role in the Divine Expedition. He uses our experiences and backgrounds to equip us to be agents of His rescue and restore mission.

The biblical master plan helped me (Linus Jr.) see that God has been at work throughout my life to equip me to reach out to others. One of my requirements to graduate from university in Graphic Design was to display my paintings, graphic design, and photography in a special art show. As I reflected upon the theme of my work, I decided upon the title "Reclamation."

The introduction to my art that I displayed at the entrance of the art show expressed how God shaped my worldview through my family, the moves we made, and even circumstances along the way. Reflecting back, I could see how God prepared me for the way forward. God was at work to shape me into the person I am and to prepare me for my role in the Divine Expedition. Following is the description I posted at the art show:

My formative years were spent in Europe. Being born in Canada, and raised in France, Holland, and America gave me different eyes to see life. I am what is referred to as a "third culture person." This has shaped my view of the world and is expressed in my art.

Along the way I have experienced some painful things with friends and family. Grieving over a close friend's tragic death, I was told by one of my sisters, "Life is painful, life is suffering—but life is also so beautiful that it catches you by surprise—at the most unforeseen moments." Ernest Hemingway once said, "Life breaks us all." I believe that. But I also believe that we can be made strong at the broken places.

My art touches upon the painful part of the human condition. Some of the themes you will see that express this in my work are:
—Man's attempts to control and quench the human spirit through politics cold as steel
—Life at times appears chaotic
—We easily fall into a mindless acceptance rather than push through to deeper truth
—People replace authenticity with performance.

Even though life involves pain and breaks us, I passionately believe that life is beautiful, so:
—Stop and look at its beauty
—Do everything you ever dreamed

—If you don't, it will pass you by
—Live soulfully
—Reach for spirituality and freedom
—Reclaim who you are and who you want to be
—Take hold of wisdom that beckons us to show us the
  Way.

Take the view expressed on one of the remaining panels of the Berlin Wall, painted after the fall of Communism: "Many small people who in many small places do many small things can alter the face of the world."
—Linus Morris, 4/24/00

Knowing the biblical master plan helps us see that God can use both pain and beauty in life to shape us for the part we are to play in the Divine Expedition. It also enables us to see where we fit in God's overall timeline. We are approaching the third great epoch of God's grand rescue plan. The first was the choosing of the nation of Israel to be a light to the nations. The second was the sacrificial death and resurrection of Jesus, and the sending of His followers to make disciples of all people. The third epoch will be a future redeemed Israel that joins in the rescue of the nations. This meta-perspective illuminates what our focus is to be.

God desires for all humanity to be rescued and restored to a relationship with Him. Our mission is to be ambassadors and witnesses of Jesus to rescue all peoples. This rescue plan is multi-cultural (both Jew and non-Jew together as the people of God), multi-racial, and multinational. The Divine Expedition is entrusted to every person who confesses and believes in Jesus as Messiah-Son-King-Lord-Savior, and it is intended for all people irrespective of race, gender, or status.

GOOD NEWS FOR THE JEWS

Does the fact that God shifted the Divine Expedition from Israel to Jesus and His followers mean that Israel is permanently set aside? Paul tells us a remnant of Jews do accept Jesus as Messiah and Lord (11:1-6). As I (Linus Sr.) write this, the chairman of the board of the ministry I am with is a Jewish follower of Jesus, as are two of the six other members of our leadership team. I have a Jewish brother-in-law who believes in Messiah Jesus and many Jewish friends who do as well. I have met Jewish followers of Jesus all over the world. The Divine Expedition calls us to proclaim the Good News of Jesus to both Jew and non-Jew alike. As we do, many respond.

A fellow worker of ours, Brian, was brought up steeped in cultural Judaism in what he calls a "self-imposed ghetto" of Long Island, a New York City suburb. His family members were "conservative" Jews, which meant that he was bar mitzvahed at age thirteen, went to temple on the High Holidays, and, as he says, "looked forward to getting presents at Hanukkah and enjoying a great meal at Passover." While culturally Jewish, he was philosophically agnostic, as was every other Jew he knew.

> The Divine Expedition calls us to proclaim the Good News of Jesus to both Jew and non-Jew alike.

Brian's journey to faith was marked by two huge events. The first was the break-up with a Catholic girlfriend because of his different religion. The second was his Jewish grandfather's death. For Brian, at twenty-years-of-age, these were the first times "God got in my way."

The break-up with his girlfriend sent Brian into an emotional tailspin. He became desperate enough to ask his older brother, who came to know Jesus several years earlier, for help. His brother recommended Brian read the Gospel of Matthew. Brian had no idea what that was!

Two months later Brian's grandfather, a well-known leader in the Jewish community in Brooklyn, died. The only person at his funeral who seemed upset about his death was Brian's Jewish-Christian brother. Brian realized that his brother's grief over their grandfather's death was because of the likelihood that he had not found peace with Christ and was lost. This gnawed at the inside of Brian.

Brian came to faith in Jesus sometime later after falling out of bed in his dorm room in upstate New York. Horribly hung over from the previous night's partying, Brian lay on his stomach, desperate for hope, having reached the end of himself. His girlfriend had dumped him, and both of his grandparents had died (his grandmother had died previously). Moreover, the only Christian in Brian's life, his brother, seemed to grasp the enormity of their deaths.

Upon reflection, Brian said half to God and half to himself, "Well, what the hell...I'll become a Christian!" and opened his life to Jesus. Brian began the journey of following Christ and says that one of the most joyous events of his life was the privilege of baptizing his mother some years later. She too embraced Jesus as her Messiah-Savior after a lifetime journey of seeking God.

DID WE ALREADY SAY, "GOOD NEWS FOR JEWS?"

Our British friend Paul is another person with a Jewish heritage who embraced Jesus. He was brought up in a Jewish community in North London, England. Paul attended synagogue with his family, studied Hebrew, and attended the annual Passover supper, all part and parcel of being Jewish. Ironically, during this time he considered himself an atheist and fully expected to be so for the rest of his life. This began to change as a Christian friend from school faithfully witnessed to Paul about Jesus and invited him to his young people's group at church. Accepting the invitation, Paul attended a church service for the first time ever.

Paul was intrigued with the Christians he met. They seemed to be people of genuine faith in God. He reasoned, "How could this be if there is no God?" Inquisitively, he began asking questions, reading books, and discussing issues related to God. His curiosity grew as he heard that Jesus lived, died, and was alive today. His response was—"Wow!" Within a few months Paul decided to find out for himself if this Good News was true, so he knelt down and invited Jesus into his life.

Paul didn't know anything would happen, but a few days later, when his parents asked him why he was different, he told them! They struggled to understand why Paul should want to be a Christian, but they saw in him a new joy and purpose. Paul's parents thought it was a phase – but some 35 years later, the phase continues! Something that surprised Paul as a follower of Jesus is a greater appreciation and understanding of his Jewish faith. "After all," he says, "I'm still Jewish!"

GOOD NEWS FOR MUSLIMS TOO

The Good News of Jesus is meant for everyone, regardless of heritage. Our friend Iman (Arabic for "faith") grew up in a Muslim home. She moved with her family from Lebanon to Australia, seeking work to "have a better life." Little did her parents know that their decision would also mean that she would find eternal life through Jesus.

God used different people to fulfill His plan in Iman's life. Following her parent's relocation to Australia, a Christian Palestinian family helped them with their immigration paperwork. Iman's parents thought this was strange, due to the fact that her parents were Muslim and the people helping them were Christians. Iman's mother was completely illiterate because, as a girl, it was not a priority for her parents to send her to school. Consequently, Iman's "mum's" goal in life was to make sure her daughter received the opportunity for the education not afforded to her.

Iman's mother was thrilled when the Palestinian Christian family's mother offered to tutor Iman in English, and at no cost. Iman was eight-years-old, struggling in school, and her mother was unable to help her. This Christian friend devoted several hours each week, listening to and correcting her as she read aloud Bible-based storybooks. This didn't bother Iman's mother, who said, "Well, these Old Testament stories are not too different from those in the Qur'an."

Iman's tutoring continued for several years, and as her reading improved, she began to read directly from her tutor's Bible. Her mother was aware of this but, yet again, didn't protest. Iman believes her mother's positive response was because the things Iman shared with her mother from the Bible touched her mom's heart as much as it touched her own.

Iman, however, started to feel confused, as she was living in a Muslim community where she was taught that Islam was the best religion in the world, and that Christians were wrong in their beliefs. Nevertheless, she looked forward to her weekly lessons with her

Christian tutor and "to reading from Christian books with beautiful stories." She frequently wondered, "What really is the truth?"

By the time Iman reached the sixth grade, her tutor moved to another State in Australia. Soon afterward, her mother became good friends with an Egyptian Muslim woman who started taking Iman's family to a nearby Mosque. It was more of a social gathering, but there was also an hour lesson on the Qur'an each week. Iman enjoyed the community aspect of the mosque and found friends who understood her. She soon believed that Islam was the best religion in the world and was proud to be Muslim.

By the time Iman finished high school, her family stopped going to the mosque regularly, due to conflicts within the Muslim community. In college she met a new group of friends who partied a lot and seemed to enjoy life. She began dating a Catholic boyfriend but told him that to marry her he would have to convert to Islam. He responded that his parents would disown him and that she needed to convert to Catholicism. She replied that her parents would kill them both, so which would he prefer?

It was at this time that Iman started to pray and seek God again. The question, "What really is the truth?" resurfaced in her heart, so she prayed and asked God to reveal the truth to her. She thought, "If the truth is found in Islam, I will break up with my boyfriend and dutifully observe the five pillars of Islam. If it is found in Christianity, then I will follow Jesus." Months passed, and no answer seemed to come. She decided to break up with her boyfriend anyway.

Soon after, Iman's best friend in college, a Lebanese Catholic Maronite, gave her life to Christ. Iman was amazed by the immediate transformation in her friend's life. Studying together one night, her new Christian friend invited Iman to attend church. She thought, "Why not? It would be a good experience to attend a church at least once in my life." As Iman entered the church, she felt God's presence in the room. When the person leading the service spoke, Iman's heart started pounding, and she thought, "How does this person know what I am thinking? How does he know what is in my heart?" She felt as if he was speaking directly to her.

Iman knew she had found the truth, because for the first time in her life she felt an incredible peace! She says, "I came to know God's love for me through Jesus in a very deep and powerful way that night." Although she wasn't sure what was required in following Christ, she asked God to guide her. Her journey as a follower of Jesus continues, and she is now a full-time participant in spreading the message of the Divine Expedition. She says, "It would take a book to express how my relationship with Jesus has developed and continues to grow." Her "mum" also embraced Jesus just ten days before she died.

MISSIONAL MARKER #10: STRATEGIC ACTION

The meta-story of the Bible is that God seeks to draw all people to a loving, intimate relationship with himself. Corresponding to God's *master plan* is the tenth marker to reach others with the message of the Divine Expedition—our *strategic action*.

Paul's own strategic action to rescue people is laid out in Romans 9-11. Paul began Romans chapter nine by expressing compassion to reach his fellow Jew (9:1-3). Unfortunately, his Jewish brethren thought they could achieve their own salvation, so were hardened to their need for a Savior (9:4, 5, 16, and 10:3). Strategically, Paul shifted his ministry to prioritize non-Jews (11:13), doing so in part because he knew God's master plan was to rescue them. Since Israel hadn't carried out this task, Paul took it on, just as we are called to do so today.

> The divine side is God's master plan; the human side is our strategic action.

_____

But Paul had another reason for prioritizing Gentiles. He knew this was the most *strategic* way to reach his fellow Jew. It seems absurd to say that the best way to reach one group of people (Jews) is to focus on a different group of people (non-Jews). It is like saying in order to reach the French we are going to launch a mission to China. Odd as it may seem, Paul, through the Holy Spirit's guidance, engages in an ingenious strategy.

We did a similar thing in our own mission to Europe. Traveling to Europe with basketball teams made up of Christ-followers, we observed that many Europeans had abandoned Christianity in its traditional form. People ceased attending church except for occasional ceremonial events such as marriage, baptisms, and funerals. Christian churches and Christianity were viewed as obsolete, relics of the past. The attitude we encountered over and over again was, "We've tried Christianity and it doesn't work."

At the halftime of our basketball games, our team members gave a brief presentation about how a relationship with Jesus was the most important thing in our lives. Over and over again people expressed interest in what it meant to have a personal relationship with Jesus. As we interacted with those who came up to us after the games, we concluded that what most Europeans rejected was not Jesus but anemic institutional forms of "Christendom," dominating the landscape of Europe for centuries.

As we moved from city to city in continental Europe, we felt an increasing concern to stay connected with those we met. Pondering what we could do to follow-up those interested in our message, we discerned that gathering people together as Christ-followers was the primary means of the spread of the early Christian movement. We knew that starting a national-language church would be difficult, due to the "We've-tried-Christianity-and-it-doesn't-work" attitude everywhere in Western Europe. After much thought, prayer, and deliberation, we decided to establish an English-speaking international community of Christ-followers in the greater Geneva, Switzerland area.

As we launched this new work, more than a few fellow-Christians expressed skepticism at our strategy. They argued that mission in Europe should focus on reaching Europeans in their national languages. We were convinced, however, that by starting with the English-speaking international community we could get a church up and running more quickly. Moreover, we believed that many bi-lingual Europeans would be attracted to Jesus once they saw a more contemporary and vibrant expression of the church, in contrast to the traditional ones they distanced themselves from. This proved to be so and a vibrant multi-national church now exists.

Our strategy was similar to Paul's: by reaching internationals (in Paul's case, Gentiles), those Europeans living around us (in Paul's case, fellow-Jews) would see God at work in a more dynamic way than that to which they were accustomed, thus creating a thirst (make jealous) to know Jesus (11:13-14). This strategy has worked, and the church that resulted in the Geneva area has reached many, many people, including Europeans from the host country.

HOLLAND TOO

Later moving to Holland, our family employed a similar strategy. Accepting the invitation of a Dutch ambassador who was part of the church we started in Geneva, we began the Crossroads International Church in Amsterdam. This church has grown to over 1000 in weekly attendance with more that sixty percent of these Dutch. We are convinced that many more Europeans (in Paul's case, fellow-Jews) have been reached than would have had we begun a national language work. This strategy has also led to the multiplication of national-language churches as Europeans caught a vision for the Christ-centered, Biblically-based, grace-oriented, outreach-focused, spiritually-vibrant, culturally-relevant church strategy we employed.

Paul knew that when Jews, who failed to reach God through their own merit, saw God working powerfully among non-Jews, who were the recipients of God's grace, his Jewish countrymen would awaken to the reality that something was missing in their own lives. Seeing God work among non-Jews made Paul's fellow-Jews desire what they didn't have. As a consequence, a greater number of Jews turned to God's grace through Messiah Jesus and were saved than would otherwise have been (11:13-14). By this means, both Jews and non-Jews were reconciled to God (11:15-16). This was not just good strategy—it was Divine strategy.

> Seeing God work in this way made his fellow-Jews desire [jealous for] what they didn't have.

SHIFTING STRATEGY

Sadly, the greater part of Israel and the Jewish community is hardened to God's plan (11:7-10), while a spiritual harvest continues among the peoples of the world. Paul makes it clear that non-Jewish followers of Jesus ought not to be arrogant about their inclusion in God's family, as they have been "grafted" into the promise given to Abraham. God loves Israel and will restore her again in the future to once again be the chief bearer of the Divine Expedition. In the meantime, it falls upon us to compassionately seek the rescue of Jew and non-Jew alike. To follow Jesus is to be an agent of the Divine Expedition to reach and rescue all peoples.

Romans chapter eleven unfolds the God's master plan in history, at the same time calling us to strategic action as agents of the Divine Expedition. The time is coming when Israel will once again be the primary Divine Expedition herald (see Revelation 7), at which time she will carry out the task to reach the nations to which she was called (11:1, 11, 12, 15, 26). God's redemptive plan will ultimately be carried out by Israel as a whole (not just a remnant, as is now the case) and all Israel will embrace Messiah-Son-King-Lord-Savior Jesus. This will result in even greater numbers of non-Jews throughout the world being rescued (11:17-32).

> The time is coming when Israel will once again be the primary agent of the Divine Expedition.

This then is God's plan to reach the maximum number of people throughout history. As we engage in strategic action and carry out our role in the mission of the Divine Expedition, we will one day look back, like Sir Edmund Hillary, and experience "a glow of achievement that made all this effort seem worthwhile."[5] We will, like Cook, have been part of a feat "unparalleled in human history."[6] Like John Aaron's ingenuity in rescuing *Apollo 13*, Paul praises God for the incredible wisdom of His plan (11:33-36). He is mercifully at work to bring the maximum number of people to faith—and we have a strategic part to play—but not alone, as we shall see in the next chapter.

CHAPTER 16

ROMANS 12:1-21
THE DIVINE COMMUNITY

Lewis had written to William Clark.... It launched one of the greatest friendships of all time and started the friends on one of the greatest adventures, and one of the great explorations, of all time. They complimented each other. In general, in areas in which Lewis was shaky, Clark was strong, and vice versa.

—*Undaunted Courage*[1]

The fiery summer of 1768 was a hectic time for Cook. Between May, when he was commissioned and took command, and August when he planned to sail, Cook had a near impossible list of tasks to accomplish. He needed sailors, warrant officers, and officers.

—*Farther Than Any Man*[2]

Lowe and I were waiting the announcement of the rest of the party with considerable interest and were very pleased indeed to hear of the inclusion of Evans, Bourdillon, and Gregory of the Cho Oyu Expedition, and Ward of the 1951 Reconnaissance. The climbing team also included Wylie and Noyce, both of whom had excellent Himalayan records; and

Westmacott and Band, who had done some fine climbing in the European Alps. The non-climbing members were our movie-cameraman, Stobart, and our old friend Dr. Griffiths Pugh, whose inclusion indicated psychological torture for some unwary climbers.

—Sir Edmund Hillary[3]

Just as each of us has one body with many members, and these members do not all have the same function, so in Christ we who are many form one body, and each member belongs to all the others. We all have different gifts according to the grace given us.

—Romans 12:4-6

LOOKING BACK ON GOD'S MERCY

Paul begins Romans 12 by looking back at where the journey has brought us thus far. The first eleven chapters can be summed up by the words "God's mercy." Reflecting upon these chapters, Paul begins his rearview look with the statement, "Therefore, I urge you, brothers (and sisters), *in view of God's mercy*, to offer your bodies as living sacrifices, holy and pleasing to God—this is your spiritual act of service" (12:1). The New Living Translation of Romans 12:1 puts it this way: "And so, dear brothers and sisters, I plead with you to give your bodies to God. Let them be a living and holy sacrifice—the kind He will accept. When you think of what He has done for you [chapters 1-11], is this too much to ask? " The success of the Divine Expedition rests upon a continual referencing of what God has done for us though Jesus;[4] that is, keeping God's mercy in view.[5]

God's mercy includes the sum of all that He has done for and made available to us.

God's mercy includes the sum of all that He has made available to us. This includes our credit of righteousness, our peace with God, our access by faith into the grace in which we stand, our hope of the glory of God, the love of God poured into our hearts by the Holy Spirit, as well as the "much mores" of Romans 5. His mercy includes our new life in Christ, our freedom from the law of sin and death, and our empowerment by the Holy Spirit of Romans 6-8. All of these things together are the restoration of the Divine Design of the first eight chapters of Romans. They are rooted in and the result of God's mercy.

But His mercy also includes the call to participate in the Divine Expedition unfolded in Romans 9-11 with the missional markers in those chapters to guide us. We have a role to play in the greatest rescue and restoration mission ever undertaken. God's mercy restores to us the Divine Design and commissions us to be participants in a global rescue mission. God's mercy engages us with a purpose more adventurous and more fulfilling than any quest for power, money, sex, survival, comfort, consumerism, or any other earthly pursuit imaginable. We are invited to be part of the Divine Expedition to rescue and restore others through the Good News of Jesus.

Because of God's mercy, we have a God-given significance and purpose in this world that calls us to action. We matter, and what we do matters. We are called to active duty. We are called to be on mission. It matters that we trust and follow Jesus. It matters that we take risks to rescue and restore others. It matters that we offer our whole selves, head, heart, and hands, to God and His mission in the world. God's mercy connects us to God, our true humanity is restored, and we are commissioned to extend God's mercy to others. What could be more exciting than that?

DEAD-END OF RETREATING INTO SELF

Offering ourselves to God and His mission to rescue and restore others is the antidote for isolation, aloneness, and meaningless-ness. On a recent flight, Sharon and I (Linus Sr.) sat next to a man who appeared quite nervous. Before take-off, he asked if he could have our flight magazine, since his was missing. We obliged, and he grasped it tightly, saying he suffered from anxiety and needed something to distract him. He proceeded to talk non-stop during the entire trip. In the course of our travel, our seatmate told us that he had a son and daughter-in-law, neither of whom had he spoken with in twenty years. He likewise had never spoken with their 14-year old daughter, his granddaughter—in fact, he had never even met her. He further added that his second son lived close to him, but he no longer saw him either because he lived with his mother, our flight-mate's estranged ex-wife.

When I asked what happened to his marriage, he replied, "We just grew apart. We developed separate sets of friends, and even when attending the same party, we took separate cars and didn't hang out together." He explained that he preferred living alone because it was too difficult to adjust to others. It was clear that our travel-mate desperately needed friendship and community, as evidenced by his talkativeness, but, for whatever reason, he retreated into a life of aloneness.

> Offering ourselves to God and His mission to rescue and restore others is the antidote for isolation, aloneness, and meaninglessness.

After our flight landed and we parted, I reflected upon how my story could have ended up like his. The difference was that I embraced God's mercy through Jesus. Jesus changed the trajectory of my life, turning me from my fears, insecurity, and self-centeredness. He healed the damaged and wounded areas of my life, giving me strength to change, forgive others, and ask others for forgiveness. Continually referencing God's mercy is what moved Sharon and me toward, rather than away from each other.

Jesus said, "Unless a kernel of wheat (metaphor for our lives) falls to the ground and dies, it remains only a single seed. But if it dies, it produces many seeds. The man who loves his life will lose it, while the man who hates his life in this world will keep it" (John 12:24-25). The two primary elements that bind Sharon and me together, helping us work through the rough patches of our marriage, are a gratitude for God's love and mercy, and a passion to impart that love and mercy to family, friends, and neighbors around us.

WALKING THE TALK

To effectively carry out the mission of the Divine Expedition, our walk must align with our talk ("walk the talk"). The more we draw upon God's mercy and the resources of the Divine Design, the more God transforms us and aligns our hearts, minds, and behavior with His holy, loving, and merciful character. To walk the talk of our faith, hope, and love (I Corinthians 13), we must continually burrow deeper into God's mercy.

The first several years of Sharon's and my marriage was filled with turmoil and conflict. During our frequent arguments, I, typically, flooded with emotion, vented my frustration, and relentlessly argued my point. After doing so I felt better. Yet the more I emoted, the more Sharon shut down emotionally. The day following one of our heated exchanges, I would forget what we argued about, but Sharon would not. Sensing something bothering her, I would probe until I drew out of her the reason for her emotional distance. She would then rehearse our conversation in detail.

> To walk the talk of our faith, hope, and love, we must continually burrow into God's mercy.

Believing that divorce was inevitable, I began keeping a record of our arguments, thinking I would need a record to prove in court why I was right and Sharon was wrong. (This was before what is now called "no-fault" divorce.) The way I recorded our exchanges looked something like this in tone: "All I said was…" (thus, minimizing my role in the conflict), then adding, "**BUT SHE SAID…**" (thereby, magnifying her role). In my mind, her responsibility for our conflict was far, far greater than mine. Looking back, I realize that the reverse was actually true some of the time—okay, most of the time. To keep Sharon from finding the record of our conflict I kept, I hid my list in a cigar box in the bottom drawer of my desk.

Following my decision to follow Jesus, I began to understand God's love and forgiveness, and was struck by what I read in Paul's letter to the Corinthians, that "love is patient, love is kind. It does not envy, does not boast, is not proud, is not rude, is not self-seeking, is not easily angered, and *keeps no record of wrongs*" (I Corinthians 13:4-5). My conscience was especially pricked by statement that love *keeps no record of wrongs*. I knew that as a follower of Jesus, this was how God loved me, and it was the way God wanted me to love Sharon.

Even though I was still unsure our marriage would survive, one evening, before I went to bed, I took the list containing the record of our conflicts and destroyed it. I decided to trust God for our marriage and asked Him to make me a more loving husband. This was a big step toward the healing of our relationship. The changes that followed were incremental, but the more I opened myself to God's love and sought to express it toward Sharon (I had to apologize a lot), the more she responded in trust and appreciation of me. I am amazed to look back and see the healing that has occurred in our marriage as my walk began to align with God's mercy.

God's holiness is not an otherworldly "super-spirituality." It expresses itself in our relationships with others in real love, joy, peace, patience, kindness, goodness, faithfulness, gentleness and self-control (Galatians 5:22-23). These are like gauges on a dashboard that indicate whether or not we are keeping God's mercy constantly in view. As we respond to His mercy toward us and draw upon the resources of the Divine Expedition, including the Holy Spirit's empowerment, we experience an internal transformation that aligns us with God's holiness, goodness, and love. The Divine Expedition makes possible an inside-out transformation, the outworking of which commends our faith in Jesus to others.

> Love, joy, peace, patience, kindness, goodness, faithfulness, gentleness and self-control are like gauges on a dashboard....

The Divine Expedition is fueled by a gratitude for the merciful action of God. This is what motivates us to repeatedly present ourselves as God's instruments in the world, and is what is meant by "being transformed by the renewing of your mind" (Romans 12:1-2).

MOVING FORWARD IN COMMUNITY

Paul encourages us to reflect back upon God's mercy, but he goes on to push forward on mission together as a band of brothers and sisters. Launching a spacecraft, climbing a mountain, or voyaging around the world requires teamwork and community. One person may lead and be more visible, but without the participation of others, expeditions are impossible.

Only Edmund Hillary and his Sherpa companion, Tenzing Norgay, made it to the top of Mount Everest, but the larger team made their ascent possible. The persons listed in the Hillary quote at the beginning of this chapter are only a part of an army of team members who expended themselves in the establishment of a string of camps up the mountain, stocking them with the supplies Hillary and Norgay would rely upon for their ultimate successful summit of Everest. Likewise, the Cook and Lewis and Clark expeditions relied upon teams who made their exploits possible. Still others were in the background sponsoring and supporting these leaders and their exploits. Every expedition is a team endeavor, none more so than the Divine Expedition. It too requires collaborative teamwork.

> Every expedition is a team endeavor.

Romans chapter twelve highlights the missional community needed to carry out the mission of the Divine Expedition. Our mission is not individualistic. Paul's statement, "Do not think of yourself more highly than you ought..." (12:3), at first glance seems to mean we should not be prideful. While this is emphasized elsewhere in Scripture, Paul connects his admonition here to our participation in a community of Christ-followers, each member of which contributes complimentary gifts (12:4-5). Following his charge *not to think* of ourselves more highly than we ought, Paul says *we are to think* of ourselves "with sober judgment, in accordance with the measure of faith God has given us." He adds, "we form one body, and each member belongs to all the others," and then goes on to list the different gifts we are to use by faith (12:6-8).

INTERCONNECTED

To carry out the Divine Expedition necessitates interconnectedness where each of us uses our supernaturally imparted gift or gifts in concert with each other. The God-given gifts of prophesying, serving, teaching, encouraging, giving, leadership, and showing mercy are complimentary and to be used in community together. Paul lists additional gifts elsewhere (I Corinthians 12:12-31;

Ephesians 4:11-16) and states in Ephesians 4:12 that the working in tandem of these various gifts is how the body of Christ is built up. Here in Romans, he tells us that Divine gifts are given by grace and are to be exercised by faith—and with diligence and cheerfulness (12:6-8).

The Divine Expedition connects us both to Christ and to the community of His followers, called the body of Christ or the church. Our effectiveness in life and ministry depends upon this interconnectedness as a body. The Divine Expedition is a team endeavor to be carried out with other Christ-followers, who by grace are given a variety of spiritual gifts, which are held together by the bond of love (12:9-10).

This points us away from the individualism, self-absorption, and isolation characterizing Western culture, and, unfortunately, many who consider themselves Christians. The Divine Expedition is not about "me, myself, and I"; it is about "us, ourselves, and we." It may be a cliché, but "there is no 'I' in team." Hugh Halter and Matt Smay address the issue of individualism in their book, *The Tangible Kingdom*, advocating "discipling togetherness," even eliminating services that allow people to remain autonomous or invisible. They say that in their Denver Christ-following community, "We never reference our relationship with God as 'personal.' We speak of it as 'communal.'[6]

One of my (Linus Jr.) favorite activities is kiteboarding, the risk factor of which goes way up if you kiteboard alone. I was kiting on the north shore of Maui when a fourteen-foot wave crashed my kite, snapped one of my lines, and tossed me into the ocean. Since I was still connected by my harness, my kite dragged me along the water's surface and then across a reef. Although bleeding and hurting, I was able to get to my kite, which I bundled together to keep me afloat. My biggest concern was what my blood might attract, as I was aware of recent reports of Tiger Shark attacks in the area. To my relief, my friend Pierre saw my dilemma, kited up and shouted, "Grab onto the back of my harness!" He then kite-pulled me with him to shore.

Kiting together with Pierre, friends Reese and Ben, or nephews Cheyne and Colin is not only safer; it is a thousand times more enjoyable. We learn from each other and teach each other new maneuvers. So it is with the Divine Expedition. As Christ-followers we also help each other as we follow Jesus and seek to rescue and restore others. My brother and sister Christ-followers encourage me when I'm struggling and challenge me when I am being selfish or feeling sorry for myself. I try to do the same with them.

THE DIVINE EXPEDITION AUDIO-VISUAL

Words alone will not attract people to Jesus. The message of the Divine Expedition is meant to be audio-visual. People need to *hear* the Good News of Jesus, but they also want to *see* the Good News. The Good News is heard when we proclaim the life, sacrificial death, resurrection, and ascension of Jesus; it is seen through vibrant, loving communities of His followers.

As the community of Christ's followers, we are called to show sincere love, honoring others above self, zealous spiritual fervor in serving the Lord, joyful hope, patience in affliction, and faithfulness in prayer (Romans 12:9-12). We are called to share with God's people in need,

> The message of the Divine Expedition is meant to be audio-visual.

practice hospitality, bless those who persecute us, rejoice with those who rejoice, and grieve with those who grieve (12:13-15). We are to live in harmony with each other, not be proud, but be willing to associate with those of low status, and avoid conceit (12:16). We are not to take revenge, but do what is right, live at peace with everyone as far as possible, and overcome evil with good. In each of these ways, we make the genuineness of our faith visible (12:17-21).

The Christ-following bar is so high and God's mission so challenging that they can only be attained by the power of Jesus transforming us in community with each other. Thus, the verbal message of our faith is underscored by the visual demonstration of serving together in a gracious, loving, merciful, humble, caring, witnessing community of Christ-followers.

Carrying out the Divine Expedition in community points us away from simply focusing on church programs, where a small percentage of people carry the bulk of the ministry load. It is essential to compliment the larger gatherings of the church with smaller groupings, emphasizing the giftedness and ministry of all believers, not just a few. This includes multiplying smaller ministry groups that connect in caring ways, not only to each other, but also to the surrounding community.

ON MISSION TOGETHER

In the old "Christendom" paradigm, the goal was to get the community into the church. In the Divine Expedition paradigm, the goal is to get the church into the community. This means an outward missional engagement with the community around us so that we reflect Jesus' words that the kingdom/church is to be like yeast, permeating everything around it. The kingdom/church is to be like a net dropping down and spreading out into the deep for a great catch (Matthew 13:33, 47-48).

All Christ's followers are called to be involved in the Divine Expedition. We are to structure the church away from members who are passive consumers. Halter and Smay put it this way: "Church gatherings were never the intended goal; they were the natural result of people finding others who were living their alternative Kingdom story. The goal of our missional life is not to grow churches. The goal of church is to grow missionaries."[7] We (both Linus Sr. and Linus Jr.) believe more so that the goal is to grow Christ-following ministers, missionaries, and multipliers, as well as ministering, missional, and multiplying Christ-following communities.

Expeditions require community, teamwork, and collaboration with others. I (Linus Jr.) am connected together with friends who live in the same apartment complex. They eat together, hang out together, have breakfasts together, and work out at the gym together. They plan Christmas parties, Thanksgiving celebrations, and lots of other celebrative gatherings because they love being together. I like spending time with them (especially one young lady). But they are not a closed group. They invite people who don't know Jesus into their circle of community and share their lives and faith with them. While most of my friends' parents are steeped in quests for financial security and live more individualistic life styles, my friends and I place a high value on community.

It is no accident that Paul addresses the need for community (Romans 12) immediately following presenting God's master strategy to reach our world with the Good News of Jesus (Romans 9-11). Moving forward as a team is the only way we can carry out the Divine Expedition. So the question is, are we moving forward with others together on mission? Romans chapter 13 describes what this is to look like in society around us.

CHAPTER 17

ROMANS 13:1-14
GOVERNMENT AND SOCIETY

When Magellan arrived at the Court of Spain, he presented King Charles V with a plan that would give the ships of the Crown of Castile full access to the lands of the Spice Islands.[1]

The proposed team will be approved by the Himalayan Joint Committee.....

—John Hunt's letter to Sir Edmund Hillary[2]

In all your intercourse with the natives, treat them in the most friendly and conciliatory manner which their own conduct will admit.

—Thomas Jefferson[3]

Bucking Cook's authority, Banks and Solander climbed out the two great cabin's large stern windows and snuck ashore by rowboat. Much to Cook's amusement the viceroy (of Rio) refused to allow the pair to land.

—Farther Than Any Man[4]

Let no debt remain outstanding, except the continuing debt to love....

—Romans 13:8

GOVERNMENT, TAXES, AND LOVE

No expedition operates in a vacuum. Expeditions do not exist without some degree of favor granted from a greater governing body and its authorities. Magellan was spurned by his native Portuguese government, but was able to sail under the banner of Spain with the backing of the Spanish king, Charles V. Edmund Hillary depended upon the support of the Royal Geographic Society of England, the New Zealand Alpine Club, the Nepalese government, and the Himalayan Joint Committee. Lewis and Clark operated under the sponsorship of President Jefferson and the United States Congress, and later benefited from good relations with frontier settlements and Native Americans along their expedition route.

As representatives of the Divine Expedition, we court the respect and good graces of the communities we seek to reach. The effectiveness of our mission depends upon our functioning as good citizens in

> Rather than disdain society, we aim to live within it with integrity and love.

the broader context of the social structure around us. Rather than disdain and remove ourselves from society, we aim to live within it with integrity and love, thus commending the message we proclaim. Romans chapter thirteen tells us that this requires submitting to the governing structure of society (13:1), paying our taxes (13:6), treating others with respect (13:7), and fulfilling our debts (13:8), especially our greatest debt—to love others (13:8-10).

Recognizing the value of government is important in carrying out the Divine Expedition. We are to respect government without conceding its all-importance. Paul reminds us that God establishes government for the welfare of its citizens, saying, "Governing authorities...have been established by God for...our good" (13:1-4). Without some form of governmental structure, chaos and lawlessness rule, as seen in countries such as Somalia, which are led by warlords with no functioning central government. Without government, many of the everyday things we take for granted would not exist, things like safe travel, safe homes, and safe streets—or even streets at all.

I (Linus Jr.) love traveling and surfing Baja, Mexico; however, I am always relieved to return home. There is much about Mexico I like, but without fail every time I cross the border back into California, I am struck by how comparatively safe and well-kept U.S. and Western European cities are. Although I question how effectively tax money is spent and grimace at tax-time, I get that it takes money to make cities safe and clean. When it is time to give to Caesar what is Caesar's, although I still wince, I reflect on the reasonably safe cities and paved streets afforded by my taxes. Doing so eases (a bit) the paying of my tax bill.

BROTHER'S KEEPER

Where we have a voice in choosing the authorities that govern us, we are to embrace our participation as a responsibility and privilege. We cannot give in to the feeling that the part we can play doesn't matter. The reform movement that led to the collapse of Communism in east central Europe and the Soviet Union, marking the end of the Cold War, is a reminder that small people in small places doing small things can alter things. Participating in the democratic processes afforded us is part of being our brother's keeper.

Our selection of government officials is not to be based simply upon self-interest, but equally upon the benefit to the wider community. While stewarding our own relational, economic, and material wellbeing, we are also to seek the furtherance of the common good. Furthering the common good includes preserving the moral character of society and caring for the powerless, marginalized, and poor. These are difficult choices. How best to encourage the common good without taking away personal responsibility and initiative is the subject of hot debate. We do not try to resolve this debate in this book but we believe that the answer lies somewhere between carrying one another's burdens (Galatians 6:2) and each one carrying his- or her-own burden (Galatians 6:5).

Caring for the marginalized and poor both locally and globally is part of the Divine Expedition. In the early 1980s, friend Mike Bagby flew A-6 Intruders in the U.S. Navy, and in his spare time was a ski bum. He visited Hawaii where he found that his cousin had become a follower of Jesus. As MIke began hanging out with the

Hope Chapel, Maui network of Christ-followers, of which his cousin was a part, he found that "they were guys like me—just not doing drugs like I was." Before long Mike became a follower of Jesus too.

Several years later, Mike joined a short-term ministry-team of Christians to bring relief supplies to Nicaraguan Miskito Indian refugees who were living in the swamps and savannahs along the Kruta and Coco Rivers in Honduras. The Nicaraguan, Communist Sandinistas oppressed the Miskitos, destroying their villages and schools, forcing them to find refuge across the border. During Mike's ministry trip, the Miskitos asked the relief team to help educate their children, as it had been five years since many had attended school.

Mike didn't realize that God would get hold of his heart for this persecuted and marginalized people group, but from that trip, *Seek the Lamb* ministries was birthed. In the years since, God has used Mike and his wife Laura to recruit many volunteers to train Miskito teachers, build schools, provide school supplies, and bring to them the Good News of Jesus. Teachers in the Miskito schools today were themselves educated in the first generation of *Seek the Lamb* schools. Several businesses (Rio Coco Beans; Rio Coco Beads) have been started in partnership with the Miskitos to fund the teachers, schools, and school children. When the Sandinista government was voted out in 1991, the new Nicaraguan regime invited the Miskito schools to join the public school system. *Seek the Lamb*, however, continues to play a vital part in the training and resourcing of the Miskitos.

Followers of Jesus know they are called to be "salt and light" in society, reflecting God's love and compassion. They also pray for and seek to influence government to promote the wellbeing of *all* those under their authority, something the Sandinistas did not do. Christ-followers submit to governing authorities but they work toward influencing a redemptive and just society (13:5).

THE DEBT OF LOVE

Our desire to rescue others leads us to live respectfully in whatever society we are in, but it also motivates us to go beyond respect to extend Christ's love to those around us. The debt of love is not one of grudging obligation; it is one of willing gratitude because of what Jesus has done for us. Once we experience God's love, it wells up inside us, and then flows out from us.

As grateful and indebted recipients of God's mercy and love, we seek to rise above the legal obligations and requirements of society. We also aim to transcend the moral obligations of God's law (such as "Do not commit adultery." "Do not murder." "Do not steal." "Do not

> We seek to rise above the legal obligations and requirements of society.

covet."). The even higher standard we aspire to is to show forth the love of Christ. Christ's love compels us (2 Corinthians 5:14). His love does no harm to its neighbor. His love is not just the negation of what is bad; it is, even more, the carrying out of what is good. We aspire to "do good to all people, especially to those who belong to the family of believers" (Galatians 6:10), and to love our neighbors as ourselves (Romans 13:8-10).

Rodney Stark writes that the enormous rise of Christianity during the first three centuries after Christ was significantly due to the involvement of Christians who cared for others. In 165 A.D., during the reign of the Roman Emperor Marcus Aurelius, a devastating epidemic swept though the Roman Empire. During the fifteen-year duration of the outbreak, between one-quarter and one-third of the empire's population died, including Marcus Aurelius himself. Pagan priests admitted ignorance of why the epidemic was happening, not knowing why the gods sent such misery, or if the gods even cared. At first onset of the plague, pagan priests pushed the sufferers away. Many pagan priests fled the epidemic, as did the highest civil authorities and the wealthiest families, only adding to the disorder and suffering.[5] The pagan priests even fled from their dearest, or threw them out into the roads before they were dead.[6]

In contrast, Christ-followers offered both explanation and comfort. Christian doctrine provided a *prescription for action*, so Christians remained, many losing their lives in heroic efforts to care for others. According to Stark, pagans behaved in the very opposite way, as they had no doctrinal basis to match Christian compassion and practice.[7] In the same way today, Christ-followers are not to cut and run in the midst of crisis but to remain and care for others. We have a debt of love that trumps personal security and survival.

WHAT ABOUT BUSINESS?

One arena to carry out the debt of love in society is in the realm of business. Ken Eldred applies his Christian faith to the world of business in a recent book entitled *The Integrated Life*.[8] Eldred was the founder of Inmac, a public company he served as CEO for over 20 years. His book presents a compelling case for for-profit business, but with the overarching objective to "serve others to the glory of God."

The Integrated Life presents a blueprint for blending faith, family, and business. However, it also challenges both socialism and capitalism. Eldred undercuts the socialistic premise "that aggregate wealth is a constant and the total economic pie is fixed. Thus, if one person is making a profit, it must come at another's expense."[9] Instead, he argues that successful commerce leads to the creation of goods and services, the growth of aggregate wealth, and the increase of standards of living. Rather than a fixed amount of wealth that must be stingily distributed between the haves and the

> Greed must give way to seeking the wellbeing of others for God's glory.

have-nots, more wealth and more jobs can be created so that there is a bigger pie to share.

Eldred undercuts the "there-is-only-so-much-to-go-around" premise of socialism, but he also challenges the *amorality* and greed characterizing much of Western capitalism. He argues that we need capitalism—capitalism with a greater heart and higher purpose. It must be a capitalism that "serves others for the glory of God." Greed, the self-serving quest for personal affluence, must give way to loving others by seeking their wellbeing for God's glory.

Cultures in which God is honored and Biblical values are ingrained generate *spiritual capital* and establish the environment for successful business and commerce. In noting that *spiritual capital* is the key to economic blessing, Eldred references the Nobel-winning work of Douglass North. North points to trust as one of the institutional factors that lead to a better economy. *The Integrated Life* points out that an amazing 80 percent of the wealth in rich countries is connected to the intangible of "spiritual capital."[10] According to Eldred, the roots of spiritual capital are Biblical values like honesty, service, excellence, respect, commitment, value, trust, loyalty, and quality.[11] We (Linus Jr. and Linus Sr.) would add the values of generosity, compassion, mercy, grace, and love. For capitalism and commerce to flourish, integrity, honesty, truthfulness, loyalty, faithfulness, trust, commitment, and much more are needed as underpinnings.

Regardless of the kind of political or economic system we live in, or whether we engage in business or not, carrying out the Divine Expedition requires that we live within society with respect and love. We are to "do good and to share with others, for with such sacrifices God is pleased" (Hebrews 13:16). We are to "live such good lives among the pagans that, though they accuse you of doing wrong, they may see your good deeds and glorify God on the day he visits us" (1 Peter 2:12). We are even to "love our enemies, and do good to them" (Luke 6:35).

"PROTECT AND SERVE"

Paul's missionary efforts largely took place in cities where there was a strong Roman governing presence, affording him the protection and safety needed to proclaim the Good News of Jesus. His choice to minister in these cities was a strategic decision on his part. Even though writing at a time when Christ-followers were a powerless minority and Rome was a totalitarian state, Paul saw Roman government as a positive force for good and, as such, God's servant.

> The role of government is to foster and protect society.

The motto of the Los Angeles Police Department, "to protect and serve," captures the God-given role of government. It is to protect society and foster its citizen's wellbeing, it is to promote good and restrain evil. Government is God's servant to reinforce what is right and to punish what is wrong. It is to preserve justice and order, protect and defend its citizens, and restrain and remedy evil.

Determining what is good and what is evil or what is right and what is wrong, requires more than social consensus or majority vote. There is a higher accountability than the decisions of a society's government, the dictates of its laws, or the wishes of its general populace. These can be manipulated or corrupted, as the story of Nazi Germany as well as other populist movements that ended in tyranny illustrate. Without a higher transcending morality to establish societal good, we are cast adrift in the sea of relativism, dysfunctional ideology, and survival of the fittest.

RESPECTFUL DISOBEDIENCE

Unfortunately, there are times when government ceases to be an instrument for good, becoming instead an instrument of oppression and evil. As the first century rolled on, the Roman Emperor perverted government by exalting himself as deity, demanding allegiance to himself as lord. Consequently, those who followed Jesus as Messiah-Son-King-Lord-Savior refused to submit to the Emperor's outrageous demand, even upon penalty of death. Jesus' followers were willing to give to Caesar what was Caesar's (taxes, respect, honor) but not give him what was God's (supreme allegiance, worship, and love with all one's heart, soul, strength, and mind).

> There are times when government ceases to be an instrument for good.

The same applies to us when government prevents us from following Jesus, carrying out His commands, or proclaiming the message of the Divine Expedition. Several years ago I (Linus Jr.) was shooting photography for a graduate program that traveled to Hong Kong and then on to Shenzhen, China. The group taking the course scheduled a visit to several underground churches in Shenzhen, where there was a lack of Bibles. Taking Bibles into Mainland China was declared illegal by the Chinese Communist government; however, the Christian group organizing our trip asked if we would carry Chinese-language Bibles in our luggage to give to our brothers and sisters in Christ. The danger of doing so was explained, but I, along with others in our group, felt a deep desire to help my Chinese brothers and sisters obtain copies of the Bible.[12] My allegiance to Jesus took precedence over the dictates of the Communist government.

With Hong Kong behind us, we approached the Mainland Chinese border. Exiting our bus, we waited nervously as stern-looking soldiers isolated each group member and sifted though his or her belongings—one person and one suitcase at a time. After passing through customs, we re-boarded the bus while those behind us still were being processed. To alleviate the tension, I directed some members of our group to the worst smelling toilet I had ever experienced, telling them we had several more hours before we would come to another rest stop (actually Shenzhen was only twenty minutes away). We had a good laugh as my companions staggered out of the toilet gasping for air and pinching their noses to keep the smell out. Happily, no one was arrested, none of the Bibles we carried was confiscated—and none of the group's members passed out. Humor helped alleviate the tension we felt, and more importantly, we were able to deliver the Bibles to deeply grateful Chinese house-church members.

> We aim to fulfill our civic duties...while maintaining our supreme allegiance to Jesus as Lord.

TRANSFORMING SOCIETY

Even in situations where our convictions lead us to disobey governing authorities (as did the early followers of Jesus in Acts 5:12-29), the Divine Expedition directs us to live in a way that wins the respect of our community. By living lovingly, respectfully, and above reproach as citizens, we increase the possibility that even the governing authorities will be attracted to our message. We seek to fulfill our civic duties with integrity in all we do, all the while maintaining our supreme allegiance to Jesus as Lord.

Our aim is not simply to comply with the rules of government, but to transform society from within. This involves much more than obeying laws and carrying out civic duties (for example, voting). It requires heartfelt love (13:8-10) to all. Love transcends duty and transforms culture. Love calls us to service and sacrifice rather than indifference and selfishness. Love calls us to go the extra mile, turn the other cheek, and actively show God's love to those around us.

God's love is viral. He infects us with His Divine love and then spreads His love further through our care and respect of others, as well as our proclamation of the message of the Divine Expedition. The greatest expres-

God's love is viral.

sion of love is that God sent Jesus to rescue us and impart to us "salvation." Once received and experienced, God's love results in a whole new trajectory of life, as seen in someone like Mike Bagby, who turned from living for self to rescuing and restoring others.

PUTTING ASIDE DARKNESS

"Being saved" is incompatible with passivity. As we awaken to the salvation bestowed upon us, we are motivated to put aside the kind of dark deeds found in the first chapter of Romans. In place of the darkness once characterizing us, we put on a new "armor of light" and clothe ourselves with our Lord Jesus Christ who works in and through us (13:11-13). Living to gratify our sensual desires leaves us dissatisfied and unfulfilled. Clothing ourselves with Jesus, however (13:14), leads us to the true meaning and fulfillment we long for. Through Him, we become light to a dark world.

The more we grasp and experience God's love, grace, and salvation in Jesus, the more we are moved to share His love and grace with others. The more we travel down the path of the Divine Expedition, the more His light and love shine in the public arena (Romans 13; Matthew 5:16; John 8:12), and the more our future salvation draws closer. We know that it is nearer now than when we first believed (13:11).

Living with integrity, respect, and love make a difference in society. Regardless of the form of government, or whether or not government looks favorably upon us as Christ-followers, we are to carry out our debt to love. This encompasses those who are culturally different from us—as we shall see in the next chapter.

CHAPTER 18

ROMANS 14:1-23
CULTURAL DIFFERENCES

Spanish authorities were wary of Magellan, who was Portuguese.[1]

Any and every duty is undertaken cheerfully and willingly and no complaint or whining is ever heard no matter what hardships or inconvenience may be encountered. The principal credit of this is due to the tact and leadership of the head of the expedition....
> —Frank Worsley, captain of the *Endurance*[2]

Roosevelt had gone to great lengths to show his Brazilian co-commander every courtesy and mark of respect that his experience and position, as well as his character, deserved.
> —*The River of Doubt*[3]

Together, under the leadership of the captains, they had become a family.
> —*Undaunted Courage*[4]

So then, let us aim for harmony in the church and try to build each other up.
> —Romans 14:19[5]

ROPED TOGETHER

Every expedition faces risks. Some are external, but equally dangerous are internal threats such as loss of morale or dissent among team members. One wonders if the outcome of Magellan's expedition might have been more successful had not two of the five ships under his command mutinied. Certainly more than the eighteen men who completed the circumnavigation of the globe and returned to Spain would have survived. Perhaps Magellan himself would have completed the voyage. Unfortunately, the Spanish captains resented serving under the Magellan, so rebelled against his leadership.

The success and survival of expeditions rest upon the ability of its participants to work in harmony. The *Endurance* crew under the leadership of Ernest Shackleton demonstrated this, maintaining their morale and unity during their January, 1915 to August, 1916 ordeal of being stranded in the Antarctic.

Former American president Teddy Roosevelt and Brazilian captain Candido Rondon also exhibited the ability to maintain harmony and morale while exploring and surviving the Amazon River of Doubt, later named the Rio Roosevelt. Roosevelt and Rondon navigated their cultural differences by mutual respect and courtesy toward each other. Roosevelt refused to take a seat unless Rondon also had a chair. "Mr. Roosevelt positively declared to me, that as long as he was in the wilderness he would accept nothing, and do nothing, that might have any appearance of special attention to his person," Rondon recalled. "And consequently just as he saw me sit, so would he sit himself."[6]

> The success and survival of expeditions rest upon the ability of its participants to work in harmony.

It is no accident that Paul deals with the issue of harmony at this stage in the sequential unfolding of the Divine Expedition. One of the greatest threats to our mission is internal strife among fellow Christ-followers, arising from differences in cultural values or preferences. The inability or unwillingness to navigate these differences derail and knock us off course. Instead of maintaining our focus on mission and manifesting Christ's love, demonstrating we are His followers (John 13:34-35), our attention shifts to personal preferences, and our energy is dissipated.

The survival of mountain climbers depends upon staying roped together. Traversing an Olympic wilderness glacier, I (Linus Jr.) stepped into a moulin, a nearly vertical shaft or cavity worn deep into the glacier. A moulin is created by a rock that the sun heats up or by water cascading through a crack in the ice. They are undetectable to the naked eye when covered by snow. The cavity that is created can sink down as far as a mile (1.6 kilometers), often connecting to an underground river. One NOLS participant disappeared into such a moulin, never to be found. Fortunately, I was roped to my teammates and saved from a similar fate.

Our NOLS (National Outdoor Leadership School) trainers hammered into us the importance of teamwork, as well as flexibility and tolerance in difficulty. They said it wasn't a matter of *if* something would go wrong, but *when*. The question they asked was, "How will you deal with it?" They further asked, "What kind of teammate will you be when things aren't going the way you would like?" NOLS leadership stresses that the critical element in dealing with things that go wrong or do not go the way we expect is to work cooperatively with teammates, to stay roped together—both literally and figuratively.

WEAK AND STRONG

The success of the Divine Expedition depends upon our staying roped together as Christ-followers. This was in jeopardy in first century Rome as cultural differences were pulling the Roman Christians apart. The immediate issue was one of dietary sensitivities. Those from strict Jewish backgrounds were kosher with regard to what they ate or drank, while those from non-Jewish backgrounds were more liberal about these matters. The former preferred expressions and practices in keeping with their Jewish cultural heritage, while the latter opted for practices that aligned with their non-Jewish cultural background.

Paul calls these differences "disputable matters" and adds, "one person's faith allows him to eat everything, but another man whose faith is weak eats only vegetables" (14:1-2). These differing cultural preferences created strife and gave rise to criticism between the two (or perhaps multiple) cultural groups.

We may not face the exact same cultural differences in our contemporary world, but the issue remains: how do we stay roped together with those whose cultural preferences differ from our own? Today, some Christ-followers do not believe it is right to celebrate Christmas with Christmas trees or celebrate Halloween at all; others do. Some think it is wrong to drink anything containing alcohol; others believe it is permissible if done with moderation. Some hold that everything in church services should be done for those who already believe in Jesus; others argue that church services should be tailored for those not presently connected to Christ, even making them a priority. Some wish to preserve past styles and forms of music and worship; others believe the church must adopt new styles to remain effective. Some believe women cannot be pastors or elders in the church; others argue they can. Some believe the church should only meet in small groups (house churches, simple churches, etc); others prefer larger, event-oriented multi-program churches. None of these are differences about core beliefs (although there are those who argue otherwise), but fall into the category of cultural or pragmatic preferences.

I (Linus Sr.) was asked to speak at a church with a culturally conservative background but had begun to include contemporary music choruses in its Sunday services. One of the songs included the phrase, "I lift my hands unto your name." Feeling a sense of connectedness to both God and the music at that moment, I raised one hand upward as the song suggested. After the service, while conversing with two men who came up to talk with me, a third man burst into our midst and aggressively charged, "So you have become a Charismatic!"

I asked why he thought that, to which he replied, "I saw you lift your hand during the worship."

Somewhat taken aback, I responded, "I don't believe Charismatic Christians have a corner on being expressive."

At that, he spun around and stormed off. He was angry with me, and I was offended by his rudeness. I wondered why he appointed himself to be the worship service watchdog, taking upon himself the task of policing the expression of others.

FOUR PRACTICES TO STAY ROPED TOGETHER

Debates over cultural expressions often get heated and polarize fellow Christians. The underlying question these issues pose is, "What is the essence of the Divine Expedition and what are merely cultural expressions of how we do things?" Romans chapter 14 instructs us in how to address cultural differences and stay roped together. In this chapter, Paul encourages four practices to help us navigate the tension between those who are more conservative and those who are more adaptable in their approach to culture.

PRACTICE ACCEPTANCE

The first practice Paul advocates is for those who are strong in faith to accept those whose faith is weaker, without passing judgment or looking down on them (14:1-3a). We are to stay roped together as fellow Christ-followers even though we come from different backgrounds and may not agree with each other. Paul understands there is a continuum of freedom. The person who is strong in faith has a high degree of freedom, while the one who is weak in faith has a lesser degree of freedom and has trouble operating outside their established tradition. Paul tells us that those who are high in freedom are not to judge or reject those who lack the same freedom.

STRONG IN FAITH (HIGH IN FREEDOM)

WEAK IN FAITH (LOW IN FREEDOM)

The same is true for rock climbing. When I (Linus Jr.) take someone climbing who has little experience, I don't push that person beyond the level that he or she is able to cope. I restrain my advanced climbing ability to accommodate and encourage the weaker or less experienced climber. They must be brought along gradually, which takes patience.

Similarly, Paul counsels the strong in faith (those high in freedom) to accept those whose faith is weaker. However, Paul also counsels the weak in faith (those low in freedom) not to condemn those whose faith is strong. Those strong in faith are not to leave behind the weak in faith, and the weak in faith are not to insist that the strong stay behind. Paul asks, "Who are you to judge someone else's servant?" He reminds us that both strong and weak will answer to the Lord, who is also able to make both stand (14:4).

I (Linus Sr.) am amazed at how much criticism there is in many evangelical churches. Finding something to criticize seems to be a sport—perhaps more so, an addiction. When our criticisms are unrestrained, no one wins, including Christ. After a recent church service I attended, I overheard several conversations in which a variety of complaints were lodged within a span of just a few minutes. One person was critical of the church's two-service format (classical and contemporary) and inflexibly lobbied for a single blended-style service. A second church member made the point that the sermon was incomplete without an invitation for not-yet believers to accept Christ (I don't think there were any there). A third person felt like the music of the contemporary service was too worldly (contemporary praise songs). Yet another argued that the church should focus on the more established residents in the community (catered to in the earlier classical service) because they were the only ones who could afford to live in the immediate area. Ironically, the contemporary service had three times as many people in attendance, mostly young. All of these complaints were expressions of cultural preferences.

The examples above are from the old guard criticizing contemporary expressions of worship. But the pendulum of criticism swings the other way too, as those preferring newer styles and expressions (such as the emerging and emergent church movements) frequently react to the more traditional and institutional cultural expressions of churches out of which they came. By doing so, they define themselves more by what they are against, than what they are for, even losing sight of core biblical beliefs and the mission to rescue others.

Paul encourages graciousness and acceptance between those who are culturally conservative and those who are culturally more adaptable. While Romans chapter fourteen strikes a conciliatory tone, Paul takes a much more confrontational approach in his letter to the Galatians. Galatians is directed toward legalists, who are rigidly low in freedom, seeking to impose their legalism on others. The legalistic emphasis on outward behavior (such as circumcision and keeping the Mosaic Law) to gain God's acceptance actually undermines the core message of the gospel of grace. Paul confronts the legalistic teaching that it is up to us to keep God's law as it undercuts the complete adequacy of Jesus' work to rescue us (Galatians 1:6). In Romans, however, the issue is not one of legalism, but one of weak believers struggling with cultural comfort, scrupulousness, and preference.

PRACTICE A "TO THE LORD" FOCUS

Paul's second practice is for both sides to keep a "to the Lord" focus. While important to follow one's personal convictions regarding what he or she thinks constitutes living for the Lord (14:5), it is essential to stay focused on Jesus and His Lordship. Living for the Lord is not merely a matter of "what" we believe but in "whom" we believe. Cultural preferences and convictions are important, but Paul puts the emphasis on relating to the Lord and maintaining a "to the Lord" focus. Six times the phrase, "to the Lord" is used in Romans 14:6-8, emphasizing that our primary focus is to be toward the Lord. This "to the Lord" focus shifts the emphasis from our cultural preferences to the dynamic organic relationship we are meant to have with Jesus as Lord. We are to maintain a constant focus toward Him.

The focus of my critical church friends, following the Sunday service mentioned above, was more on their cultural preferences than it was on Jesus and His mission to the world. Sadly, if they got their way, the church would eventually die with them. Only those willing to conform to their cultural preferences would be able to hurdle the barrier these preferences erected. Unwittingly, they were sacrificing their children and others in the community around them for their traditions and preferences.

The essence of staying roped together is more vertical than horizontal. We are to keep focused upward on Jesus, rather than horizontally on our preferences. The real measure of spirituality is not the way we do things, but a passion to "live to the Lord" and keep Him central (14:8). The more we focus on Jesus, the more we yield our insistence that others be like us culturally and the more we are able to transcend our differences with other Christ-followers.

> The essence of staying roped together is more vertical than horizontal.

Our harmony with other believers does not rest upon agreement on style of ministry. It rests upon mutual faith in the person and work of Jesus, as well as a desire to live to and from Him to carry out His mission in the world around us. We experienced this kind of harmony in the multinational churches our family helped launch in both Geneva and Amsterdam. Attending these churches are people from many different cultural backgrounds: Asian, African, European, North American, South American, and more. The congregations are comprised of people from Anglican, Baptist, Catholic, Lutheran, Reformed, Orthodox, Pentecostal and non-Pentecostal backgrounds.

The central thing that holds these diverse people together is faith in the person and work of Jesus, and a desire to be His ambassadors to those around them. There are all kinds of differences, which sometimes cause friction. One member expressing concern about these differences said, "We are always in the process of falling apart," to which another replied, "To the contrary. We are always in the process of holding together." This is possible because of the overall "to the Lord" focus held by these churches' leadership and the majority of their members.

Paul reminds us that whether we live or die, we belong "to the Lord" (14:8). He then adds a sobering reminder that one day we will stand before God to give an account for ourselves (14:9-11). Because of this, we are to keep our primary focus on the vertical (to the Lord), not the horizontal (judging our brothers and sisters in Christ). Jesus is the Lord of the dead and the living, as well as the strong and the weak. Our primary accountability is *toward Christ* (14:9-10). We are to look *up to* Him rather than look *down upon* those who don't agree with us, knowing that, one day, both strong and weak will appear before God, and each will give an account to Him. Until then, our perspective is to be one of devotion and humility toward Jesus, not judgment and criticism toward each other (14:11-13).

PRACTICE LOVE

The third practice to navigate differences with our fellow Christ-followers is that of love. It is possible for the strong in faith to be high in freedom but low in love. Paul argues that it is better to be high in love and suspend our freedom than to be low in love and hurt the faith of another. This does not mean that we give up our convictions, but it does mean that we not act in ways destructive to others (14:14-15).

HIGH IN LOVE ———————————————— LOW IN LOVE

The focus of the Divine Expedition is not one of insisting upon our freedom; it is on exhibiting righteousness, peace, and joy through the Holy Spirit's empowerment (14:16-18). We are to make every effort to do what leads to peace and to build each other up (14:19-21), even if it means suspending our own freedoms.

This does not mean those more conservative in their backgrounds and convictions can demand their way under the guise of being weaker in faith, or that the failure to accept conservative cultural practices will cause a weaker brother to fall. Paul admonishes the weak in faith to refrain from imposing his or her convictions upon others (14:3). They are to grow stronger in their faith by developing and allowing more freedom, at the same time maintaining their core convictions. In living "to the Lord," (14:8) both strong and weak are to avoid judging each other (14:13). They are, instead, to act in love and make every effort to do what leads to peace and the strengthening of one another (14:15, 19).

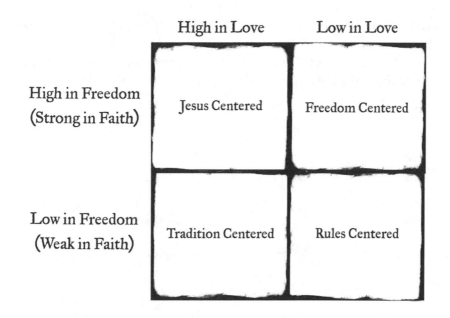

	High in Love	Low in Love
High in Freedom (Strong in Faith)	Jesus Centered	Freedom Centered
Low in Freedom (Weak in Faith)	Tradition Centered	Rules Centered

PRACTICE FAITH

If the strong in faith are to suspend their freedom in order to keep others from stumbling, then the weak in faith are to keep their cultural convictions between themselves and God, and not to impose their preferences on others (14:22-23). The Divine Expedition is about a missional community of Christ-followers from diverse cultural backgrounds with different cultural preferences roped together to rescue and restore others.

Whether strong or weak, it is the responsibility of all to live by faith and lead with love. Not to do so is sin. Although our consciences may be bound by certain cultural conditioning, the Divine Expedition orients us away from insisting upon personal preferences. Instead, it re-orients us toward loving and building the faith of others. The only way we can stay on course is to remain roped together by practicing acceptance, a "to the Lord" focus, love, and faith. By observing these, we can both encourage new expressions and styles of worship, and at the same time honor, respect,

> Whether strong or weak, it is the responsibility of all to live by faith and lead with love.

and love those who are more culturally conservative. How this works out is tricky, but the success of our expedition depends on it.

Paul emphasizes this more in the next chapter, while moving us further toward the global mission to which we are called.

CHAPTER 19

ROMANS 15:1-33
MISSION, MERCY, AND GENEROSITY

For ten days we climbed and explored country that men had never seen. We crossed difficult passes and visited great green glaciers. And at the end of it, it wasn't so much our achievements I remembered, exciting as they had been, but more the character of Eric Shipton: his ability to be calm and comfortable in any circumstances; his insatiable curiosity to know what lay over the next hill or around the next corner; and above all, his remarkable power to transform the discomfort and pain and misery of high-altitude life into a great adventure.

—Sir Edmund Hillary[1]

I know a good fellow....

—Thor Heyerdahl[2]

But well-led men working together can do far more than they ever thought they could.

—*Undaunted Courage*[3]

The first rule of the Caird was that there would be no swearing. Everyone had to be positive. Shackleton knew the trip was going to be hell and they had to pull together.

—*Shackleton's Way*[4]

Therefore I will praise you among the Gentiles....
—Romans 15:9

GOOD CHARACTER

It is easy to be drawn to expeditions for personal glory and fame, or to meet some deep inner ego need such as the approval or acclaim of others. Often the motivation is a search for significance, or sometimes just the sheer thrill of adventure. The greatest expeditions, however, draw upon higher values and ideals. Glory, acclaim, and adventure may be a significant part of the motivation, but typically more noble motives and character are mixed in or emerge. Hillary notes that he was drawn to Shipton's calm and curious character, and his ability to "transform the discomfort and pain and misery of high-altitude life into a great adventure." The nobility of Hillary's own character comes out in the way he leveraged his fame to work for the wellbeing of the Nepalese Sherpas, who made his ascent up Everest possible.

The importance of good character is seen in the basis Norwegian Thor Heyerdahl's used to choose his five crew members for the 4,300 nautical miles voyage from Peru to Polynesia on the balsa raft *Kon-Tiki*. Heyerdahl recruited his sailing mates on the basis both character and need, commenting, "No storm clouds with low pressure and gusty weather held greater menace for us than the danger of psychological cloudburst among six men shut up together for months on a drifting raft. In such circumstances a good joke was often as valuable as a life belt."[5]

Both humor and life belts were important for the success of the *Kon-Tiki*, but so was the kind of character that risks self for the welfare of others. During the voyage, *Kon Tiki* crewmember Herman Watzinger fell overboard in a storm. Although an excellent swimmer, he had no hope of catching the raft being driven rapidly onward by currents and wind. The attempt to throw him a life belt/rope was thwarted by the strong wind pushing the boat forward, at the same time blowing the rope back toward the boat. Suddenly, raft-mate Knut Haugland grabbed the life belt and plunged into the sea, swimming to Herman. Risking his own life, Haugland reached

Watzinger with the rope, enabling the rest of the crew to pull them both back to safety on board.[6]

Expeditions call for noble character and challenge us to give ourselves for a greater good. Meriwether Lewis on his 31st birthday wrote, "This day I completed my thirty-first year...I reflected that I had as yet done but little, very little indeed, to further the happiness of the human race, or to advance the information of the succeeding generation. I viewed with regret the many hours I have spent in indolence." He went on to resolve, "in future, to live for mankind, as I have heretofore lived for myself."[7]

> Expeditions challenge us to give ourselves for a greater-good.

Great expeditions call forth sacrificial and selfless character. Unfortunately, it is possible to lose sight of the greater goals and ideals beckoning us and yield to less noble motives or the weaknesses of our character. Such was the case of Captain James Cook. Cook became driven by self-aggrandizement, eventually contributing to his death.[8]

> Great expeditions call forth sacrificial character.

INVINCIBLE?

Success frequently leads to feelings of invincibility and vulnerability to character weaknesses. Christ-followers are not immune to this. Many Christian leaders gain prominence and acclaim due to their giftedness and charisma, and develop an over-inflated sense of importance. In doing so, they fail to address hidden character flaws and cease developing the deeper spiritual strength needed for the long haul. They begin thinking "more highly of themselves than they ought" and lose their connectedness to community. At some point they give in to the weight of unattended wounds or character flaws. Sadly, they do not draw upon the resources of the Divine Design, and they end up relinquishing their passion to engage in the Divine Expedition.

One such leader gave a message to a leadership gathering I (Linus Sr.) attended. His talk was entitled, "Ten Lessons I've

Learned in Ministry." Two years later it was discovered that he was having an affair. Knowing he resigned but not knowing the reason for his resignation, I (Linus Sr.) met with him and asked what he would add to the ten points he presented earlier. His advice was for leaders to make sure they dealt with childhood issues. He went on to tell me how his father, also a pastor, assembled his two sons in the "guest only" room of their home. There, he emphasized that this was the only room in the house where non-family members were permitted. It was the "show room." He then directed his two sons that they were not allowed in the show room, and guests were never allowed in the rest of the home. The show room was always kept neat and tidy—unlike the other rooms of the house.

Lamentably, my soon to be disgraced pastor-friend internalized a message that you only let people into the "show room" of your life; you don't allow them to see the real you. He developed a charismatic public persona that didn't accord with his real internal self, publically showing and impressing people with the "guest room," but hiding from view the messy part inside.

PRESSING ONWARD

In Romans 15, Paul continues to guide us toward Divine Expedition outcomes and practices, calling us to seek the wellbeing of others. He continues the emphasis of Romans chapter fourteen: to bear with the failings of the weak, and not live to please our selves (15:1-2). We are to expend ourselves on behalf of others to build them up, just as Jesus did. He did not live to please Himself but took the abuse and insults of others in order to give us hope (15:3-4).

Paul reminds us that God gives endurance and encouragement....

Paul reminds us that God gives endurance and encouragement to strive for a spirit of unity. Unity—or staying roped together—comes by following Christ Jesus and focusing on living to honor and glorify God. The purpose of our staying roped together is to carry out the apostolic mission of the Divine Expedition so that with one heart and mouth we may "glorify the God and Father of our Lord Jesus Christ" (15:5-6).

Unity is not an end in itself. It is unity for a purpose. The purpose of unity is missional, that others "may glorify God for his mercy" (15:8). To accomplish this we must accept one another as Christ accepted us. This brings praise to God (15:7).

GRACE AND STRENGTH IN LIFE'S DUNGEON

Glorifying God does not mean the absence of conflict, struggle, or difficulty. It means that God will encourage and sustain us in the midst of these things. In the early years of our ministry, it was discovered that one of our more prominent staff members was sexually involved with several women other than his wife. His response to our attempt (as well as the attempt of the elders of the church he was leading at the time) to address this with him was met with anger and defensiveness. He ended up leaving his wife, his children, the church, and our training and outreach ministry. Typical of those in denial, he blamed everyone but himself.

I was part of the gathering where the church members were informed of the immorality of our friend and fellow worker. The aim of the announcement, as well as previous efforts to talk with this leader, was to get him to stop his harmful behavior and get help. Since repeated earlier attempts were met with resistance and an unwillingness to change, the decision was made to make his infidelity known to the larger body.

The setting for the meeting that took place was on the beach where the church met regularly (it seldom rains in Southern California). The presentation by the stand-in pastor was done sensitively, without any explicit detail, following the biblical guidance of Matthew 18:15-17. The leader being exposed was told in advance that this would take place. During the meeting, he arrived and stood disapprovingly some distance above and behind the beach where the cars were parked. His arms were folded in anger, and upon the conclusion of the brief explanation, he defiantly roared off in his Porsche. The impact on those who trusted him was devastating. His emotional, physical, and spiritual abandonment of his wife and children left them to fend for themselves.

His dismissal from the church left deep wounds in many who looked up to him, his departure changed the course of our ministry organization. Due to his visibility as an author and well-known speaker, he was the primary draw of students to our work. Without this, we were forced to merge the training part of our work with another organization and shut down the university student part of our ministry. What remained was a fledgling church-planting initiative. In the midst of our disappointment, the breakup of our team, and the struggle to sort out the direction we should go, those of us who remained sought and found "grace and strength in the dungeon."

We especially found endurance and encouragement in the promises of Scripture. In the days and months that followed, we relied upon God's promise that He would never leave us nor forsake us (Joshua 1:5; Hebrews 13:5). We turned to the Biblical promise that God would strengthen, help, and uphold us (Isaiah 41:10). We claimed God's promise that He causes "all things" to work together for good for those who love him (Romans 8:28). Uncertain of the future, we looked to God for the "endurance and encouragement" He promises in Romans 15:5. As we did, these promises became a reality. We were encouraged, found strength to endure, and God gave us new direction for our ministry.

Unity can be shattered—but it can also be rebuilt as we look to God and His promises, follow Jesus, and seek to honor and glorify God. Though there may be loss, through God's grace and strength, we can form a renewed unity with those who remain, grow in character through conflict and struggle, and re-engage in the Divine Expedition.

ULTIMATE OBJECTIVE

The ultimate objective of the Divine Expedition is that the world around us will glorify God for His mercy (15:7-9). This is what motivates us to accept those whose cultural preferences are different than ours. Our objective in mission is what causes us to persevere in building each other up spiritually and relationally. It is what causes us to let go of past hurts and wounds, and seek the wellbeing of those who have hurt or wounded us. It is what stretches us to show patience with others, knowing that we all are works in progress. But our sense of mission is also what emboldens us to confront those harming others by their actions and attitudes.

Our desire for others to glorify God for His mercy helps us maintain a "to the Lord" focus. It is what leads us to restrain our selfish impulses, knowing we are to follow Christ's example instead of seeking to please ourselves. Our passion to see others give God glory for His mercy compels us forward in mission and is a marker of where we are in the unfolding of the Divine Expedition in the book of Romans. The essence of the Divine Expedition is that God poured out His mercy on us by sending Jesus to bear our sins and give us hope. Infected as we are with the virus of God's mercy and hope in Jesus, we become carriers of that virus to others (15:10-13).

> Our sense of being on mission together is what causes us to persevere.

I (Linus Jr.) was driving in my pickup truck along the California coast listening to the radio when I heard the news of a climber's death on Mt. Everest. I knew of other stories of teams and individual climbers who perished attempting to climb their way to "the top of the world," but this accident particularly struck me as more tragic than most. A thirty-four-year-old British man named David Sharp lay on the mountain in crucial need of rescuing. Unable to move and barely breathing, nearly forty people walked past him in pursuit of the summit—but none stopped, leaving him to die.[9]

I was horrified that personal accomplishment was more important than the rescue of this dying man. Sir Edmund Hillary articulated my sentiments when he later said, "I think the whole attitude towards climbing Mount Everest has become rather horrifying. People just want to get to the top. They don't give a damn for anybody else who may be in distress and it doesn't impress me at all that they leave someone lying under a rock to die." I pondered, "Is this a metaphor for our world today? People trying to climb to the top without regard for others?" Even more troubling, I wondered, "Can this be the attitude of many Christians to the condition that people around them who are dying are in need of another kind of rescue?"

A few days later I was in my car again when I heard a report that another man lay dying on Everest. Lincoln Hall spent an entire night high on the mountain without a sleeping bag. This time, however, a climbing team led by Dan Mazur came across Hall and immediately began an effort to rescue him. In doing so, Hall and his team gave up their own aspirations to make it to the summit. Mazur embodies the mercy and compassion to which the Divine Expedition calls each of us.

MERCY AND MISSION

The more we grasp God's compassion and mercy toward us, the more we are moved to extend His compassion and mercy to others. God's love compels us to reach out, not only to those who are like us culturally, but also to those who are not. We are commissioned to rescue all people regardless of status or importance from our human perspective. The scope of the Divine Expedition encompasses "all you Gentiles;" that is, every person, race, culture, and nation (15:9-12). Rather than insulate and protect ourselves from those around us, we strive to reach them with the joy and peace that comes from trusting Christ and drawing upon the overflowing hope by the power of the Holy Spirit (15:13).

> Rather than insulate ourselves from those around us, we strive to reach them.

DUTCH SON

Our family has provided a home for a number of students over the years. One was a seventeen-year-old Dutch basketball player who lived with us for two years. He wanted to play basketball in America and live with a Christian family so we opened our home to him. It was great to have him live with us, and he in effect became our "Dutch son." Following his time with us, he went on to play basketball for a Christian college, one that could be characterized by a negative view of culture, and every other group that didn't line up with their separate-from-culture stance. This kind of thinking gradually began to characterize our Dutch son. The longer he attended this school, the more he became critical of our attempt to engage culture in order to rescue others with the good news of Christ. (To do this we sought to be "in the world but not of it.") Our Dutch son's criticisms and withdrawal from our family were hurtful, but we continued to maintain contact and communicate our love for him.

Several years after graduating from college, marrying, and working in business, he called to apologize. He explained that his views were changing, and that he had begun to see that the college he attended was itself culturally bound. It was a sub-culture known more for what it was against than what it was for, thus making the rescue of others more difficult. He followed with an email:

Linus,

I read your book, *The High-Impact Church* last month. I had plans on reading it before, but never was much of a reader until about 3 months ago. I actually grabbed the copy you gave to my parents when I was back in Holland for my mom's funeral, and read most of it on the way back from Holland on the plane.

It was really challenging. I believe that I have not been active enough as a Christian, and based on your book, I wrote a proposal to my church's pastor to illustrate my idea of community outreach, with the church as the centerpiece.

I do believe church is for believers as it is characterized as the bride Christ will come back for. But I am also convinced that church needs to be relevant culturally and that people need to get out of the pews and into the community to rescue the lost. I hope that the outreach event I am trying to organize will spur my church to grow in a qualitative and quantitative way.

I liked your 5-point analysis that churches are either seeker-driven, seeker-sensitive, seeker-friendly, seeker-insensitive, or seeker-hostile. I believe that our church should [strive to] be in the middle category (seeker-friendly), but that it lingers in the 4th stage (seeker-insensitive).

I do see a paradigm shift in our senior pastor. He has been here for 20+ years, but as he nears retirement he wants to prepare the church to reach the next generation. He's switched his Bible translation to the ESV (English Standard Version), which was a big deal for him, since he's solely preached from the NASB (New American Standard Bible) his whole life. He is also looking to open up the church during the week to make the front lobby a lounge for students to come and get free coffee, Wi-Fi, and books. He's even looking to infuse more media and up-to-date music to speak to the people in a contemporary way.

My heart is heavy for the lost and I foresee a role for me in this church now, but later on, my desire is for full-time ministry after I complete seminary. My passion is for the glory of God and to hold fast to His truth, the Bible and to see His Word go forth. My passion is for the church as the bride of Christ and for its outreach to a lost and dying world.

Anyway, I want to pick up more dialogue with you as I admire all that you have done for the Kingdom, and more specifically in bringing me to the US and providing a way for me to grow in my relationship with God, my love for the Savior, my growth through the Spirit, and the blessing of a wife and two children. Thanks to you and Sharon and your family for guiding me early in my journey with Jesus, and thanks for your continued thoughts and prayers.

Bastian (Bas)

Our family rejoiced upon receiving Bas' letter, and we are grateful that we were able to play a role in his spiritual journey. We are most excited that he is pressing forward on the Divine Expedition. Paul reiterates in Romans 15 (as in Romans 9) that God's plan is to pour out His mercy on the whole world (15:9-12— quoting 2 Samuel 22:50, Psalm 18:49, Deuteronomy 32:43, Isaiah 66:10, Psalm 117:1, and Isaiah 11:10). By God's grace and because of His mercy, we are empowered to be ministers of Jesus Christ and proclaim the good news about Him. This is what we want to be *known for*, and it is this that will lead to others becoming acceptable to God and also set apart ("sanctified") for the purpose of the Divine Expedition (15:15-16).

GO GLOBAL

The sequential unfolding of the Divine Expedition leads us to a global missional passion, to carry the Good News of Jesus to every place and to every person on the planet. We are to "go global." Paul models this in his letters, as well as his missionary journeys. All followers of Jesus are called do the same. By the time Paul wrote the book of Romans, he had already proclaimed the message of the Divine Expedition in Syria, Israel, Turkey (Asia Minor), and Greece (Macedonia and Achaia). He was preparing to visit Italy (Rome), with the intent of establishing a mission base-camp there. He purposed to continue on from there to spread the message of the Divine Expedition to Spain (15:16-24).

> The sequential unfolding of the Divine Expedition leads us to a global missional passion.

Paul's missional strategy was to establish mission base-camps from which the message of the Divine Expedition would radiate outward to surrounding areas. Mission centers were already established in Jerusalem, Antioch, Ephesus, and Corinth, and now Paul's intent was to multiply them in Italy and Spain. Wherever a church is located, and whatever size it might be, it is intended to be a missional community, reaching out to the world around it. This is part of the unfolding of the Divine Expedition, and where we are in the book of Romans.

Paul did get to Rome—but not in the way he expected. Before traveling to Rome, his intent was to make a brief stop in Jerusalem even though he knew that as he made his way there he faced imprisonment and hardship in every city (Acts 20:23). Upon reaching Jerusalem, he was arrested and handed over to the custody of the Roman occupying forces. He was then incarcerated in Caesarea for two years before being taken as a prisoner to face trial in Rome (Acts 21-27).

ON TO SPAIN

It is not known whether or not Paul ever made it to Spain, but he inspired others to spread the gospel there. Christian Associates has launched two churches in Madrid called Mountainview and Oasis. Mountainview's purpose is "to establish a vital church in Madrid that is radically devoted to God, relentlessly committed to authentic community, and remarkably passionate for lost people." Located in the northwest township Las Rozas de Madrid, it has a vision to unleash God's power and multiply churches across the greater northwest region and beyond. Oasis is located in the urban center of Madrid and is "a Christ-centered community that helps people follow Jesus." The church has a vision to birth similar works in other university centers in Spain and is already giving rise to a daughter work in the nearby Malasaña area of the city, famous for its trendy alternative scene.

The Divine Expedition calls us to broaden the scope of our vision beyond our own immediate families and communities to encompass a concern for all peoples. Our hope is that every person, in every place on planet Earth will embrace the good news of Jesus and His redemptive, life-giving and transforming power. Like the mandate given by Jesus to the early church (Acts 1:8), our mission is multinational (Jerusalem, all Judea, and Samaria, and to the ends of the earth) and multicultural (Jew and Gentile; all peoples). Carrying out such a daunting global mission cannot be done in our own strength. To overcome the many obstacles along the way necessitates Christ's blessing and our prayer (15:29-32).

GRACE FLOWING INTO GENEROSITY

Though globally minded, Paul did not forget those in material need. He believed that the essence of the gospel of grace was that Jesus Christ, though He was rich, yet for our sakes He became poor that we through His poverty might become rich (2 Corinthians 8:9). Paul viewed this not only spiritually, but also materially. Understanding and experiencing God's grace flows over into generosity. Before going to Rome and then on to Spain, Paul planned to deliver a generous financial contribution to the impoverished

Christians in Jerusalem (15:25), bearing a gift he was to collect from the Macedonia and Achaia churches.

The members of the church in Corinth gave with overflowing joy. Even though they were impoverished, they contributed generosiy, even beyond their ability. They saw it as a privilege to give to other Christians in need (2 Corinthians 8:1-4). The churches from the Galatia region (an area in the highlands of central Anatolia in today's modern Turkey) contributed to this fund as well by regularly setting aside a sum of money. The gifts were accounted for, and checks and balances were put in place to make sure the money got to its intended destination (1 Corinthians 16:1-4).

> Paul did not forget those in material need.

Grace flowing into generosity in giving is also seen in the support Paul received from the Philippi church. Their financial support allowed him the freedom to concentrate fully on his apostolic ministry (Philippians 4:15). Paul indicates that those who work hard at preaching and teaching deserve to be supported by those who are benefiting from their efforts (1 Timothy 5:17-18). Those who are wealthy are admonished "to be rich in good deeds, and to be generous and willing to share. In this way they will lay up treasure for themselves in heaven" (1 Timothy 5:17-19).

Paul encourages giving, especially giving ourselves to the Lord. But giving includes giving of financial means. We are to "excel in the grace of giving" (2 Corinthians 8:7). Giving thusly is a grace or gift (charisma), not only to those who receive the gift, but also to those who give it. Giving does something in the life of the giver. The saying, "You can't take it with you but you can send it ahead," is true.

> Giving is a mark of where we are in the book of Romans.

Giving is a mark of where we are in the book of Romans. Paul's heart was to give himself to spread the gospel, as well as to give help to the needy he left behind (15:26-29). The Divine Expedition includes passion for the lost and compassion for the needy. It calls for and calls forth noble character that risks and sacrifices to rescue others. It is about grace, mercy, mission, and generosity. It is about leadership-multiplication, as we will see in the next chapter, the next step in the Divine Expedition.

CHAPTER 20

ROMANS 16:1-27
REPRODUCING LEADERS
AND CHURCHES

By the time the Endurance sailed in 1914, Shackleton was forty-years-old and an experienced leader. He no longer had illusions about the perfection of men and supplies; he knew that the ice could destroy either, and that the ultimate success or failure of the venture rested with him. He had matured into a more confident, shrewder, and much more decisive leader.

—Shackleton's Way[1]

Lowe, Gregory and Ang Numa cut a stairway up the firm, steep snow of the couloir. Tenzing and I followed these tracks and were able to conserve our strength and make faster time.

—Edmond Hillary[2]

How both men overcame the torments of those harrowing days is an epic tale of fear, suffering, and survival, and a poignant testament to unshakable courage and friendship.

—Touching the Void[3]

...she has been a great help to many people...my fellow workers...the church that meets at their house...they are outstanding among the apostles...our fellow worker in Christ...those women who work hard in the Lord.
—Romans 16:2, 3, 5, 7, 9, 12

MULTIPLY LEADERS AND CHURCHES

It is said of Ernest Shackleton, "He led; he did not drive."[4] Expeditions require leaders, and leaders develop qualities that attract others to follow and engage in the task at hand. Leaders command respect, confidence, and even affection. Moreover, they have the ability to identify others capable of fulfilling the various roles needed to carry out the expedition.

Leaders sometimes err in their selection of team members, but they learn from their mistakes. Shackleton chose poorly on his earlier expedition to Antarctica on the *Nimrod,* hiring men who didn't fit the bold, risk-taking culture of exploration. He mistakenly picked two captains who appeared well qualified but proved unfit for the unique challenges of the Antarctic.[5] Learning from his mistake, Shackleton chose a crew for the *Endurance* that held up under the extreme conditions they encountered.

Notwithstanding the possibility of choosing the wrong people, leaders recognize they need others. Hillary and Norgay were part of a larger team, without which they would not have made it to the summit of Everest. Their success was due to a collective effort.[6] Similarly, the carrying out of the Divine Expedition is a collective endeavor, and impossible without a team.

> Everywhere Paul went he prioritized reproducing new churches and leaders.

The Divine Expedition task of "making (rescuing and restoring) disciples of all people" (Matthew 28:18-20) is enormous in scope, encompassing every people group in every nation of the world. It can only be accomplished through the multiplication of other missionally minded workers, leaders, and churches. Everywhere Paul went he prioritized reproducing new communities of Christ-followers and leaders to lead them.

The two lists of people in Romans chapter sixteen (16:3-16 and 16:21-24) give us insight into Paul's emphasis on church and leadership multiplication. He not only proclaimed Christ (1:15; 15:20) and strengthened those who responded (1:11-12), but he also gathered them together in communities (16:3, 5, 16) and raised up leaders to guide them. The church in Rome seems to have consisted of a network of house churches (clusters of believers, not buildings), led by "lay leaders."

The first list of lay leaders is found in Romans 16:3-16, made up of those who were ministering in Rome and to whom Paul's letter was intended. Priscilla and Aquila are addressed as "fellow workers" (16:3). A church met in their house. Mary is commended as someone who "worked very hard" for the church in Rome (16:6). Andronicus and Junias were "relatives" of Paul engaging in apostolic ministry (16:7). Urbanus was a "fellow worker in Christ" (16:9). Tryphena and Tryphosa were two women commended for their work in the Lord (16:12). Persis, another woman, worked "very hard in the Lord" (16:12). Twenty-seven people in all are addressed in Paul's first list. They were workers and leaders in Rome. Gender wasn't a criterion, seen in the fact that one third of the names are women.

The second list of lay leaders is recorded in Romans 16:21-24, and is comprised of the leadership network or community Paul was connecting with in Corinth. It was from here that he wrote his letter to the Romans. The Corinth leadership community included Timothy (a fellow worker), Lucius, Jason, and Sosispater (relatives), Gaius (hosted a house church), Erastus (city director of public works), and Quartus (also part of the leadership community in Corinth).

Not to be overlooked is Phoebe, mentioned in Romans 16:1. Paul calls her "our sister, a minister in the church in Cenchrea." Cenchrea was a harbor town nine miles (14.5 kilometers) east of Corinth and part of the overall Achaia (today's southern Greece) church network. Phoebe was a recognized servant-leader in that network. Paul commends her to the Roman leadership and is likely the person Paul entrusted to deliver his letter to the church in Rome.

MORE LEADERS

These two lists point to Paul's emphasis on multiplying workers and leaders. It is difficult to read Romans chapter sixteen and not be impressed with the number of people he recruited and trained for ministry and leadership. Paul mentored many of those named in the first list of this chapter before they migrated to Rome, as is obvious by the comments he makes about them. He was active mentoring those mentioned in the second list during a three-month stay in Corinth recorded in Acts 20:2-3. In both lists we see that wherever Paul went, he prioritized mentoring and multiplying leaders. We must do the same.

Our friend Lance Pittluck has a similar commitment to multiply leaders and churches. Lance grew up on Long Island, New York, where he was raised with a Jewish background but no religious training. At eighteen, he moved to Los Angeles, where he came into contact with our family, met Jesus Christ, and became involved in the Jesus Christ Light and Power House, a training center and campus outreach ministry of which we were a part. After university and seminary, Lance led a church in the Los Angeles area when he had a vision one nightof a fire burning in the center of a map of Long Island. As the fire burned, it spread out and engulfed the whole Island.

From this vision, Lance sensed God's call to return to New York to multiply churches. In the years that followed, Lance led a movement of new missional churches, impacting Long Island and the greater northeastern United States. Lance is now seeking to do the same thing in Anaheim, California. To multiply churches, Lance emphasizes the importance of reproducing leaders, saying, "My purpose in life is to influence people to follow Jesus and to raise up other influencers."[7]

CHRISTENDOM OR MISSIONAL?

Multiplying workers and leaders in Western culture is critical, but it is also challenging. One of the hindrances is individualism. People are consumed with personal demands and individual interests and pursuits. Nevertheless, there is a longing for community, meaning, and the adventure of being part of a "larger purpose or story." Individualism and its twin, consumerism, cannot deliver these. The Divine Expedition can. Multiplying workers and leaders begins by inviting people into the community, meaning, and larger story of the Divine Expedition.

To multiply laborers for the Divine Expedition requires that we invite people into a greater vision than the quest for personal peace, affluence, or security. The Divine Expedition invites us to enter community with others and participate in the story of God's master plan to rescue and restore others. Multiplying ministers and leaders begins with lifting up and calling others to this vision.

But it is not enough to simply call people to this vision. We must structure the church in such a way that it encourages participation in mission. This requires a shift from viewing the church through the lens of the "Christendom" paradigm, focused as it is on gathering people for programs and events. It starts with envisioning the church as a missional-movement, one in which every Christ-follower is a missionary connected with others in a net-like structure. Romans chapter sixteen points to this, as Paul references multiple house/household churches and leaders linked together locally (16:1, 4, 5, 10,11, 16, 23), regionally (Rome with Corinth), and beyond (15:24). The interconnections were not institutional; they were relational and missional.

CONTROL OR EMPOWER

The "Christendom" paradigm of the church is structured on the basis of a hierarchical leadership, where a few leaders do most of the ministry. Christendom leadership typically holds on to ministry and restricts it, wittingly or unwittingly, to a relatively few number of people. While clearly defined leadership is needed, the missional-movement paradigm seeks to mobilize and equip all Christ-followers to do the work of ministry. Missional-movement leadership cultivates a mentality of giving ministry away, as well as prioritizing the training and empowerment of other workers and leaders. This requires an organizing structure that allows and encourages others to participate in the grander mission of God.

I (Linus Sr.) have observed many Christendom-structured churches over the years. One of their characteristics is that the ministry of the church predominantly takes place in the Sunday service. Often, the lead pastor is wary of possible rivals to his position. The main service is dominated by the pastor and is primarily a monologue. The only time others take a turn in the pulpit is when the pastor is on vacation. In this Christendom model of the church, the role of the typical church member is to support the Sunday program by attending and giving. Other leadership roles are designed to support the program-oriented structure. Unfortunately, most members are passive and feel useless, even invisible.

In contrast, I am encouraged by the emergence of more and more missionally minded pastors, seeking to empower, mobilize, and multiply other workers and leaders. One of these pastors is a Vineyard pastor-friend, Brad Bailey. Brad leads a multi-racial, mixed-gender preaching team that regularly rotates speaking in the church's Sunday services. Leadership multiplication is encouraged rather than stifled. Instead of being threatened by other gifted leaders, Brad encourages and sees the multiplication of leaders as a gauge of his effectiveness. Brad's church also engages a large number of its members in community groups and outreach to the community

On the other side of the United States, pastor Tim Holt in Myrtle Beach, South Carolina is committed to developing leaders who start new churches. In the past two years Seacoast Vineyard has started four new churches. The same is true of New Community in Spokane, Washington, previously led by Rob Fairbanks (now President of Christian Associates). Leaders developed within New Community have launched seven new churches in the greater Spokane area in the past several years. Brad Bailey, Tim Holt, and Rob Fairbanks have each broken through the Christendom paradigm and think in terms of mission, movement, and multiplication.

LEADERSHIP MULTIPLICATION STAGE 1

The book of Romans points to the importance of the multiplication of churches and leaders and can be used as a grid for leadership development. The question, "Where are you in the book of Romans?" is based on the belief that there is a sequential unfolding of spiritual development outlined in this book. It culminates in

Romans chapter sixteen, pointing to the importance of developing other leaders to join us in the Divine Expedition. As we move to this last stage, we can use Romans as a template to develop others. The process of mentoring others means taking them through the various stages in Romans we have been through.

The first stage of leadership multiplication is to guide people to understand and embrace the Gospel (Romans 1-4), activate the spiritual dynamics of the Divine Design (Romans chapters 5-7), and experience the Holy Spirit's empowerment (Romans 8). Leadership multiplication connects people to Jesus and encourages them to access the spiritual resources He imparts. You can only pass on to others what you possess yourself. Leadership development begins with recognition of the need for Christ and the resources He provides.

> You can only pass on to others what you possess yourself.

An aspect of connecting people to the spiritual resources of the Divine Design is to help emerging leaders face those things that hinder them from accessing them, including the invasive power of sin-within. Only by learning to live by the Spirit can the power of sin-within be diminished. Another hindrance that emerging leaders must face are wounds inflicted upon them by others. The effect of these can be diminished as we embrace Jesus and draw upon the resources He makes available in community with others.

Some wounds require specialized counsel and guidance to free us from their effects. I (Linus Jr.) am involved in a ministry called "Adventures of the Heart." One of the things we emphasize is a shift from following Jesus as a matter of sin-management, duty, or obligation, to one of intimacy with Him. We seek to help people address the kinds of emotional and spiritual wounds inflicted upon us all in life's journey. Unattended to, these will keep us from experiencing intimacy with God and health in relationships with others.

I was fortunate to address such a wound that I felt my father (yes, Linus Sr.) inflicted (albeit, unwittingly) on me growing up. I had a longstanding, gnawing sense that my dad was disappointed with me. On an Adventure of the Heart retreat that my dad and I attended together, I was able to express to him my sense of woundedness and receive his apology. His lack of defensiveness and subsequent affirmation of me freed me to disarm my woundedness and move forward with renewed confidence that God's heart (my dad's too) toward me was good. It fortified in me the assurance that I have what it takes to wholeheartedly pursue the adventure of the Divine Expedition and to lead others to do the same.

RELEASING GRACE AND STRENGTH

Leadership multiplication addresses the kinds of hindrances that prevent us from intimacy with God and accessing the resources of the Divine Design. By the encouragement and empowerment of the Holy Spirit, as well as help of those we are in community with, we can disarm both the power of sin and our internal wounds. This frees us to experience God's grace and go forward in His strength.

> Leadership multiplication grounds people in God's grace and strength.

Leadership multiplication starts with the leader being grounded in God's grace, so that he or she can ground others in grace. Every epistle in the New Testament begins and ends with a focus on God's grace. We are told that God saves us by His grace (Ephesians 2:8-9), that where sin abounds grace abounds more (Romans 5:20), and that Jesus came in grace and truth (John 1:17). Paul states his task as that of "testifying to the gospel of God's grace" (Acts 20:24). Thus, the good news of Jesus is the good news of grace. Our ministry is one of seeing lives transformed from the inside out by the grace of God through our Jesus Christ.

Leadership multiplication also roots others in God's strength. Scripture speaks of the Lord as "our strength and our song" (Exodus 15:2). We are told that God arms us with strength (2 Samuel 22:33). The Psalms declare that the Lord is our strength and our shield, as well as our refuge and our strength (Psalm 28:7; 46:1). Paul assures us that we can do *all things* through Christ who gives us strength (Philippians 4:13). The scope of the mission of the Divine Expedition is impossible without God's strength—but possible with it.

Someone humorously said that in the early years of Christian Associates, Sharon was the Christian and I (Linus Sr.) was the associate. This is not far from the truth in that Sharon was indeed the Christian, and I was not during the first three-and-a-half years of our marriage. Then, God rescued me and transformed our marriage by His great grace and strength. Over the years, Sharon and I have faced many challenges, which at times seemed insurmountable. The story of our life together has been one of experiencing God's grace and strength both in and through us. Effective and enduring leadership begins and ends with drawing upon God's grace and strength. So does leadership multiplication.

LEADERSHIP MULTIPLICATION STAGE 2

The second stage to multiply Divine Expedition leaders is to equip them to reach, rescue, and restore others (Romans 9-11). This includes mentoring the emerging leader in how to communicate Jesus effectively with not-yet Christ-followers. A Divine Expedition leader is someone who is being *transformed* him-or herself and who is in *proximity* with others who need rescue.

> Multiplying Divine Expedition leaders involves equipping them to reach, rescue, and restore others.

The Divine Expedition leader is someone who is full of *conviction* and *compassion*, and is able to give a *clear reason* for the hope they have in Jesus.

A Divine Expedition leader is also someone who is *persistent* and *passionate* and can *proclaim* the good news of Christ in a compelling way. He or she is someone who grasps God's *master plan* and who acts strategically (*strategic action*) to reach the culture of which they are a part.

Leadership development seeks to move the above missional markers from being aspiration to actual skills and practices in the emerging leader's life. As a new follower of Jesus, I (Linus Sr.) was fortunate to be mentored by a mature Christ-follower named Ron Thurman. Ron pointed me to Scripture and connected me with other more seasoned Christians who were following Jesus. Ron then coached me in how to share my new faith in Jesus with those who were not-yet Christians. The first part of this training was to help me explain succinctly who Jesus was and what He did. Ron next coached me to share what I did to accept Jesus (prayed to receive Him as my rescuer and Lord) and the effect this was having in my life (changes in my thinking and marriage). Following a brief session of training, Ron had me accompany him as he shared the gospel of grace with others on our university campus—but he didn't allow me to just observe; he called on me to tell my story too.

Although scared at first, I gradually became more and more confident in sharing my faith in Jesus openly with others. I discovered that people were searching for God and open to talk about Jesus, if approached respectfully and genuinely. Sharing with others was like learning to swim. I didn't learn to swim until I was fourteen-years-old, as I was afraid of deep water. It wasn't until I was with friends at school who were jumping in the deep end of a swimming pool that I got enough courage and jumped too. When I did, rather than drown as I expected (I jumped near the edge so I could grab the side of the pool or someone could grab me), I bobbed up to the surface and realized I wouldn't sink. I am grateful that Ron Thurman helped me plunge into the deep of telling others about my faith in Jesus.

The sequence of the Book of Romans moves us from understanding and embracing the gospel, to activating God's grace and strength in our lives, to then reaching out to others around us. The sooner we get over the hurdle of learning to share our faith with others, the better. We might not be able to argue as clearly and persuasively as Paul does, but nothing will motivate us more to learn to give "the reason for the hope within us" than jumping in the waters of engaging others with the Good News of Jesus.

LEADERSHIP MULTIPLICATION STAGE 3

A third stage of multiplying leaders is to guide the emerging leader to practice continual renewal in Christ, and not conform to the culture surrounding them. Spiritual vibrancy is rooted in the "renewing of your mind." Divine Expedition leaders learn to keep God's mercy in view (12:1-2), to "abide in Christ" (John 15:4), and to "set apart Christ as Lord" in their hearts (1 Peter 3:15). This is mental and volitional. It involves practicing spiritual discipline or what are called "spiritual disciplines." But continual renewal is not just a matter or discipline; it is a matter of the Holy Spirit's guidance and empowerment. Paul admonishes us to "be filled with the Spirit" (Ephesians 5:18), to "live by the Spirit" (Galatians 5:16), to "keep in step with the Spirit" (Galatians 5:21), to "live in accordance with the Spirit" (Romans 8:4, 5), and to "be controlled by the Spirit" (Romans 8:9).

Continual renewal includes the activity of both the mind and the heart of the follower of Christ. It also involves action and activity. Paul urges us to offer our bodies "as living sacrifices" (12:1). We are to engage in actions and practices that further God's design and purpose for our lives, families, and world. Thus, continual renewal involves head, heart, and hands,

> Developing new leaders guides them to practice continual renewal in Christ.

aligning all three in concert with the Holy Spirit who resides in us. In doing so we "test and approve God's good, pleasing, and perfect will" (12:2).

At a recent conference I (Linus Sr.) attended, two speakers spoke on the topic of renewal. Neither knew in advance what the other was going to communicate, nor did either hear the other speak. The first speaker referred to spiritual renewal in terms of "getting alone with God." This person advocated that we can do more for God's kingdom when ceasing from all activity, other than to pray and listen to God.

I was agitated by this speaker's emphasis on the equating of spirituality with the cessation of activity. It seemed too reductionistic and monastic. It seemed too impractical for those with significant responsibilities. Some of those in attendance, however, were encouraged by the message, as they felt it gave them permission to slow down from the unceasing rigors and demands of their lives and ministry.

The second speaker's emphasis was almost the opposite from the first. He spoke of how he never hears from God when he is still or silent. God speaks to him and he senses God's presence when he is "on the move doing something for Christ." He said, "That's when God shows up."

As an action-oriented person, I related more to the second speaker's action connect–with-God-on-the-move message. Others related more to the contemplative hear-God-in-stillness-and-quietness emphasis of the first speaker. The first speaker held a *heart-head-hands* approach to renewal—in that order. The second speaker's order of emphasis was *hands-head-heart*. Continual renewal involves the integration of all three, the order depending upon how we are wired. The important thing in leadership multiplication is to help each person continually be renewed by the power of the Holy Spirit.

REMEMBERING AND CONNECTING

The offering of our bodies as continual sacrifices as well as the renewing of our minds in Romans 12:1-2 are based upon remembering the mercies of God found in chapters 1-11. But renewal doesn't just look back; it looks forward. Paul connects renewal to what follows in Romans 12:3-21; that is, using our gifts in community with others.

Fast forwarding to Romans chapter 16 shows that Christ-followers are connected together on both a micro and a macro scale. The early church was made up of multiple house churches or gatherings networked together. Smaller settings (micro scale) allow for transparency, belonging, life sharing, and accountability. They are ideal places for emerging leaders to grow spiritually and discover, develop, and use their spiritual gifts in harmony with other Christ-followers.

> Christ-followers are connected together on both a micro and a macro scale, locally and trans-locally.

Paul addresses "all in Rome who are loved by God and called to be saints" (Romans 1:7). This points to the connection believers and churches had on a citywide level (macro scale), whether formally or informally. These churches were also connected on a multi-city level (Rome and Corinth)— and even on an international level, as Paul speaks of "all the churches of Christ" sending their greetings (16:16). The early church was networked locally and trans-locally.

Therefore, Divine Expedition leaders are to be kingdom builders rather than empire builders.

Leadership multiplication encourages the discovery and use of spiritual gifts and structures the church in a way that allows these gifts to be exercised. Leadership multiplication also encourages qualities such as hating what is evil, clinging to what is good, being devoted to one another in brotherly love, honoring one another above ourselves, and keeping our spiritual fervor in serving the Lord, joyfulness in hope, patience in affliction, faithfulness in prayer, and sharing with fellow Christ-followers in need and hospitality (12:9-13). These are but some of the character traits we seek to impart in multiplying leaders.

LEADERSHIP MULTIPLICATION STAGE 4

A fourth stage of leadership multiplication is to guide emerging leaders to live with integrity and love in the midst of the society around them (chapter 13). This includes learning to be financially responsible and respect governing structures. It means, above all, leading with love, which "is the fulfillment of the law."

Divine Expedition leaders are to exhibit a loving presence in both a local body of Christ-followers (Leadership Development Stage 3), as well as engage the culture and society around them in a loving way. Community engagement can range from holding a job to participating in some kind of community activity or service. In both cases it involves learning to build positive, loving relationships with others around them.

> A fourth stage is to guide emerging leaders to live with integrity, love and a sense of urgency.

This stage of leadership development encourages a sense of urgency and an eternal perspective, recognizing that "the night is nearly over; the day is almost here" (13:12). Knowing that this life is not all there is motivates us to "put off the deeds of darkness and clothe ourselves with the Lord Jesus Christ" (13:12-14). We have a sense that the clock of history is ticking and that it is urgent that we invest ourselves in carrying out the Divine Expedition.

Jesus instructed, "As long as it is day, we must do the work of him who sent me. Night is coming, when no one can work" (John 9:4). For many years I (Linus Sr.) have pushed myself purposefully (not frenetically), as I know that I have a stewardship of the time, money, gifts, and opportunities God gives me. As I have grown older, the little aches, pains, and gradual changes in my physical body (such as hair graying), remind me that my days on earth are limited and motivate me to live with a future orientation. Even though I believe some of my best days are ahead, these physical changes are reminders that the "night is over; the day is almost here" in terms of my time to accomplish what God has for me.

LEADERSHIP MULTIPLICATION STAGE 5

A fifth stage of multiplying leaders is to encourage the emerging leader to practice patience, love, acceptance, and respect toward other Christ-followers whose cultural preferences are different from those of the leader (chapters 14-15). This requires a growing maturity, discernment, and wisdom. The mature leader is strong in freedom but knows when to restrict that freedom in order to encourage the faith of others.

The Apostle John lists three levels of spiritual maturity in the first of his small letters, appearing toward the end of the New Testament. The three levels are "children", "fathers", and "young men" (1 John 2:12-14). John actually addresses each of these three categories of believers twice, first in 1 John 2:12-13a, and then in I John 2:13b-14. Both times he addresses each of the three levels in the same order: children, fathers, and young men.

> A fifth stage of multiplying leaders is to encourage the practice of patience, love, acceptance, and respect

In his first address to *children* (young believers), John reminds them that their sins have been forgiven on account of His (Jesus) name. In his second address to them, he affirms they "have known the Father" (God). These two statements together reveal the features that are characteristic of a new believer in Jesus—forgiveness and a relationship with God as Father.

John's addresses *young men* by commending them for over-coming the evil one. His follow up statement to them acknowledges, "you are strong and the word of God lives in you, and you have overcome the evil one." Young men are those who overcome evil, grow strong in their faith through applying God's word (Scripture), and engage in the spiritual battle of rescuing and restoring others.

John says something different in each of his two statements to both *children* ("your sins are forgiven;" "you have known the Father") and *young men* ("you have overcome the evil one;" "you are strong and the word of God lives in you"). But curiously, he says exactly the same thing in both of his statements to fathers (spiritual fathers): "I write to you fathers because you have known him who is from the beginning." This repeated phrase points to the enduring depth of knowledge, intimate relationship, and life-long walk with God, characterizing a spiritual father (or spiritual mother).

Of special interest is the positioning of *fathers* between *children* and *young men* in both sequences (1 John 2:12-13a and 2:13b-4). The expected developmental order would be *children*, *young men*, and then *fathers*. However, John places *fathers* between *children* and *young men*, and then repeats the same order again. Is this accidental? This positioning appears intentional, emphasizing that spiritual fathers (and mothers) serve as a buffer between young believers who are more vulnerable in their faith, and more zealous young-leaders who, left to themselves, might wreck havoc on the younger believers. Leadership multiplication encourages growth toward maturity, depth of faith, and intimacy with God over time, thus, becoming a spiritual father or mother.

FATHER AND MOTHER PRACTICES

Romans chapter fourteen points us to the kinds of prac-tices needed for young leaders to develop into mature "fathers." Maturing leaders learn to practice acceptance, a "to the Lord" focus, love, and faith. They aspire to build the faith of others and stay roped together, even when the cultural preferences of a fellow Christian differs from their own. Combining John's view of "fathers" with Paul's counsel for those "strong in faith," mature leaders are high in freedom and high in love.

I (Linus Jr.) consider myself to be at the "young man" stage of maturity. I am passionate about rescuing and restoring others and am engaged in a number of endeavors to do so. I am glad for the "fathers" in my life, including my own dad who in addition to being my biological father is a spiritual father to me as well.

I know many "young men" who lack any healthy role model. One example is a friend who was abandoned by his mother when young. His father remarried and eventually died, leaving everything he owned to his second family. His son from his first marriage was left completely out of his will. The abandonment he experienced scarred him deeply, resulting in a diminished inability to trust. He desperately needs a "father."

LEADERSHIP MULTIPLICATION STAGE 6

A sixth stage of leadership multiplication is growth in mercy and generosity. This includes a passion to reach out to those not-yet connected to God's mercy as well as a compassion for those in material need (chapter 15). Divine Expedition leaders align themselves with the heart of God for all people to know His mercy. To be a minister of Jesus is to have the "priestly duty of pro-claiming the gospel of God" (15:16) that others may "glorify God for His mercy" (15:9). God's mercy spurs us to engage in the global mission to proclaim Christ where he is not known (15:20).

> A sixth stage of leadership multiplication is growth in mercy, mission, and generosity.

Aligning with the heart of God expresses itself in compassion for those in social and economic need, especially other Christ-followers. The Western church in the 20th century was polarized between mission and social compassion. Paul holds the two together. I (Linus Sr.) lead a Bible study group of men who work in business. I am impressed by their efforts to integrate their faith in their personal lives, their families, and their work. We interact about how God's word applies to each of these areas, and we pray for one another. But following Christ doesn't stop with their personal lives, families, or work for them. Several are on the Board of a rescue mission that provides recovery programs that change the trajectory of the lives of those who have been trapped on the streets of Los Angeles.

Divine Expedition leadership expresses itself in stewardship and generosity with our time, energy, and money. God intends for us to expend ourselves in more than the pursuit of personal survival, comfort, and security. The real meaning of our lives is found in mercy, mission, and compassion. The Christ-followers in Macedonia and Achaia left an example for us to follow: generosity, even in poverty (15:26; 2 Cor. 8:1-7). Developing Divine Expedition leaders involves encouraging generosity toward both the lost and needy. The saying, "If someone's money is not in the boat, they are not in the boat," is true.

LEADERSHIP MULTIPLICATION STAGE 7

The seventh and final stage to multiply and develop leaders is for the emerging leader to multiply even more leaders. Paul's two lists of leaders in Romans chapter 16 show that he prioritized leadership multiplication. He speaks of Phoebe who was a servant of Christ is Cenchrea (16:1), of Priscilla and Aquila, fellow workers who risked their lives for him and led a church in their home (16:3), of Mary who worked hard on behalf of the church at Rome, of Andronicus and Junias,

> The final stage to develop leaders is for them to multiply even more leaders.

who had an apostolic ministry, and of many others. Paul's two leadership lists in Romans 16 highlight that Divine Expedition leaders multiply other leaders.

Multiplying leaders includes identifying, recruiting, training, mentoring, and mobilizing others to participate in the mission of the Divine Expedition. In conversing with a leader in a fast growing church planting movement, I (Linus Sr.) asked why the movement was growing so rapidly. He replied, "a criterion for leadership is for every leader to identify three other people to mentor from the outset of their area of ministry." The vision of the church was not just to plant other churches; it was to multiply them. Leadership multiplication was the key for this to happen.

But there is another element of leadership development and multiplication highlighted in Romans 16. Paul addresses the problem of those who cause divisions and put obstacles in our way (16:17). These are self-serving people who are driven by their appetites and deceive others with smooth talk and flattery (16:18). To counter these people and the disharmony and confusion they create, leaders need discernment and wisdom regarding "what is good" and "what is evil" (16:19).

> Paul connects trouble-making and deceptive people with unseen spiritual forces.

Paul connects trouble-making and deceptive people with unseen spiritual forces. Behind such people is a malevolent being named Satan who leads a host of demonic beings. Although these forces hinder our mission, Divine Expedition leaders know they will ultimately prevail as they draw upon God's grace and strength. We can take heart in the certainty that "the God of peace will crush Satan under our feet." Multiplying and developing Divine Expedition leaders includes training in how to discern people's toxic agendas and Satan's demonic stratagems. We must be on the lookout for those who cause divisions and are driven by their own appetites, while staying focused on the God of peace and the grace of our Lord Jesus Christ (16:20).

Our mission is to see Christ's followers established by the gospel and to see all the nations believe and obey by our proclamation of Jesus. Although the message of Jesus as Messiah-Son-King-Lord-Savior was a hidden mystery in ages past, it was revealed and made known through the Old Testament prophetic writings and the proclamation of Jesus Christ, so that now all nations might believe and obey God. This is the task of the Divine Expedition: to spread the Good News so that the glory of God through Jesus Christ is made known everywhere (16:25-27).

The seven sequential stages above, following the outline of Romans, provide a pathway for us to develop and multiply Divine Expedition leaders. Because the process is organic, the stages will overlap. Some leaders will develop more rapidly and some stages will go by more quickly. We will have to cycle back to earlier stages from time to time. Sometimes progress will be two steps forward, one step back. Leaders will develop in different ways, but there is a sequential dimension involved—the sequence of the book of Romans. Whatever the pace, we must not lose sight of the overall Divine Expedition goal: to multiply leaders and churches so that all nations might believe and obey Messiah-Son-King-Savior-Lord Jesus, and, thus, be rescued and restored.

CHAPTER 21

CONCLUSION
WHERE ARE YOU IN THE BOOK OF ROMANS?

Ellen MacArthur endured stormy seas, 65-mile per hour winds, a broken sail, burns, bruises and exhaustion. The payoff: a solo around-the-world sailing record. The 28-year-old English woman completed the 26,000-mile circumnavigation in 71 days, 14 hours, 18 minutes and 33 seconds, 32 hours and 35 minutes ahead of the previous record.

—*USA Today*[1]

But I'd had many great moments in the last few weeks, and I couldn't help feeling a touch of sadness at the thought that it was all over.

—Sir Edmond Hillary[2]

They had made it! Their ordeal was over, though they were left with nothing but the soaking wet clothes on their backs. They felt a flood of emotions—relief, gratitude, joy—mixed with more profound thoughts of their greatness, their insignificance, and to what they owed their victory.

—*Shackleton's Way*[3]

Fellows, we're home.

—Jim Lovell[4]

Now to him who is able to establish you by my gospel and the proclamation of Jesus Christ, according to the revelation of the mystery hidden for long ages past, but now revealed and made known through the prophetic writings by the command of the eternal God, so that all nations might believe and obey him—to the only wise God be glory forever through Jesus Christ! Amen.

—Romans 16:25-27

MISSION ACCOMPLISHED!

Expeditions come to an end. Looking back on them leaves us in awe. Upon completion of her around the world sailing record, Ellen MacArthur exclaimed, "I feel absolutely exhausted, but I'm elated to be here." Since her journey began, she slept an average of four hours a day, living in an area measuring five feet by six-and-one-half feet (1.52 by 1.98 meters).[5]

Edmond Hillary reflecting back on his successful summit of Everest, exclaimed, "I could remember so clearly Charles Evans and Tom Bourdillon, weary to death, dragging themselves down to the South Col; and John Hunt's lined and indomitable face as he handed me his tiny cross while the wind battered our tent; and the feeling of terrible loneliness as George Lowe and Gregory left us high on our little ledge; and then, at the last, Tenzing's smile of triumph on the summit. And now our adventure was finished!"[6]

Shackleton too paid an eloquent tribute to the whole experience of the journey to rescue his stranded crew in *South: The Endurance Expedition.*[7] Paraphrasing Robert Service's poem, *The Call of the Wild,* he wrote, "We have pierced the veneer of outside things. We had 'suffered, starved, and triumphed, groveled down yet grasped at glory, grown bigger in the bigness of the whole. We had seen God in his splendors, heard the text that Nature renders. We had reached the naked soul of man."[8]

Nothing is more satisfying than seeing an expedition through to the end—and so it is with the Divine Expedition. The Divine

Expedition is the greatest mission ever given: to rescue others from their brokenness and separation from God, and to restore to them God's grand design and purpose.

THE UNFOLDING SEQUENCE OF THE DIVINE DESIGN

The book of Romans invites us on an unfolding expedition. Where are you in this expedition? Where are you in the book of Romans? Romans 1:18-3:20 reveals humanity's most basic problem: separation from God and His design for us. Incredibly, undeservedly, and only possible by God's grace, a solution to our estrangement from Him is provided. The solution is that God rescues us by providing a credit of righteousness for us through the death and resurrection of Jesus Christ. This alone removes our alienation from God caused by the defect of sin-within. Only this puts us in right standing with God (Romans 3:21-4). This credit of righteousness becomes ours when we embrace Jesus and put our trust in Him for taking upon Himself the guilt and blame that was ours.

The portal into the rescue of the Divine Expedition is God's grace and forgiveness. Being put right with God by faith in Jesus as Messiah-Son-King-Lord-Savior initiates the restoration of the Divine Design of peace with God, access to His grace, hope of inner transformation, and the Holy Spirit's love poured into our hearts. It also releases the "much mores" of the reversal of wrath, salvation through Christ's life, overflowing grace, and the reign of the life of Jesus in and through us (Romans 5). These, along with being connected to Jesus in a mystical, intimate, and inseparable way (Romans 6), are the resources we must access to reach and rescue others.

Although we have access to incredible spiritual resources, the residual presence of sin-within trips us, and hinders us from fully activating them and benefiting from our new life in Christ (Romans 7). The only way to break the stranglehold of sin-within is through the transforming power of the Holy Spirit. As we live from the Spirit, are controlled by the Spirit, set our minds on what the Spirit desires, and walk by the Spirit, we are empowered to overcome the downward pull of sin.

By "operationalizing" the Spirit's power within, we are liberated from the bondage of sin and death, and put to death the dark thoughts and deeds that otherwise control us. The Spirit helps us in our weaknesses and gives us the assurance that nothing can separate us from God's love (Romans 8). In all of this, God's grace and mercy in Jesus (rather than religion or law) and the Holy Spirit's empowerment become the modus operandi of our lives.

THE UNFOLDING SEQUENCE OF THE DIVINE EXPEDITION

The first eight chapters of Romans unfold the map of our rescue and restoration. This readies us for participation in the Divine Expedition, the subject of the second half of the book of Romans. The second half of Romans (Divine Expedition) is dependent on the first half (Divine Design). Drawing upon the Spirit's power releases the spiritual resources outlined in Romans 3-8. Thus, our participation in the rescue mission of the Divine Expedition begins with our own *transformation*.

With this underway, we are then ready to set out to help rescue and restore others. This begins with proximity, with those who are near us, and involves *conviction, compassion, clear reasoning, perseverance*, and *passion* (Romans 9). At the center of the rescue mission is the *proclamation* "that if you confess with your mouth, 'Jesus is Lord,' and believe in your heart that God raised him from the dead, you will be saved" (Romans 10:9).

To keep from getting lost in our journey, it is imperative that we keep in view God's *grand plan* to reach the greatest number of people throughout history (Romans 9-11). This helps us

> The second half of Romans [Divine Expedition] is dependent on the first half [Divine Design].

engage in *strategic action* to reach those around us with the message of God's mercy.

To carry out the Divine Expedition requires the continual renewing of our minds. We renew our minds by constantly reviewing God's mercy outlined in the restoration of the Divine Design in chapters 1-8. This leads us to offer ourselves as living sacrifices, as well as use our gifts synergistically with others. It is as a missional Christ-following community that we most effectively draw others to Jesus and God's love, grace, and mercy (Romans 12).

The Divine Expedition directs us to engage government and society with integrity, respect, and love. By doing so, God's salvation is commended to the culture we live in the midst of and are seeking to influence (Romans 13). The Divine Expedition further instructs us in how to stay roped together with those whose backgrounds and cultural preferences are different that ours. We stay "roped together" by practicing acceptance, a "to the Lord" focus, love, and faith. Practicing these things enable us to edify and encourage other believers (Romans 14).

While the success of the Divine Expedition rests upon how we live in society and relate to others, it preeminently involves extending God's love and mercy in mission, compassion, and generosity to the lost and broken. Our mission is a global one: to reach all people, near and far, with the message of God's grace and mercy in Jesus. This includes compassion toward those who are lost and generosity to those in need (Romans 15).

Finally, the completion of the Divine Expedition requires mobilizing others for ministry and developing leaders to multiply more Christ-following communities and leaders to spread the Good News of Jesus to the whole world. Our task is not finished until all nations and cultures have the opportunity to respond to Jesus, and thereby glorify the "only wise God" (Romans 16). Only the multiplication of more Jesus-reflecting, Jesus-following communities and leaders will accomplish this.

THE BIG QUESTION

So the big question each of us must ask is, "Where am I in the book of Romans?" You may be reading this as someone who has never come to know Messiah-Son-King-Lord-Savior Jesus in a personal way. You may have been oblivious of, or indifferent to, His saving work and the credit of righteousness He makes available to you. You may have assumed

The question each of us must ask....

_____

that by being a moral or religious person God would reward you and accept you. If these statements describe you, you fit somewhere within the first three chapters of Romans. No matter how successful, moral, or religious you may be, you are still separated from God because of the defect of sin-within and missing out on an intimate relationship with the One who created you and loves you.

TAKE A STEP TOWARD JESUS

Without Jesus, the "wrath of God" is playing out in your life. Life will not work the way God designed and likely the way you hope. You can never have the assurance that God accepts you, nor will you be able to experience the purpose for which He created you. As you realize the difference between relying upon self-merit and receiving the scholarship of righteousness provided through Jesus, we encourage you to take the step of placing your faith in Jesus. You can do so by simply praying "God, I know I am separated from you because of my sin. I open my life to Jesus and place my trust in Him for the forgiveness, righteousness, and new life that only He provides. I ask your Holy Spirit to empower me to follow Jesus and experience God's Divine Design for my life." Open your life to Jesus, the renewal of the Divine Design, and the adventure of the Divine Expedition (see John 1:12; Romans 10:9; Revelation 3:20).

TAKE A STEP TOWARD GOD'S DESIGN

If you are a follower of Jesus, you may not have progressed beyond the "righteousness from God by faith" stage of Romans 3:21-4:25. You believe in Jesus and know that He has credited you with the righteousness you need to be accepted by God, but you are not experiencing the peace, grace, hope, and love of the Divine Design in Romans 5. You are not yet drawing upon the "much more" resources also available to you in this chapter. You may be like the baby Christians Paul speaks of in his first letter to the Corinthians, who are still drinking milk and have not yet begun to eat meat. If this is true of you, ask God to make the 4x4 resources of Romans chapter five fully real in your experience. Each of these resources is activated and experienced incrementally by faith. Our experience of these is enhanced as we join with others engaging in the Divine Expedition.

TAKE A STEP TOWARD THE HOLY SPIRIT

If you are experiencing the peace, grace, hope, and love and the "much mores" of Romans chapter five, you may not be experiencing the new life in Jesus in Romans chapter six. Furthermore, you may find you are doing things you don't want to do and are not doing the things you would like, and feel trapped in Romans chapter seven. If so, dive into Romans chapter eight and ask the Holy Spirit to teach you, guide you, and empower you. Open yourself to the Holy Spirit's presence and empowerment. Pray, "Holy Spirit, I need your power and life to flow through me. I need your guidance and provision. I choose to be filled by you."

TAKE A STEP TOWARD REACHING THOSE NEAR YOU

You may have progressed beyond Romans chapter seven and are experiencing the Holy Spirit's empowerment of Romans chapter eight—but you are not on mission to rescue others. It is easy for Christians to become insulated from not-yet Christians, and for life to be consumed with survival or escapism. Romans chapters nine through eleven challenge us to be in proximity with not-yet believers and to reach out to them in purposeful, compassionate, and strategic ways. Are you there yet? Who can you reach out to in love and kindness? Commit yourself to be a living sacrifice because of God's mercy, and reach out and share the message of the Divine Expedition with those around you.

TAKE A STEP TOWARD COMMUNITY WITH
OTHER BELIEVERS

You may be reaching out to others but are not connected with a local gathering of Christ-followers. If so, it is less likely that you will see others become fully devoted followers of Jesus ("make disciples"). The Divine Expedition couples the verbal message of the Good News of Jesus with a visual manifestation of God's love and mercy through a body of Christ-followers. To effectively engage others in the Divine Expedition requires the discovery and use of our spiritual gifts in collaboration with a loving and "missional" community of believers (Romans 12). Search out a local gathering of Christ-followers where your gifts will be used in concert with those of others. Find a church where members are passionately and lovingly missional, not merely content with attending a weekly program or event.

TAKE A STEP TOWARD SOCIETY

You may be actively involved in a body of believers but not engaging with your surrounding neighborhood or community as a fellow-citizen, showing respect, honor, and love to those around you (Romans 13). Are there unpaid bills, debts, or taxes you need to take care of? Is there a neighbor you can show God's love to in some tangible way? Is there a way you can engage as a good citizen in your community? The Divine Expedition stretches us to live beyond consumerism, selfishness, isolation, and individualism. It moves us instead to become responsible participants in society, seeking the wellbeing of others for the glory of God.

TAKE A STEP TOWARD THOSE DIFFERENT THAN YOU.

It may be that you are a good citizen but are having a hard time relating to some hard-to-get-along-with fellow Christ-followers. One of the greatest challenges for all of us is to relate to those who profess to follow Jesus but have different cultural convictions and preferences from ours (Romans 14). It is understandable that Paul saves this issue toward the end of Romans. Nothing is harder. The challenge is to accept people who are different and keep our focus "to the Lord" and building others up (first part of Romans 15). What step do you need to take in this regard?

TAKE A STEP TOWARD BEING MISSIONAL

If you are this far along, then are you playing a role in world mission? For some it will involve a prayer role, for others a support role, and for still others it may mean moving across town, moving to another city, moving to another country, or reaching out to another culture. For all, it means we are to keep in view the global scope of the Divine Expedition (second half of Romans chapter fifteen). What part in world-missions might God have you play? But mission isn't just world-missions. It is being missional wherever we are. There is a difference between the church sending missionaries and the church being sent. Many churches think they are missional simply by sending some of their members as missionaries to other countries. While worthwhile, every Christ-follower is called to be missional, actively seeking to rescue and restore others both near and far.

TAKE ONE MORE STEP: TOWARD MULTIPLYING LEADERS AND CHURCHES

Finally, there is one more step to fully carrying out the Divine Expedition. Are you helping mobilize and multiply additional Christ-followers, workers, and leaders? What steps can you take to mentor someone else? What steps can you take to develop another leader? The rescue of our world will take an army of missional followers of Jesus and the multiplication of workers, leaders, and churches.

EVERY PERSON, EVERY LEADER, EVERY CHURCH

Where are you in the book of Romans? What is the next step you need to take? Every person must take stock of where he or she is along the journey presented in Romans. This question must be asked not only by every Christian but also by every leader and by the leadership of every church and ministry. Leaders of ministries or churches must ask, "Where is my ministry or church in the book of Romans?" Is my ministry or church reaching others and engaging them in the Divine Expedition? Is it restoring to them the Divine Design? Is it outfitting them to reach, rescue, and restore others? Is it mobilizing them for the Divine Expedition? Is it developing leaders? Is it multiplying other churches? Is it structured to do so?

> This question is not only to be asked by every Christian but also by every leader.

If you are a leader, ask, "Is our Christ-following community a global, missional one?" Are we pursuing empire building or kingdom building? To finish the task Christ has given us requires that every church be structured to multiply disciples, leaders, and churches. Are you ready to play a part in this?

This is the Divine Expedition, outlined from Romans 1:1 to 16:27. Many have become stranded somewhere along the way, often because they are unaware of the overall master plan God outlined through His apostle Paul in Romans. The Divine Expedition calls us to keep stretching beyond our comfort level and to keep risking, growing, developing, and pushing onward. As we stretch and reach out, God will guide and empower us. We will experience a close and abiding relationship with Him and attract others into His Kingdom. The result is that they too will join us in the greatest mission ever revealed: the Divine Expedition.

In the journey we have undertaken in this book, we have explored the River of Doubt with Roosevelt, traveled the world's oceans with Shackelton, Cook, and Magellan, crossed the American frontier with Lewis and Clark, summated the world's highest mountain with Hillary and Norgay, and flown into space and back to earth with the crew of *Apollo 13*. Hopefully, your heart leaps, as do ours, as you read about such explorations and expeditions—but even more as you recognize it is the call of God to every man and woman to engage in the Divine Expedition and be caught up in the rescue of humanity in collaboration with God. This expedition isn't a call to duty. It is a call to destiny. God has placed in each of us a desire for such an exploit.

Where are you in the book of Romans? What is the next step you need to take? Don't stop until you complete the journey.

ENDNOTES

Chapter 1

1. William Marsden, *The Travels of Marco Polo* (Ware, Hetfordshire: Cumberland House, 1997), p. 8.
2. Laurence Bergreen, *Over the Edge of the World: Magellan's Terrifying Circumnavigation of the Globe* (New York: Harper Collins, 2004), p. 127.
3. Marco Polo (September 15, 1254– January 9, 1324 at earliest, but no later than June 1324) was a trader and explorer from the Venetian Republic who gained fame for his worldwide travels, recorded in the book Il Milione ("The Million" or The Travels of Marco Polo) also known as Oriente Poliano (the Orient of the Polos) and the Description of the World: http://en.wikipedia.org/wiki/Marco_Polo.
4. Ferdinand Magellan (Spring 1480 – April 27, 1521) was a Portuguese maritime explorer who, while in the service of the Spanish Crown, tried to find a westward route to the Spice Islands of Indonesia. He thereby became the first person to lead an expedition across the Pacific Ocean. This was also the first successful attempt to circumnavigate the Earth in history. Although he did not complete the entire voyage (he was killed during the Battle of Mactan in the Philippines), Magellan had earlier traveled eastward to the Spice Islands, so he became one of the first individuals to cross all of the meridians of the Globe: http://en.wikipedia.org/wiki/Ferdinand_Magellan.
5. Bergreen, pp. 2-3.
6. "Christ" is the Greek equivalent of the Hebrew word "Messiah," the one promised by the Old Testament Prophets.
7. The story of Paul's conversion is found three times in the New Testament book of Acts: chapter nine, chapter twenty-two and chapter twenty-six. More

details are also found in Philippians chapter three and Galatians chapters one and two

8. John Eldredge, *Wild at Heart* (Nashville: Thomas Nelson Publishers, 2001), p. 9.

9. *Wild at Heart*, p.xi.

10. John & Stasi Eldredge, *Captivating* (Nashville: Thomas Nelson Publishers, 2005), p. 8.

Chapter 2

1. *High Adventure: the True Story of the First Ascent of Everest* (Oxford: Oxford University Press, 1955), p. 5.

2. Margot Morrell and Stephanie Capparell, *Shackleton's Way: Leadership Lessons from the Great Antarctic Explorer* (New York: Penguin Books, 2001), p. 55.

3. *High Adventure*, p. 1.

4. Acts 17:1-10.

5. For example, Luke remained in Philippi after Paul's visit (as indicated by the "we" sections in Acts 16:6-17:1, 20:1-6, and 27:1-28:16, comparing these with the list of names in Colossians 4:14). Colossians was one of four letters Paul wrote during his imprisonment in Rome following his harrowing sea voyage described in the last several chapters of Acts. The others are Philippians, Ephesians and Philemon.

6. Acts 19:1-10.

7. II Corinthians 6:3-10; 11:23-28.

8. Acts 2:10-11.

9. Acts 2:14-40.

10. Acts 2:41.

Chapter 3

1. Martin Dugard, *Farther Than Any Man: The Rise and Fall of Captain James Cook*, (New York: Washington Square Press, 2001), p. 67.

2. Candice Millard, *The River of Doubt: Theodore Roosevelt's Darkest Journey*: (New York: Broadway Books, 2005).

3. *The Holy Bible*, New International Version (Nashville: Broadman & Holman Publishers), 1996.

4. *Farther Than Any Man*, p.2.

5. Candice Millard, *The River of Doubt: Theodore Roosevelt's Darkest Journey:* (New York: Broadway Books, 2005), p. 2.
6. Candice Millard, pp. 15, 17.
7. Candice Millard, pp. 18, 21.
8. 1 Timothy 1:15.
9. 1 Corinthians 9:22-23.
10. I Corinthians 9:3-18.

Chapter 4

1. Stephen E. Ambrose, *Undaunted Courage: Meriwether Lewis, Thomas Jefferson, and the Opening of the West* (New York: Simon and Schuster, 1996), p.14.
2. Ambrose, p. 31. See also page 280.
3. Ambrose, p. 13.
4. Ambrose, p. 14.
5. Genesis 3:15 (Adam and Eve); Genesis 12:2-7; 13:4, 14-17; 14:4-6; 17:3-8; and 22:17 with Romans 4 (Abraham).
6. Psalm 2; see also Mark 12:35-37 with Psalm 110.
7. See 2 Samuel 7:11-14 along with the genealogies in Matthew 1 and Luke 3 that both trace Jesus' lineage to king David, thus qualifying him to inherit the promise to David.
8. Zechariah 11:12 with Matthew 26:14-15; Psalm 55:12-14, Psalm 41:9 and Zechariah 13:6 with Matthew 26:49-50; Zechariah 11:13 with Matthew 27:5-7; Zechariah 13:7 with Matthew 26:56; Psalm 35:11 with Matthew 26:59-60; Isaiah 50:6 with Matthew 26:6-7; Psalm 22:16 with Luke 23:33 and John 20:25-27 and Isaiah 53:5-7 with Matthew 27:12-29; Isaiah 53:12 with Mark 15:27-28 and Luke 23:24; Psalm 109:24-25 with John 19:17, Luke 23:26 and Matthew 27:39; Psalm 22:8 and 17-18 with Matthew 27:41-43, Luke 23:35 and John 19:23-24; Psalm 22:1 with Matthew 27:46; Psalm 69:21 with John 19:28-29; Psalm 31:5 with Luke 23:46; Psalm 38:11 with Luke 23:49; Psalm 34:20 with John 19:33, 36; Zechariah 12:10 with John 19:34-37; Amos 8:9 with Matthew 27:45 and Isaiah 53:9 with Matthew 27:57-60.
9. See especially Psalm 22 and Isaiah 53.
10. See the prophetic reference to this in 2 Samuel 7:14 and Psalm 2:7-12.
11. See 1 Corinthians 15:3-8.

12. Isaiah 9:6-7. See also Isaiah 7:14; Romans 10:9, 13; 1 Corinthians 12:3; 15:57; Galatians 6:14; Philippians 2:11; Colossians 2:6; 1 Peter 3:15; Revelation 17:14.
13. New Living Translation.
14. http://thinkexist.com/quotation/there_is_a_god_shaped_vacuum_in_the_heart_of/166425.html.
15. http://www.maniacworld.com/Phone-Salesman-Amazes-Crowd.html.

Chapter 5
1. *High Adventure*, p. 182.
2. *Shackleton's Way: Leadership Lessons from the Great Antarctic Explorer*, by Margot Morrell and Stephanie Capparell (New York: Penguin Books, 2001), p. 55.
3. Martin Dugard, *Farther Than Any Man*, p. 190.
4. Note by Chris McCandless who perished in the Alaska wilderness, quoted from *Into the Wild* by Jon Krakauer (New York: Anchor Books, 1997), p. 12.
5. *High Adventure*, p. 182.
6. http://en.wikipedia.org/wiki/Into_the_Wild.
7. Psalm 14; Psalm 53.
8. Anonymous, quoted from Richard Stearns, *The Hole in the Gospel* (Nashville: Thomas Nelson, 2009), p. 161.
9. Dr. Larry Crabb, *66 Love Letters: A Conversation with God that Invites You Into His Story* (Nashville: Thomas Nelson, 2009), p. xxiii.
10. Vishal Mangalwadi, *Must The Sun Set on The West: An Indian Explores the Soul of Western Civilization* (Pasadena: Revelation Movement LLC, 2008). Part of a ten lecture series given at the University of Minnesota.
11. While there are no doubt cases of genetic sexual confusion, most homosexuals are socialized into this life style or come from families with one or more dysfunctional and overbearing parent, creating a sense of identity insecurity.
12. http://www.brainyquote.com/quotes/quotes/f/fyodordost176819.html.

Chapter 6
1. Cited from http://www.has.vcu.edu/group/thinair.htm, commenting on the failed expedition chronicled in *Into Thin Air* by Jon Krakauer (New York: Random House, 1997).
2. Cited from http://en.wikipedia.org/wiki/William_Grant_Stairs.
3. Jon Krakauer, p. 213.

4. http://en.wikipedia.org/wiki/William_Grant_Stairs.

5. Sources: Daniel Liebowitz, M.D. and Charles Pearson, *The Last Expedition: Stanley's Mad Journey through the Congo*, (New York: W.W. Norton & Co., 2005): http://en.wikipedia.org/wiki/Henry_Morton_Stanley, and http://en.wikipedia.org/wiki/William_Grant_Stairs.

6. Mark 7:15.

Chapter 7

1. Margot Morrell and Stephanie Capparell, p. 28. The event referred to was Ernest Shackleton's reading the fascinating news that the *Belgica* had left Punta Arenas, Chile, in December, 1897, with plans to become the first scientific expedition to the Antarctic and to take the first photographs of the region.

2. *Undaunted Courage,* p. 80.

3. *High Adventure*, p. 44.

4. New Living Translation.

5. *Undaunted Courage*, p. 230 ff.

6. "Discovering Lewis and Clark:" http://www.lewis-clark.org/content/content-channel.asp?ChannelID=262.

7. Romans 4:3, 4, 5, 6, 9, 10, 11, 21, 23, and 24.

Chapter 8

1. An ad, which Shackleton placed in a London newspaper seeking recruits for his 1914 Imperial Trans-Antarctic Expedition: http://www.pbs.org/wgbh/nova/shackleton/1914/team.html.

2. *Undaunted Courage*, p. 95.

3. *High Adventure*, p. 9. During a 1952 trip in the Alps, Hillary and his friend George Lowe were invited by the Joint Himalayan Committee for the approved British 1953 attempt on Everest. Shipton was named as leader but was replaced by Hunt. Hillary considered pulling out, but both Hunt and Shipton talked him into remaining. Hillary was intending to climb with Lowe but Hunt named two teams for the assault: Tom Bourdillon and Charles Evans; and Hillary and Tenzing.

4. *Shackleton's Way*, p. 69.

5. "Hillary of New Zealand and Tenzing reach the top," Reuter (in The Guardian, June 2, 1953): http://en.wikipedia.org/wiki/Edmund_Hillary#cite_note-guard1-10.

6. http://www.beargrylls.com/biography.html.

Chapter 9

1. Stephen Ambrose, pp. 52-53.
2. *Undaunted Courage: Meriwether Lewis, Thomas Jefferson, and the Opening of the American West.* (New York: Simon and Schuster, 1996), p. 79. Jefferson was giving his reasons for selecting Meriwether Lewis to lead the expedition across the North American Continent.
3. Simon Robinson, Sir Edmund Hillary: Top of the World, Time Magazine, 2008-01-10. Accessed 2008-01-14: http://en.wikipedia.org/wiki/Edmund_Hillary#cite_note-Time_obit-3.
4. *Undaunted Courage*, p. 25. Note: There were no public schools in eighteenth-century Virginia. Planter's sons, which Lewis was, got their education by boarding with teachers, almost always preachers or parsons, who would instruct them in Latin, mathematics, natural science, and English.
5. *Undaunted Courage*, p. 19.
6. http://teacher.scholastic.com/activities/hillary/climb/climb01.htm.
7. http://teacher.scholastic.com/activities/hillary/climb/climb02.htm.

Chapter 10

1. *Farther Than Any Man: The Rise and Fall of Captain James Cook* by Martin Dugard (New York: Washington Square Press, 2001), p. 117. Captain James Cook (1728–1779) was an English explorer, navigator and cartographer, rising to the rank of Captain in the Royal Navy. He was the first to map Newfoundland prior to making three voyages to the Pacific Ocean during which he achieved the first European contact with the eastern coastline of Australia and the Hawaiian Islands as well as the first recorded circumnavigation of New Zealand.
2. Laurence Bergreen, pp. 127, 272. Magellan was born in 1480. Like Columbus before him, he believed he could get to the Spice Islands by sailing west toward the east coast of South America where he found a passage to the Pacific Ocean. After befriending a king in the Spice Islands, Magellan foolishly got involved in the natives' tribal warfare and was killed in battle on [April 27, 1521]. Source: "Ferdinand Magellan and the First Circumnavigation of the World:" http://www.mariner.org/educationalad/ageofex/magellan.php
3. "Sir Edmund Hillary Achievement:" http://www.achievement.org/autodoc/page/hil0bio-1.
4. New Living Translation.

5. The object of Cook's third voyage was to find out whether there existed a northeast passage from Pacific to Atlantic. This eventually took him to Hawaii.

6. Edmund Hillary returned to Britain with the other climbers and was knighted by Queen Elizabeth II.

7. Laurence Bergreen, p. 127. In April of 1520, the captains of three of the other four ships plotted against Magellan. Unfortunately, Magellan terrorized his men and ruled by fear (Bergreen, p. 151).

8. "Captain James Cook the Navigator", by Guy Pocock: http://www.geocities.com/TheTropics/7557/page1.html

9. 1 Corinthians 12:13 (NIV).

10. Romans 8:9 (NIV).

11. John 15:1-4.

12. New Living Translation.

Chapter 11

1. John Robson, *The Captain Cook Encyclopædia*. Random House Australia, 2004 quoted from "James Cook:" http://en.wikipedia.org/wiki/James_Cook.

2. Margot Morrell and Stephanie Capparell, p. 131.

3. From John Hunt's diary; Colonel John Hunt was the leader of the successful Mount Everest expedition that Edmund Hillary and Tenzing Norgay were part of in May 1953. Quoted from "Everest By Storm" in *Travel in Dangerous Places*, edited by John Keay,(London: Constable and Robinson, 1993), p. 99.

4. Stephen Ambrose (*Undaunted Courage, p. 216)* describing Meriwether Lewis' entry into the Rocky Mountains, which heretofore no American had ever seen.

5. *Farther Than Any Man*, pp. 124-128.

6. M. Scott Peck, *The Road Less Traveled: A New Psychology of Love, Traditional Values and Spiritual Growth*(New York: Simon & Schuster, 1978).

7. M. Scott Peck, pp 15-17.

8. David Kinnaman and Gabe Lyons, *UnChristian: What a New Generation Really Thinks about Christianity...and Why it Matters* (Grand Rapids: Baker Books, 2007). Kinneman and Lyons, found that most of the lifestyle activities of born-again Christians were statistically equivalent to those of non-born-again people in areas like gambling, pornography, theft, hostility, abuse, misuse of drugs and alcohol, gossip and other areas (pp. 24-25).

Chapter 12

1. *Touching the Void*, p. 147.
2. Margot Morrell and Stephanie Capparell, p. 187.
3. *Touching the Void*, by Joe Simpson, back cover.
4. *Touching the Void*, back cover.
5. Ernest Shackleton, *Escape from the Antarctic* (New York: Penguin Books, 1999), p.72.
6. *Farther Than Any Man*, p. 128.
7. New Living Translation.
8. Selwyn Hughes, "Every Day With Jesus" (Crusade for World Revival, November/December 1982).

Chapter 13

1. *Escape from Antarctic*, p. 87.
2. Candice Millard, *River of Doubt*, p. 31.
3. *August 11, 1905, Friday.* Source:http://query.nytimes.com/gst/abstract.html?res=F6071FF93C5912738DDDA80994D0405B858CF1D3.
4. *Apollo 13* by Jim Lovell and Jeffrey Kluger (New York: Pocket Books, 1994), cover.
5. New Living Translation.
6. God, knowing Pharaoh's heart, states to Moses that He is going to Pharaoh's heart (Exodus 7:3). The first few hardenings are Pharaoh hardening his own heart as noted in the passages above. There seems to have been a point of no return as Exodus 9:12 says, "The Lord hardened Pharaoh's heart." Thus there is an interaction between Pharaoh defying God (through Moses) and God pushing the matter toward its cause and effect conclusion.

Chapter 14

1. *Apollo 13*, by Jim Lovell and Jeffrey Kluger (New York: Pocket Books, 1994), p. 293.
2. Georg Wilhelm Steller, "Stranded on Bering Island" in *Travel in Dangerous Places* (London: Constable and Robinson, 1993), p. 7.
3. *High Adventure*, p. 187.
4. Thomas Curwen, "A hike into horror and an act of courage" (*Los Angeles Times*, April 29, 2007), p. A25.
5. http://en.wikipedia.org/wiki/Georg_Steller.
6. http://en.wikipedia.org/wiki/Georg_Steller.

7. 2 Corinthians 5:14.

Chapter 15

1. *Apollo 13*, p. 311.
2. *High Adventure*, p. 194.
3. Martin Dugard, p. 138.
4. John Aaron was a flight controller during the Apollo program. He is widely credited with saving the Apollo 12 mission when it was struck by lightning shortly after liftoff. He played an important role during the Apollo 13 crisis. Aaron was off duty when the Apollo 13 explosion occurred, but was quickly called to Mission Control to assist in the rescue and recovery effort. Flight Director Gene Kranz put Aaron in charge of the Command Module's power supply. He was in charge of rationing the spacecraft's power during the return flight. He is also credited with developing the innovative power up sequence that allowed the Command Module to reenter safely while running on very limited battery power. Going against existing NASA procedures, he ordered the instrumentation system to be turned on last, just before reentry, rather than first. The call was a calculated risk. Without the instrumentation system, the crew and controllers would not know for certain if the cold startup had been successful until the last possible moment before reentry. However without this sequence change, the capsule would have exhausted its battery supply before splashdown. The procedure was a success, and the crew was recovered safely. Source: http://en.wikipedia.org/wiki/John_Aaron.
5. *High Adventure*, p. 194.
6. Martin Dugard, p. 138

Chapter 16

1. Stephen Ambrose, p. 97.
2. Martin Dugard, p. 57.
3. *High Adventure*, p. 118.
4. New Living Translation
5. New International Version
6. Hugh Halter and Matt Smay, *The Tangible Kingdom*, (San Francisco: Josey-Bass, 2008), p. 151.
7. Halter and Smay, p. 168.

Chapter 17

1. http://en.wikipedia.org/wiki/Ferdinand_Magellan#Origins_and_first_ voyage. Magellan first proposed this to the Portuguese king, Manuel I, but was rebuffed. (Laurence Bergreen, *Over the Edge of the World, p. 23.)*
2. Letter to Sir Edmund Hillary 16[th]October, 1952 by John Hunt in *High Adventure,* p. 117.
3. *Undaunted Courage*, p. 95.
4. Martin Dugard, p. 75.
5. Rodney Stark, *The Rise of Christianity.* (San Francisco: HarperCollins Publishers, 1997), p. 79.
6. Stark, p. 88.
7. Stark, p. 88.
8. Ken Eldred, *The Integrated Life.* (San Francisco: Manna Ventures, 2010).
9. Eldred, p. 84.
10. Eldred, p. 69.
11. Eldred, p. 60.
12. The Chinese government allows a limited printing of Bibles, available for "registered churches," but the limited number and the expense make them inaccessible for those involved in the house church movement.

Chapter 18

1. http://en.wikipedia.org/wiki/Ferdinand_Magellan. Even though Magellan had the full support of King Charles V of Spain, cooperation and respect of Magellan by the Spanish was undermined even before he set sail, serving as a warning that the Spanish under his command posed a danger as great as the sea (Laurence Bergreen, *Over the Edge of the World*, p. 46). The mistrust of the Spanish sailing with Magellan turned to a full-scale mutiny in Port Saint Julian, off the coast of what is now Argentina (Bergreen, pp. 133ff.)
2. *Shackleton's Way*, p. 81.
3. *The River of Doubt,* p. 106.
4. Stephen Ambrose, p. 246.
5. New Living Translation.
6. Candice Millard, *River of Doubt,* p. 106.

Chapter 19

1. *High Adventure*, p. 40.

2. Thor Heyerdahl, *Kon-Tiki: Across the Pacific by Raft*, (New York: Washington Square Press, 1984), p. 31. Heyerdahl was speaking of Herman Watzinger whom he recommended for the *Kon-Tiki* balsa raft expedition from Peru to Polonesia. Watzinger served in the Norwegian underground with Heyerdahl during the German occupation of Norway.

3. Stephen Ambrose referring to Lewis's and Clark's ability to get more out of their men than the men themselves ever thought they could give, including ascending up the Missiouri in a keelboat, portaging the Great Falls, and the incredible labor getting the canoes up the Jefferson River. Even in life-threatening situations Lewis knew his men had more in them than they thought, and he knew how to bring out the best in them. (*Undaunted Courage,* p. 273.)

4. Margot Morrell and Stephanie Capparell, p. 174.

5. *Kon Tiki,* p. 61.

6. *Kon-Tiki,* pp. 160-161.

7. *Undaunted Courage,* p. 31.

8. *Farther Than Any Man,* p. 194.

9. http://www.progressiveu.org/015809-two-men-left-for-dead-the-ethics-of-everest

Chapter 20

1. Margot Morrell and Stephanie Capparell, p. 83.

2. "Everest by Storm," in *Travel in Dangerous Places,* p. 104.

3. *Touching the Void,* back cover.

4. *Shackleton's Way,* Margot Morrell and Stephanie Capparell, p. 105.

5. *Shackleton's Way,* p. 59

6. "Hillary of New Zealand and Tenzing reach the top," Reuter (in The Guardian, June 2, 1953): http://en.wikipedia.org/wiki/Edmund_Hillary#cite_note-guard1-10.

7. Lance Pittluck, *Simple Thoughts on Leadership,* (Anaheim: Vineyard Anaheim, 2009), p. 12.

Chapter 21

1. "British woman weathers record sail," *USA Today* (Tuesday, February 8, 2005), p. 1.

2. *High Adventure,* p. 241.

3. *Shackleton's Way* by Margot Morrell and Stephanie Capparell, p. 190.

4. *Apollo 13,* p. 360. Lovell said this upon Apollo 13's safe splashdown in the waters of the South Pacific.

5. "British woman weathers record sail," *USA Today* (Tuesday, February 8, 2005),

6. *High Adventure*, p. 241.
7. *South: A Memoir of the Endurance Voyage,* by Rt. Hon. Lord Shackleton.
8. *Shackleton's Way* by Margot Morrell and Stephanie Capparell, p. 190.